AF844162

The Social Impact of Custody on Young People in the Criminal Justice System

"This is an important book that deserves a wide readership. While there is an emerging consensus among policy makers, academics and practitioners that children should only be imprisoned as a last resort, the evidence base in relation to the experiences of children deprived of their liberty remains underdeveloped. This work goes a considerable way to filling that gap by adopting a rigorous approach to measuring outcomes for children held in the secure estate. Drawing on extensive interviews with children and staff in a secure training centre, the authors make a compelling case for limiting the use of child incarceration to a minimum and for radical reform for provision of support to those children in secure settings."

—Dr Tim Bateman, *Reader in Youth Justice, University of Bedfordshire, UK*

"In a wider societal system which in so many ways fails children and young people, the Youth Justice system is expected to rectify the mess. With the Taylor report criticising its focus on punitive and ineffective approaches, we have lacked the cohesive linking up of well-evidenced research to provide an alternative. Science shows us that 'shame' and 'guilt' approaches don't work with victims of developmental and other trauma: yet they continue to form the foundation of the YJ approach. This volume draws together the lessons from the past, and a realistic view of the present, and the current and past research, in a coherent narrative that simply lets the evidence talk sense. I hope we can all read it and build on it."

—Jim Clifford OBE, *Co-founder of IAAM, The Adoption Bond, UK*

Claire Paterson-Young •
Richard Hazenberg • Meanu Bajwa-Patel

The Social Impact of Custody on Young People in the Criminal Justice System

palgrave
macmillan

Claire Paterson-Young
University of Northampton
Northampton, UK

Richard Hazenberg
University of Northampton
Northampton, UK

Meanu Bajwa-Patel
University of Northampton
Northampton, UK

ISBN 978-3-030-18421-6 ISBN 978-3-030-18422-3 (eBook)
https://doi.org/10.1007/978-3-030-18422-3

Cover illustration: Alamy ABC98D

This Palgrave Macmillan imprint is published by the registered company Springer Nature Switzerland AG
The registered company address is: Gewerbestrasse 11, 6330 Cham, Switzerland

Acknowledgements

We wish to thank our friends and colleagues for their support and advice in developing and writing this book. We would like to thank Frederick Seddon and Annette Batchelor for providing excellent reviews and feedback on the book. We wish to give a special thank you to the young people and staff who participated in the original research. Without your views, we would not have been able to capture the challenges and complexity of measuring social impact in Secure Training Centres.

We would also like to thank the following authors and publishers for permission to reprint material:

In Chapter Two

Taylor, C. (2016). *Review of the Youth Justice System in England and Wales.* London: Ministry of Justice.

Youth Justice Board. (2015a). *Youth Offending Teams: Making the Difference for CYP, Victims and Communities.* London: YJB.

Ministry of Justice. (2010). *Breaking the Cycle: Effective Punishment, Rehabilitation and Sentencing of Offenders.* London: Ministry of Justice.

The Lammy Review. (2017). *An Independent Review into the Treatment of, and Outcomes for Black, Asian and Minority Ethnic Individuals in the Criminal Justice System.*

In Chapter Three

Clifford, J., Hehenberger, L., & Fantini, M. (2014). Proposed Approaches to Social Impact Measurement in European Commission Legislation and in Practice Relating to: EuSEFs and the EaSI, European Commission Report 140605 (June 2014).

Hazenberg, R., Seddon, F., & Denny, S. (2014). Programme Recruitment & Evaluation: The Effect of an Employability Enhancement Programme on the General Self-efficacy Levels of Unemployed Graduates. *Journal of Education & Work*, *28*(3), pp. 273–300.

In Chapter Four

HM Chief Inspector of Prisons. (1999). *Suicide Is Everyone's Concern: A Thematic Review by HM Chief Inspector of Prisons for England and Wales*. London: Home Office.

Ofsted. (2018). Inspection of Secure Training Centres – Inspection of Oakhill Secure Training Centre.

In Chapter Six

DfE. (2017). Exclusion from Maintained Schools, Academies and Pupil Referral Units in England Statutory Guidance for Those with Legal Responsibilities in Relation to Exclusion. Retrieved from https://assets.publishing.service.gov.uk/government/uploads/system/uploads/attachment_data/file/641418/20170831_Exclusion_Stat_guidance_Web_version.pdf.

Taylor, C. (2016). *Review of the Youth Justice System in England and Wales.* London: Ministry of Justice.

OFSTED. (2007). Establishing Successful Practice in Pupil Referral Units and Local Authorities.

Houses of Parliament. (2016). POSTNOTE: Education in Youth Custody. Number 524. May 2016.

Home Office Research, Development and Statistics Directorate. (2004). *The Role of Education in Enhancing Life Chances and Preventing Offending*. London: Home Office.

In Chapter Eight

Beal, C. (2014). Insider Accounts of the Move to the Outside: Two Young People Talk About Their Transitions from Secure Institutions. *Journal of Youth Justice, 13*(1), 63–75.

In Appendix A

STC. (1998). Rules [Online]. Retrieved from http://www.legislation.gov.uk/uksi/1998/472/contents/made.

Contents

1	**Introduction**	1
2	**Youth Justice: The Impact of Policy on Current Practice**	7
3	**Social Impact Measurement and Youth Justice**	27
4	**Health and Wellbeing**	47
5	**Relationships**	63
6	**Education**	83
7	**Independence and Attitudes**	109
8	**Rehabilitative Environment**	139

9 The Future of Youth Justice Rehabilitation 167

Epigraph 179

Appendix A: Secure Training Centre Rules 1998 (STC 1998) 181

Appendix B: Secure Training Centre Statement of Purpose (2015) 183

References 187

Index 215

Acronyms

BAME	Black and Minority Ethnic
BYC	Beyond Youth Custody
CHAT	Comprehensive Health Assessment Tool
CPD	Continuing Professional Development
EHCP	Education, Health and Care plans
FSM	Free School Meals
GECES	Groupe d'Experts de la Commission sur l'Entrepreneuriat Social
ICAP	Integrated Cognitive Anti-social Potential
ITT	Initial Teacher Training
KS2	Key Stage 2
LAC	Looked After Children
MoJ	Ministry of Justice
NEET	Not in Education Employment and Training
SEND	Special Educational Need and Disability
SIM	Social Impact Measurement
SLSS	Students' Life Satisfaction Scale
STC	Secure Training Centre
YJB	Youth Justice Board
YOS	Youth Offending Service
YOT	Youth Offending Team
YP	Young Person
YRO	Youth Rehabilitation Order

List of Figures

Fig. 3.1	'Multi-theory' intervention programme design and evaluation (Adapted from Hazenberg et al. 2014)	33
Fig. 3.2	Young person Centred, Theory-led SIM Framework for Youth Offending (Authors' Own). Nb. As was noted earlier, ICAP theory identifies three main impact areas for youth offending. 1. economic factors: such as low income/unemployment; 2. relational factors: such as delinquent families/peers and living in high-crime neighbourhoods; 3. psychological factors/impacts: such as family breakdown/poor parenting and internal functions	40
Fig. 4.1	Responses to factors associated with mental well-being (N)	55
Fig. 5.1	Pro-criminal relationships and desire to apologise to their victim	66
Fig. 6.1	KS2 attainment of matched young offender cohort sentenced in 2014, based on data from the Youth Justice Board and MoJ (2018)	89
Fig. 6.2	Key Stage 4 Attainment for 2014 matched young offender cohort by youth justice disposal type at the end of Key Stage 4 in academic year 2012/13	90
Fig. 6.3	Framework of improved educational provision in STC	103
Fig. 8.1	Resettlement Pyramid (Authors' Own)	142

List of Tables

Table 4.1	Descriptive statistics on life satisfaction (n = 68) [Scale 1–7]	54
Table 6.1	A summary of the educational backgrounds and characteristics of young people sentenced across England and Wales in 2014	91
Table 6.2	Current provision in youth justice	100
Table 7.1	Young people's understanding of factors for independence (n = 65)	116
Table 7.2	Independent life skills for young people in custody	121
Table 8.1	Social impact measurement factors for young people in STCs	144

1

Introduction

This book focuses on the experiences of children and young people, referred to from now on as young people in the interest of brevity, in custody in England, through analysis of a series of interviews with young people and staff in a Secure Training Centre (STC). The authors also analysed questionnaires, case files and observational data collected during a doctoral research study. The authors are a multi-disciplinary team with a wealth of expertise across the fields of youth and restorative justice, child sexual exploitation, policing and education, which is combined with a common interest and experience in Social Impact Measurement (SIM)[1]. The book explores the data by combining Integrated Cognitive Anti-social Potential (ICAP) theory and desistance theory with SIM to demonstrate the importance of measuring social impact for policy and practice. The authors hope that where allegedly evidence-based (Smith 2007), counterproductive and inhumane policy has failed, a recognition of the social and economic cost of this failure will prompt change, discussion and dialogue.

[1] This refers to the measurement of impacts generated for the young people and society at large, both in terms of monetised savings, but also softer outcomes for the individual i.e. improved well-being. A full discussion of SIM is carried out in Chap. 3.

C. Paterson-Young et al., *The Social Impact of Custody on Young People in the Criminal Justice System*, https://doi.org/10.1007/978-3-030-18422-3_1

This book is rooted in research conducted by Paterson-Young (2018) that explored how social impact measurement as a form of organisational performance management can enhance outcomes for children and young people in custody. The authors use this research throughout the book, drawing on quantitative (questionnaires) and qualitative (semi-structured interviews, case analysis and observations). Drawing on this research the book presents a framework, rooted in the Taylor (2016) report, based on the diverse needs of young people, with chapters on youth justice, health and wellbeing, relationships, education, independence and attitudes and resettlement, all hung on a social impact measurement approach which opens the book. The research conducted by Paterson-Young (2018) employed a sequential mixed method approach that promoted the active participation of young people, as well as staff members, in STCs. The quantitative data, presented in this book, was generated from questionnaires completed by young people (n = 68) and staff (n = 74) and qualitative data was generated from semi-structured interviews with young people (n = 15) and staff (n = 15). The quotes presented by the authors throughout the chapters from any 'young person' or 'staff', are directly from the research, with pseudo names used to protect identity.

A recent report (Taylor 2016) exploring the experiences of children in custody emphasises how the roots of youth offending are embedded in our social institutions, our health care, housing and education systems, as well as our social care agencies. Systems whose existence should underpin and support those deemed 'at risk' and 'vulnerable' in our society, end up criminalising and incarcerating them which results in young people playing out a dual role as 'threatening' hooligans (Pearson 1983) or 'folk devils' (Cohen 1972). The punitive approaches that underpin policy and practice across youth justice in England today has resulted in the creation of the 'twin goals of welfare and justice' (Muncie et al. 2002: 1), with 'justice' emerging as the primary goal whenever high profile youth justice cases create moral outrage amongst the public (a situation the media does little to minimise) (Franklin and Petley 1996).

Programmes to empower young people within the youth justice system needs to be underpinned by an outcomes-based approach, grounded in theory relating to evaluating impact. The issue of power (Weber 1978) is central to any discussion of issues related to recidivism within social structures. Power mediates the flow of resources, personal agency and narratives; it shapes policy interventions and the rules that govern the young people and staff in the STCs, both under the glare of public perception and the dominant societal discourse of the time, all of which shape the outcomes for the young people contained within the STC. Weber links power to class structures that embed a lack of resources (economic and otherwise) for disadvantaged sections of society, from where many incarcerated young people emerge. The authors position Weberian ideas of power with ICAP theory and desistance theory, to create a SIM framework that explores the impact of custody on young people. ICAP theory (Farrington 2005) explains offending behaviour in young people from disadvantaged backgrounds, by showing how economic, relational and psychological factors lead to anti-social potential and potentially criminal behaviour. Analysing social impact within youth justice in relation to overcoming this lack of power, by focusing on those outcomes that matter most to young people, turns the traditional discourse on its head. ICAP theory presents factors, such as family disruption, poverty and poor school attainment, as risk factors while desistance theory presents the personal narrative. This allows the book to present a model that has strong theoretical underpinnings, whilst also developing a holistic overview of offending behaviour that acknowledges the individual, institutional and societal causes.

Placing the wellbeing of and positive outcomes for young people at the heart of measuring impact in the youth justice system is essential to solving what many in society view as the issue of 'problem' children. Before we explore social impact measurement and its implications for empowering young people in Chap. 3, we review the recent history of youth justice in Chap. 2, with a summary of approaches to youth offending and its reactive nature and contradictory history. The chapter culminates with a discussion of the Taylor Review (2016) of the youth justice system that recommended the creation of child-focused secure schools. Secure schools aim to give head teachers autonomy to recruit and train staff, to commission the necessary support services, such as mental health, and create a culture where behaviour is effectively managed, and rehabilitation is promoted. This generates a child centred culture that recognises that these are vulnerable young people who would benefit from a therapeutic environment and specialist care. The Taylor report (2016) was followed by an announcement at the Conservative party conference in 2018 that Medway STC, an STC with a chequered and highly controversial past, would be repurposed as the first secure school pilot. Chapter 2 closes by questioning if Secure Schools will offer the innovated child-first approach necessary for supporting children and young people, or instead repeat a cycle of failure.

Chapter 4 considers the health and wellbeing of young people in the secure estate, an area considered by many as of significant concern. This is particularly pertinent when considering the isolation and lack of adequate services experienced by young people. Such inadequacy of provision is compounded by the fact that many young people enter the STC having suffered trauma and health inequalities, as well as having special education needs and disability (SEND). Substance abuse also represents a factor for many young people, who use it as a coping mechanism for their traumatic past experiences. Indeed, data from the STC research shows how, in some cases, the STC environment exacerbates trauma with little or no thought given to transition upon release.

Chapter 5 focuses on the importance of relationships when it comes to the successful resettlement of young people. Relationships, within the STC and with family and peers outside, can be a significant influence on young people in custody and upon release, with positive relationships helping them to make smooth transitions and desist. This chapter explores the many facets of relationships for the young people in custody. It highlights the importance of building strong, positive relationships based upon trust, both with staff in the STC and with others outside in the community. Such relationships help to empower young people and involve them in co-producing their own rehabilitation strategies, despite the isolation of their custodial sentences. This relational approach recognises how a sense of belonging and feeling a part of a family, can help begin the move away from offending behaviours.

As well as relationships, education is also a key factor in promoting desistance and in Chap. 6, we look at the role of education on recidivism. The chapter begins with the responsibilities that schools have in relation to young people and exclusion, which is especially relevant given the higher prevalence of exclusions amongst Black, Asian and Minority

Ethnic (BAME), Looked After Children (LAC) and Free School Meal (FSM) students (and to be over-represented in the youth justice system). The Taylor Review (2016) reported how many young people in custody have missed a great deal of their schooling and stated that education must be central if reoffending rates are to come down. Our research data shows that many young people feel disillusioned with education both prior to and during their incarceration in the STC. Therefore, we conclude the chapter by making recommendations designed to improve educational provision in STCs.

When it comes to transitioning successfully from custody and to adulthood, a range of personal skills critically effect transitions. Chapter 7 explores these issues under the broader heading of independence and attitudes. Independence refers to the development of the personal and social skills that support children and young people in their transition to adulthood (Montgomery et al. 2006), including communication, employability and emotional regulation. The role of independence and attitudes to the successful transition and resettlement of young people from custodial environments is paramount, with the research data and prior literature both suggesting that these skills are not being successfully developed within the STC.

Chapter 8 focuses on resettlement and the need to ensure young people transitioning from secure environments also have secure accommodation, employment/education/training placements, financial know-how and good awareness of their health and wellbeing. Analysis from previous chapters, along with a review of the literature, is positioned within a SIM framework, based upon an understanding of the impacts of custody and used to develop a five-phase Resettlement Pyramid. This Pyramid outlines the building blocks necessary for achieving successful transition for young people by helping them build resilience and pro-social attitudes. The Resettlement Pyramid is explored in relation to both possible social outcome measures and data from the STC, so as to provide a multi-stakeholder, multi-intervention design. This design combines ICAP, desistance and SIM theories to provide a holistic overview of how young people in custody should be supported and how relevant outcomes can be effectively measured. The final chapter (Chap. 9) reviews the previous chapters in relation to SIM, empowerment, ICAP and desistance, and proposes key recommendations for effective rehabilitation of young people in STCs.

References

Cohen, S. (1972). *Folk Devils and Moral Panics: The Creation of the Mods and Rockers*. London: Routledge.

Farrington, D. (2005). *Integrated Developmental and Life-Course Theories of Offending. Advances in Criminological Theory*. New Jersey: Transaction.

Franklin, B., & Petley, J. (1996). Killing the Age of Innocence: Newspaper Reporting of the Death of James Bulger. In J. Picler & S. Wagg (Eds.), *Thatcher's Children? Politics, Childhood and Society on the 1980s and the 1990s*. London: Falmer Press.

Montgomery, P., Donkoh, C., & Underhill, K. (2006). Independent Living Programs for Young People Leaving the Care System: The State of the Evidence. *Children and Youth Services Review, 28*, 1435–1448.

Muncie, J., Hughes, G., & McLaughlin, E. (2002). *Youth Justice: Critical Reading*. London: Sage.

Paterson-Young, C. (2018). *'Inspiring Futures' – How Social Impact Measurement as a Form of Organisational Performance Management Can Enhance Outcomes for Young People in Custody*. PhD Thesis, University of Northampton.

Pearson, G. (1983). *Hooligan: A History of Respectable Fears*. London: Macmillan.

Smith, R. (2007). *Youth Justice: Ideas, Policy, Practice*. Devon: Willan Publishing.

Taylor, C. (2016). *An Interim Report of Emerging Findings From the Review of the Youth Justice System*. London: Ministry of Justice.

Weber, M. (1978). *Economy and Society: An Outline of Interpretative Sociology*. Berkley, CA: California University Press.

2

Youth Justice: The Impact of Policy on Current Practice

Youth justice remains a highly visible 'domain', with political, academic and media attention on the behaviour of young people persisting for centuries. Developments in approaches to dealing with young people led to the introduction of a dedicated youth justice system, dominated by Government strategies tackling the emerging issues rather than the root cause of the problem. The Taylor (2016: 3) report demonstrated this:

> Almost all of the causes of childhood offending lie beyond the reach of the youth justice system. It is vital that health, education, social care and other services form part of an integrated, multi-agency response to a child's offending, but it is more desirable that these same services intervene with at-risk children and families before their problems manifest themselves in offending.

Taylor's (2016) report was commissioned by the Ministry of Justice with the aim of reviewing and improving the youth justice system. It outlined the wider causes of childhood offending, with recommendations for developing an integrated multi-agency system for supporting children, young people and families. Despite the recommendation in this report, the Government's response was described as an opportunity

C. Paterson-Young et al., *The Social Impact of Custody on Young People in the Criminal Justice System*, https://doi.org/10.1007/978-3-030-18422-3_2

missed (Bateman 2017), with progress in implementing recommendations from the report moving at a glacial pace. But what does this mean for youth justice practice? This chapter intends to explore these missed opportunities and cycle of failure within the youth justice system, by exploring the impacts of contemporary policy on current practice. Contextualising developments in contemporary policy, a brief history of youth justice in England and Wales shows how modern approaches to dealing with young people are ambiguous and influenced by the historically residual punitive and welfare foundations underpinning the youth justice system. Such conflict and ambivalence explain the "missed opportunities" for improving procedures, legislation and initiatives that effectively fail some young people. It explores how the dominance of punishment and justice approaches are influenced by the societal insistence that young people are 'threatening' (Pearson 1983). The perception of young people as 'threatening' is influenced by 'respectable fears', which Pearson (1983) described as the unfavourable comparisons of present with past. These 'respectable fears' are created, amplified and mobilised by media representations of young people, which often results in public outcry for punishment and justice. This societal focused punitive approach is central to the arguments presented in this book, as it demonstrates how current policy and practice in the youth justice field is not focused on young people, but on justice and the perceived needs of wider society. Such an approach severely limits positive outcomes for young people both in terms of recidivism and wider life chances. Throughout this chapter, our arguments are informed by analysis of current practice in managing young people in England and Wales, with a specific focus on the secure estate.

2.1 Learning from the Past—How Did We Approach Youth Justice?

We need look no further than the histories of the youth justice system to identify the punitive approaches underpinning our youth justice system today. Interest in youth justice peaked in the late nineteenth and early twentieth centuries, after the introduction of the 1819 and 1833 Factory

Acts. This process culminated in an acknowledgement that childhood was a developmental period, whilst the growth in urban youth populations resulted in the creation of the concept of the 'Delinquent Child' (Hendrick 1997). Not only are the behaviours of young people viewed as a social problem, but so too is the very nature of childhood and youth. This focus on young people as a 'social problem' has appeared in political discourse for centuries (Pearson 1983; Muncie 2015), contributing to the expansion of the youth justice system and specifically services dedicated to managing delinquent young people. Academic literature analysing the history and development of the youth justice system already exists (see: Hendrick 2006; Muncie 2009; Bateman and Hazel 2014; Case 2018), so rather than repeat this analysis, a brief history is offered from the late 1950s onwards. Exploring this snapshot of youth justice developments serves to contextualise the structural foundations of youth justice, which impact on contemporary policy and current practice.

Early developments in the youth justice system were founded on competing punitive and welfare principles, shaped by societal perceptions of young people as 'threatening'. Public confidence in Government responses to young people reduced, resulting in the Home Office commissioning the Ingelby Report (1956) to examine the law in England and Wales. A key recommendation from this report was to increase the age of criminal responsibility from 8 years-old to 12 years-old. This recommendation was partially implemented in the Children and Young Persons Act 1963, which increased the age of criminal responsibility in England and Wales from 8 years-old to 10 years-old (Bateman and Hazel 2014). This partial implementation of the Ingelby (1956) recommendation illustrates the Government's reluctance to challenge societal views of threatening young people. Developments in 1964 culminated in the Longford Report entitled *Crime: A Challenge to Us All,* which recommended that the government abolish juvenile courts and instead establish expert panels (Bateman and Hazel 2014). Recommendations for establishing expert panels were also found in the Kilbrandon report (1964), which led to the creation of Children's Panels in Scotland. Despite this implementation of the recommendations in Scotland, recommendations from the Longford report (1964) were dropped in England and Wales (Bateman and Hazel 2014).

Reform of the Youth Justice System continued in 1965 with the launch of the White Paper titled *The Child, the Family and the Young Offender* and the introduction of the 1969 Children and Young Persons Act (Muncie et al. 2002). Proposals in the Children and Young Persons Act 1969 were viewed at the time as radical and contributed in part to the loss of electoral support for Labour administration. The subsequent election of the Conservative Government in 1970 marked a divergence from welfare principles, with partial implementation of the aforementioned 1969 Children and Young Persons Act and the introduction of strategies for the intensive monitoring and control of young offenders (Goldson 2002). This shift from welfare principles was strengthened by proposals to re-introduce strict regimes in Detention Centres. At this time, international developments in the United Nations Standard Minimum Rule for the Administration of Juvenile Justice (introduced as the Beijing Rules in 1985), focused on limiting the use of custody for young people (Goldson 2002). This encouraged a shift in youth justice policy in England and Wales, with provisions for restricting custodial sentences for young people introduced in the 1988 Criminal Justice Act (Goldson 2002). However, provisions in this Act were contradictory, with restrictions in the use of custodial sentences implemented side-by-side with the introduction of Youth Offending Institutions. Youth Offending Institutions were introduced with the aim of helping young people prepare for their return to the community, but it remains to be seen how effective they have been in achieving this (further discussions on the use of custody can be found in Section 2.3). Therefore, developments in the youth justice system represent a revolving cycle of welfare and punitive principles influenced by societal perceptions of 'threatening' young people.

Negative societal perceptions of young people remained at the heart of developments in policy and practice in the 1990s, as evident following the murder of two year-old James Bulger by the two 10 year-olds Jon Venables and Robert Thomson. This tragic event resulted in policy that sought to further the divergence from welfare to punitive approaches that was discussed earlier. Such events result in acute societal pressures for governments to prevent a perceived deepening of offending that the public sees as being the result of increasingly persistent and young offenders (Graham and Moore 2008). The Government's response was to intensify the return to punitive principles for managing young people, culminating in the commencement of the 1993 Criminal Justice Act and the 1994 Criminal Justice and Public Order Act. This legislation increased powers for courts to impose harsher sentences on young people, extend long-term detention orders and introduce Secure Training Orders, representing not simply a return to punitive principles, but also an unravelling of welfare initiatives.

In response to increasing anxieties over the generation of 'threatening' young people, the Audit Commission examined the youth justice system; publishing the *Misspent Youth* report in 1996 (Audit Commission 1996, 1998). This report concluded that the youth justice system was an ineffective and expensive service with limited impact and recommended the implementation of a new model of youth justice. Critics of the report viewed the presentation and interpretation of evidence as questionable. However, the report was formalised in the New Labour Government's 'No More Excuses' White Paper. With the move back and forth between punitive and welfare principles, recommendations in the Misspent Youth report promised to overcome this crisis of identity by introducing a new youth justice system, but this has not proved to be the case over the last twenty years.

2.2 Repeating the Past—How Do We Approach Youth Justice?

Since the 1996 Audit Commission report, developments in youth justice include the creation of Secure Training Centres (STCs), the Youth Justice Board and multi-agency Youth Offending Teams. So, have these changes overcome the problems identified in the Audit Commission *Misspent Youth* report? STCs were created to accommodate young people aged 12 to 14 years-old receiving Secure Training Orders, complimenting existing secure estates. The first centre opened in 1998, underpinned by notions of control and security as influenced by societal concerns over the management of persistent young offenders. The original purpose was for *"accommodating trainees in a safe environment within secure conditions; and helping trainees prepare for their return to the outside community"* (Appendix A—

STC Rules 1998) (further discussions on the use of custody can be found in Section 2.3). Following the introduction of STCs, the 1998 Crime and Disorder Act was published with provisions for introducing the Youth Justice Board and Youth Offending Teams. This led to the 'new youth justice' system, with responses to young people focused on responsibilisation, prevention, risk-based early intervention and community sentences (Case 2018). Case (ibid) stated that this new youth justice system is largely devoid of welfare and justice philosophies, with increased focus on responsibilisation of young people, families and communities. Shadows of the punitive youth justice foundations, intertwined with notions of welfare, remain influential in this new youth justice system, creating the dichotomous environment that we see today.

As part of this reform, the Youth Justice Board was introduced to oversee the youth justice system in England and Wales. Within this role, the Youth Justice Board are expected to develop consistent standards and approaches for managing young people engaged in criminal activity. The functions of the Youth Justice Board were outlined in the Crime and Disorder Act 1998:

- Monitoring and evaluating the youth justice system;
- Developing guidance on effective practice for preventing offending by young people;
- Allocating funding grants to Youth Offending Team and other organisation to develop and sustain effective practices;
- Commissioning and arranging custodial placements for young people (Secure Children's Homes, Secure Training Centre's and Youth Offending Institutions),

As overseeing body, the Youth Justice Board dealt with the strategic direction of the youth justice system, with the newly created Youth Offending Teams managing the day-to-day operation (Case 2018). The introduction of Youth Offending Teams marked a shift in the management and delivery of youth justice services, with a multi-agency partnership at the core. Services delivered by Youth Offending Team are funded by statutory partners in the local authority, with annual grants received from central government. The Youth Justice Board sets standards in youth justice services and monitors Youth Offending Teams' performance. A report from the Youth Justice Board (2015b) concluded that Youth Offending Teams were key to preventing offending and recidivism, due to their multi-stakeholder approach to working with young people.

Success, as defined here, is based on the reduction in the number of young people entering the youth justice system, but what about young people still entering the system? Paterson-Young (2018) explored young people's perceptions of Youth Offending Team, finding that some view the Youth Offending Team process as a 'game', 'waste of time' and 'pointless'. For young people in custody, the Youth Offending Team process was viewed as ineffective with the process, essentially geared towards supporting some young people. Young people participating in this research described the Youth Offending Team process as 'pointless', 'rubbish' and 'boring', with one young person stating: *"…they don't work, because I'm here now"* (Paterson-Young 2018: 204). This is not to say that Youth Offending Team services do not work, but rather that some Youth Offending Team services are ineffective for the young people routinely described as 'prolific offenders'.

Developments in the new youth justice system were characterised by apparent shifts in cultural, structural and systematic approaches to young people; however, this approach was underpinned by contradictions and ambivalence (Case 2018). Such incongruities are represented in the Youth Crime Action Plan published by the Home Office in 2008 (Case 2018). The Youth Action Plan outlined New Labour's approach to 'tackling youth crime' with emphasis on enforcement and punishment to challenge unacceptable behaviour (Bateman and Hazel 2014). The Plan aimed to reduce the numbers of young people dealt with in the criminal justice system by 2020 (Bateman and Hazel 2014), by focusing on enforcement and punishment, as well as prevention and support. This contradicted the abolition of the offences, 'brought to justice' targets and diversionary practices by placing emphasis on punitive responsibilisation, net-widening and criminalisation (Case 2018). Following publication of the Youth Action Plan, Youth Rehabilitation Orders were introduced in the 2008 Criminal Justice and Immigration Act offering statutory alternatives to youth custody. This placed additional accountability on the courts to justify the imposition of custodial sentences over alternatives.

Since the Misspent Youth (1996) report, developments in youth justice from the Misspent Youth Report (1996) have been rooted in contradictory principles, with competing notions of support and punishment, diversion and intervention, prevention and justice (Case 2018).

A Coalition Government led by the majority Conservative Party and minority Liberal Democrat Party replaced the New Labour Government in 2010. This Coalition Government inherited a youth justice system with a decrease in proven offences (−19%) and custodial sentences (−16%) between 2008/2009 and 2009/2010 (Youth Justice Board 2011). This new Government approach to crime was evident from Conservative Leader David Cameron's (2008) speech outlining the 'so-called' causes of crime, notably substance use, family breakdown, debt, inappropriate housing and inadequate education failure. Cameron's focus on the 'Big Society' within this speech that empowers communities and promotes social solidarity, was reminiscent of New Labour's communitarianism and responsibilisation approach. In 2010, the Coalition Government's Green paper 'Breaking the Cycle: Effective Punishment, Rehabilitation and Sentencing of Offenders' was published (Ministry of Justice 2010). This paper set forth plans to change the Criminal Justice System, with informal intervention at the forefront, and the encouragement of 'trust' in professionals working with stakeholders on the front-line (Ministry of Justice 2010). The report outlined the need to:

1. Prevent more young people from offending and divert them from entering a life of crime, including by simplifying out-of-court disposals;
2. Protect the public and ensure that more is done to make young offenders pay back to their victims and communities;
3. Ensure the effective use of sentencing for young offenders;
4. Incentivise local partners to reduce youth offending and re-offending using payment by result models;
5. Develop more effective governance by abolishing the Youth Justice Board and its freedoms and flexibilities for local areas.

(Ministry of Justice 2010: 67)

Shortly after the 'Breaking the Cycle: Effective Punishment, Rehabilitation and Sentencing of Offenders' Green Paper, the Legal Aid, Sentencing and Punishment of Offenders Act (2012) was introduced to extend the use of youth conditional cautions for 12–17 year-olds across England and Wales (Bateman and Hazel 2014). This Act resulted in the application of the care-planning processes for children remanded to the secure estate, re-emphasising the need for a holistic approach to young people in the youth justice system. The Act established proportionate responses to young people's behaviour with the introduction of flexible disposals for first time offenders and the repeated use of referral orders for young people pleading guilty.

Further developments in youth justice were initiated by Youth Justice Board Chief Executive John Drew in 2010, with a consultation exercise seeking to evaluate the effectiveness of the scaled approach (Case 2018). The consultation resulted in a revised assessment and intervention framework culminating in the introduction of 'AssetPlus' in 2013, which introduced a new outcomes-based approach (Youth Justice Board 2014b). The AssetPlus aimed to present a holistic approach to assessment and management with emphasis on moving from a risk-based to a strength-based approach, promising to ensure young people's lives are central to the process, and promoting positive outcomes. The AssetPlus core assessment framework comprises information gathering, explanations and conclusions, pathways and planning, and modules. It provides a single assessment and plan for young people and was described as 'dynamic and iterative in nature' (Youth Justice Board 2014b). The AssetPlus may present a holistic, dynamic and iterative process for assessing and managing interventions for young people in comparison to the scaled approach, but implementation is challenging. Indeed, does the approach to AssetPlus promote this holistic, dynamic and iterative process or is it simply a rebranding of the existing Asset structures?

2.3 Child Imprisonment: The Legacy of a System Developed on Punitive Principles

Secure estates for young people in England and Wales consist of three distinct categories: Secure Children's Homes Secure Children's Homes, Secure Training Centres (STCs) and Youth Offending Institutions. Each estate is managed and operated distinctly, with local authorities managing Secure Children's Homes, private companies managing STCs (with the exception of Medway) and Youth Offending Institutions managed by the prison service. The distinct management of secure estates illustrates confusion in England and Wales in the approach to youth justice, with punitive principles overshadowing the welfare principles recommended internationally. Reports from the United Nation's Committee on the Rights of the Child (2002; 2008; 2016) have criticised the high average custody rates in England and Wales in comparison to other European countries. In 2003, the Joint Committee on Human Rights released a report in response to concerns over the use of custody in England and Wales, sharing concerns with the UN Committee over the use of imprisonment for young people. This report recommended devoting resources to community alternatives, as well as improving rehabilitative opportunities for young people. Criticisms of the approach in England and Wales demonstrate its failure to tackle the issue of youth custody, resulting in approaches that lack direction, purpose and social impact. With England and Wales maintaining the lowest age of criminal responsibility in Europe and the highest rates of incarceration, the youth justice system is failing some of the most vulnerable young people in society.

Secure Children's Homes were introduced to accommodate between 8–40 male and female young people aged 10–14 years-old. Placements in Secure Children's Homes are for young people on youth justice placements and those on welfare placements, costing on average £212,000 per year (The Parliamentary Office of Science and Technology 2016). Since 2010, accommodation on welfare grounds has increased with 51% of young people accommodated in Secure Children's Homes in 2017, in comparison with 37% in 2010 (Department of Education 2017). This reverses previous trends, with reductions in the number of young people placed on youth justice placements coinciding with increases in the number of welfare placements. Given increased demand for welfare placements, there are fewer placements available for young people engaged in criminal activity, which may result in the inappropriate placement of this group. The placements offer young people a range of services within a secure environment, with provisions tailored to individual needs. Young people have access to education and training, health provision, specialist provision, mental health and learning difficulty services.

As an alternative to Secure Children's Homes, STCs were introduced to accommodate males and females aged 12 to 14 years-old receiving Secure Training Orders (or Detention Training Orders), costing on average £178,000 per year (The Parliamentary Office of Science and Technology 2016). The age of young people accommodated in STCs was reviewed in 2000, following the death of two young people in custody (both Kevin Henson aged 17 years-old and David Dennis aged 17 years-old died in custody in 2000) (Youth Justice Board 2014a). As a result of welfare and safety concerns, the age of young people accommodated was extended to include 12–17 year-olds, with provision for the continued accommodation of young people aged 18 years-old where they have additional vulnerabilities (Pitts 2001). Each STC accommodates between 50 and 80 young people, separated into 'units' of 6 to 8. The centre aims to accommodate *"trainees in a safe environment within secure conditions; and helping trainees prepare for their return to the outside community"* (Appendix A—STC Rules 1998). This purpose was directed by the following guiding rules:

- Provide a positive regime offering high standards of education and training;
- Establish a program designed to tackle the offending behaviour of each trainee and to assist in development;
- Foster links between the trainee and the outside community;
- Co-operate with the services responsible for the trainee's supervision after release.

Recognition that young people in custody have complex needs resulted in the development of a new statement of purpose, expanding the original rules. For example, the STC (1998) Rules 3.1(a) on safety are complemented by the STC (2015) Statement of Purpose 2 (See Appendix A and B). Although the statement of purpose expands on the rules, recognition of the changes in age, sentence length and offence of young people are non-existent. If you explore the age profile of young people accommodated in STCs, you can observe the dramatic changes that have occurred over time. Initially, STCs were introduced to accommodate 12–14 year-olds receiving Secure Training Orders (or Detention Training Orders). This was reviewed in response to welfare and safety concerns after the death of Kevin Henson (17 years-old) and David Dennis (17-years-old) in 2000 (Youth Justice Board 2014a), leading to a change in the age of young people accommodate in STCs. The changing profile of young people accommodated in STCs has resulted in an approach reminiscent of Youth Offending Institutions, rather than the welfare approach that was targeted. Youth Offending Institutions were introduced to accommodate male young people aged 15–21 years-old, costing on average £65,000 per year (The Parliamentary Office of Science and Technology 2016). It was introduced with the aim of helping young people prepare for their return to the community. Primarily underpinned by punitive principles, it mirrors the traditional adult secure estate, accommodating a larger number of young people than Secure Children's Homes and STCs. Young people accommodated in Youth Offending Institutions are separated by age group, with under-18s accommodated in separate buildings. Each Youth Offending Institution accommodates between 60 and 400 young people, separated into 'wings' of 30 and 60.

Since 2006, the number of young people entering the youth justice system has reduced, with noticeable reductions in the numbers accommodated in the secure estate. Between 2007 and 2017, an 81% decrease was noted in the number of cautions or convictions received by young people (Youth Justice Board 2018). Recent statistics illustrate that the average population in youth custody (for the year ending March 2017) was 868, with an average custodial sentence length of 16 months (Youth Justice Board 2018). The number of young people entering custody has a declining trajectory with 0.4 per thousand 10–17 year-olds in custody in 2016, a 68% decrease compared with 2006. Despite the positive shift represented by this reduction, concerns over the treatment of young people and the lack of provision in custody have persisted. In 2016, the BBC's Panorama television programme (current affairs and investigations) broadcast an exposé on the physical and emotional abuse young people suffered at the hands of staff at Medway STC (BBC 2016). In response, the Government appointed an Independent Improvement Board to investigate allegations and recommend changes to policy and practice. Recommendations from the Independent Improvement Board include introducing:

- A new vision for STCs, or other arrangements, that focuses on education and rehabilitation, and cultural values that promote a nurturing and safe environment.
- An Independent Governing body to oversee and scrutinise safeguarding.
- A new leadership and governance structure, with reporting links to the Governing Body.
- A cross-departmental working group to address inconsistencies in the treatment and placement of children across secure estates.
- A review of safeguarding policies and procedures in relation to suicide and self-harm.
- An individual educational needs package for each child (rather than focusing on the number of hours spent in education).
- A formal mechanism to ensure each child's voice is heard.

The report and subsequent recommendations illustrate not only shortcoming in Medway STC, but shortcomings in the wider youth secure estate. The shortcomings of custody were outlined by staff working with young people in STCs:

> *I think the centre brings young people who are potentially here for a first offence and the kids learn how to offend. Because they are in an environment with 7 other young people, potentially one in for murder who has been here 3 times, and you put a vulnerable young person that is naïve….and they learn how to commit crime.* (Karen, Staff Member)

> *I think most of the boys that leave and don't offend probably wouldn't offend again if they went to a different establishment or received a community sentence. Obviously, a lot of the stress here is on teaching the boy's education like Maths and English rather than on rehabilitation. I'm not sure it even puts them off being in custody and I don't think it teaches them—in my experience—to rehabilitate and change their way of thinking or anything like that.* (Harry, Staff Member)

No, we definitely don't [help children desist]. We don't provide offending intervention, so the kids just leave with the same attitude. The only time we make a difference is with the kids that have only offended once, but honestly, I don't think those kids would offend again. For the ones that have multiple offences, they just laugh it off. For them, the world is a different place and they commit crime to survive. We should be teaching them to survive without crime but instead we put them on units with other kids like them and they learn from each other. (Val, Staff Member)

I think we teach young people here the worst you behave, the more you get. We got a young person that will smash up a classroom.... punch a teacher. They will put him on the unit, they will keep him separate for a little while and then he will be allowed. We had one young person here who was on X and he destroyed his room completely, I mean completely, he lifted the floor up, he got down to bare plaster.... And he lived in a corridor where the louder he shouted, the more he got. There has to be a consequence for your behaviour, it's like the louder you scream... the more you get. (Rich, Staff Member)

The above sentiments of staff were also reiterated by professionals in the community:

Custody has significantly.... impact on the trajectory of young people. So, it's difficult to be positive about the use of custody when we know that it will negatively impact of the life chances of any young people involved in it. I do, however, understand that the public want to see deterrence in our justice system. And that the use of custody, today, perhaps achieves that for them. But I think that, that's the role of government and policy to help the public understand the most effective approach to reducing crime is prevention and prevention is delivered through the delivery of support. (Ethan, Young Person)

Going back to custody, I think that sending a young person to custody has a really negative effect on their future and outcomes. For young people that have suffered traumatic childhoods, spending time in custody will have increasingly negative effects. I sometimes wonder, why did this young person end up in custody? I mean, we have all these services so why did it get to that point? Why has this young person's life come to this point? In my role, I have read reports from the police, social care and education that highlight a multitude of issues the young person has been presenting with for years, yet they have only received

> *limited support. And then we wonder why they go to custody.* (Del, Young Person)

> *Custody should be a last resort or for those serious offences like murder. If we continue to send children to custody for theft and burglary, then all we are doing is creating a revolving door in and out of custody. Recently, we had a young boy about 13 that ended up receiving a 24-month custodial sentence for burglary offences he committed with older lads in a gang. I mean 24 months at age 13, he will spend 12 months in custody and then end up back in the same environment with the same issues. He shouldn't have even got to that stage but instead of exhausting all other options, the judge wanted to make an example of him.* (Faisal, Young Person)

> *I think custody is needed for some young people, but I think what happens in custody, how they are treated and what support they receive is not good. And also, I think, you know, professionally and personally, there isn't enough transition phases for young people on realise.... (support) that you get when you come out of prison or custody—there isn't a direct link into a youth offending service.* (Anthony, Young Person)

> *Erm, I think it should be a last resort as for it. I don't think they can get the support they need to change and the opportunities for intervention are very limited. And if there is an intervention, it is very hard for them to practice what they have been taught while in that environment, so I think there can be issues with it.* (Jack, Young Person)

These quotes illustrate the views of professionals working with young people in the community. When combined with the views from staff in the secure estate, it is evident that there are questions over the appropriateness of custody, and in particularly the social impact of custody. The impact of custody on young people is extensive, with young people entering and leaving custody experiencing the highest levels of social disadvantage.

Despite the fall in custodial sentences for young people in England and Wales, young people from minority ethnic communities are over-represented in custody (Youth Justice Board 2018). Young people from minority ethnic communities represent 18% of the general population, while accounting for 45% of the population in custody. The Lammy Review (2017) found that BAME young people represented 19% of first-time entrants to the criminal justice system in 2016, an increase from 11% in 2006. This represents a wider social issue, with the Review (ibid., 2017: 7) calling for *'explain or reform'*, which places a requirement on agencies to provide evidence-based approaches. The Review concluded that individuals from BAME communities still experience bias, both unconscious and conscious, within the criminal justice system. Recommendation for managing the over-representation of BAME communities relies on principles of fair treatment, trust and responsibility (The Lammy Review 2017). The over-representation of BAME communities in custody and the wider criminal justice system represents one of several issues in youth justice. Research has demonstrated that several young people entering STCs had experienced exposure to parental separation (68%), pro-criminal family members (65%), domestic abuse (51%), bereavement (25%) and/or experiences in the care system (43%) (Paterson-Young, Hazenberg, Bajwa-Patel and Denny 2017).

The trauma resulting from experiencing child abuse, domestic abuse and bereavement can hinder the development of young people (Kitzmann, Gaylord, Holt and Kenney 2003; Holt, Buckley and Whelan 2008; Cohen, Mannarino and Deblinger 2017). Some young people experience only limited and/or brief trauma symptoms as a result of development level, resilience and external support; however, young people experiencing prolonged exposure to abuse and/or bereavement could experience enduring trauma (Cohen et al. 2017). One question arising from the above is whether the behaviours of young people are due to rational choice, mental wellbeing or manifestations of trauma?

Rather than labelling young people with conditions such as personality disorders or psychosis, qualified professionals should support young people to address their traumatic experiences. This approach empowers young people and helps professionals understand the root cause of behaviours, rather than simply focusing on the symptoms. For example, Paterson-Young (2018) found high-levels of substance use (87.4%) for young people entering STCs. Several of the young people participating in the research viewed substance use as a coping mechanism. Research conducted by Lawson, Back, Hartwell, Maria and Brady (2013) found that the prevalence of substance use was higher in groups experiencing traumatic events or adverse childhood experiences. Despite the prevalence of substance use for young people experiencing trauma, services operate in isolation, with a focus on reducing problem behaviours rather than exploring the trauma experiences leading to such behaviours. Indeed, the adverse and traumatic experience of young people entering custody demonstrates the need for a child-focused approach to practice.

2.4 Summary

The creation of dedicated systems for dealing with young people in the criminal justice system have been influenced by societal perceptions of young people as 'threatening', combined with the presentation of selective evidence (Case 2018). Early youth justice developments were underpinned notions of punishment and justice, interwoven with competing welfare principles. Whilst the residues of punitive principles remain influential in youth justice policy (intertwined with welfare principles), the positive developments in youth justice are vulnerable to change (Bateman 2017). From our review of youth justice policy in relation to the Misspent Youth (1996) and Taylor (2016) reports some twenty years later, what is apparent is that the youth justice system represents a catalogue of 'missed opportunity' (Bateman 2017). The chapter presented a review of the youth justice system noting that progress and change has remained glacial. Rather than repeat this cycle, a new approach to youth justice that acknowledges the current state of Government finances is required[1]. This book seeks to do this by presenting a new model for supporting young people in custody (and beyond), which seeks to empower them by utilising a holistic social impact measurement framework that focuses on outcomes for offenders themselves. In doing so, we propose a model of intervention that seeks to limit the institutional barriers that exist to reducing recidivism, whilst enabling personal agency amongst young people in their transition back into the community and adulthood.

[1] The authors do not wish to debate the need, merits or validity of austerity; merely, we acknowledge that the current policy paradigm is one dominated by limits to public expenditure.

References

Audit Commission. (1996). *Misspent Youth: Young People and Crime Summary*. London: Audit Commission.

Audit Commission. (1998). Misspent Youth '98 – The Challenge for Youth Justice. Retrieved April 12, 2018, from http://webarchive.nationalarchives.gov.uk/20090415152538/http://www.audit-commission.gov.uk/Products/NATIONAL-REPORT/7C38F5A0-C744-4362-A6C6-90A12D52258D/archive_misyth98.pdf.

Bateman, T. (2017). *The State of Youth Justice 2017 – An Overview of Trends and Developments*. National Association for Youth Justice – Justice for Children in Trouble.

Bateman, T., & Hazel, N. (2014). *Youth Justice Timeline*. Retrieved June 5, 2016, from http://www.beyondyouthcustody.net/wp-content/uploads/youth-justice-timeline.pdf.

BBC. (2016). *Teenage Prison Abuse Exposed*. Retrieved September 12, 2016, from http://www.bbc.co.uk/programmes/b06ymzly.

Cameron, D. (2008). *Fixing Our Broken Society*. Retrieved February 28, 2019, from https://www.webarchive.org.uk/wayback/archive/20080907225219/http://www.conservatives.com/tile.do?def=news.story.page&obj_id=145626&speeches=1.

Case, S. (2018). *Youth Justice: A Critical Introduction*. Oxon: Routledge.

Cohen, J. A., Mannarino, A. P., & Deblinger, E. (2017). *Treating Trauma and Traumatic Grief in Children and Adolescents* (2nd ed.). London: The Guildford Press.

Department of Education. (2017). *Children Accommodated in Secure Children's Homes at 31 March 2017: England and Wales*. SFR 23/2017.

Goldson, B. (2002). Children, Crime and the State. In B. Goldson, M. Lavalette, & J. McKechnie (Eds.), *Children, Welfare and the State*. London: Sage.

Graham, J., & Moore, C. (2008). *Beyond Welfare Versus Justice: Juvenile Justice England and Wales*. In J. Junger-Tas & S. H. Decker (Eds.), *International Handbook of Juvenile Justice*. New York: Springer.

Hendrick, H. (1997). Constructions and Reconstructions of British Childhood: An Interpretative Survey, 1800 to the Present. In A. James & A. Prout (Eds.), *Constructing and Reconstructing Childhood: Contemporary Issues in the Sociological Study of Childhood* (pp. 33–60). London: Routledge.

Hendrick, H. (2006). Histories of Youth Crime and Justice. In B. Goldson & J. Muncie (Eds.), *Youth Crime and Justice*. London: Sage Publications.

Holt, S., Buckley, H., & Whelan, S. (2008). The Impact of Exposure to Domestic Violence on Children and Young People: A Review of the Literature. *Child Abuse & Neglect, 32*(8), 797–810.

Kitzman, K., Gaylord, N., Holt, A., & Kenney, E. (2003). Child Witnesses to Domestic Violence: A Meta-Analytic Review. *Journal of Consulting and Clinical Psychology, 71*(2), 339–352.

Lawson, K. M., Back, S. E., Hartwell, K. J., Maria, M. M., & Brady, K. T. (2013). A Comparison of Trauma Profiles among Individuals with Prescription Opioid, Nicotine, or Cocaine Dependence. *The American Journal on Addictions, 22*(2), 127–131.

Ministry of Justice. (2010). *Breaking the Cycle: Effective Punishment, Rehabilitation and Sentencing of Offenders*. London: Ministry of Justice.

Muncie, J. (2009). *Youth and Crime* (3rd ed.). Oxford: Sage Publication Ltd.

Muncie, J. (2015). *Youth and Crime* (4th ed.). Oxford: Sage Publication Ltd.

Muncie, J., Hughes, G., & McLaughlin, E. (2002). *Youth Justice: Critical Reading*. London: Sage.

Paterson-Young, C. (2018). *'Inspiring Futures' – How Social Impact Measurement as a Form of Organisational Performance Management Can Enhance Outcomes for Young People in Custody*. PhD Thesis, University of Northampton.

Paterson-Young, C., Hazenberg, R., Bajwa-Patel, M., & Denny, S. (2017). *Developing a Social Impact Measurement Framework to Enhance Outcomes for Young People in Custody—What to Measure?* British Society of Criminology – Conference 2017.

Pearson, G. (1983). *Hooligan: A History of Respectable Fears*. London: Macmillan.

Pitts, J. (2001). *The New Politics of Youth Crime: Discipline or Solidarity*. Dorset: Russell House Publishing.

STC. (1998). Rules [Online]. Retrieved June 8, 2016, from http://www.legislation.gov.uk/uksi/1998/472/contents/made.

Taylor, C. (2016). *Review of the Youth Justice System in England and Wales*. London: Ministry of Justice, The Parliamentary Office of Science and Technology (2016) *Education in Youth Custody*. Post note: 524.

The Lammy Review. (2017). *An Independent Review into the Treatment of, and Outcomes for Black, Asian and Minority Ethnic individuals in the Criminal Justice System*. Retrieved June 26, 2018, from https://assets.publishing.service.gov.uk/government/uploads/system/uploads/attachment_data/file/643001/lammy-review-final-report.pdf.

Youth Justice Board. (2011). *Youth Justice Statistics 2009/10 – England and Wales*. London: Youth Justice Board.

Youth Justice Board. (2014a). *Deaths of Children in Custody: Action Take, Lessons Learnt*. London: Youth Justice Board.

Youth Justice Board. (2014b). *AssetPlus Model Document*. London: Youth Justice Board.

Youth Justice Board. (2015a). *Youth Justice Statistics 2013/2014*. London: Youth Justice Board.

Youth Justice Board. (2015b). *Youth Offending Teams: Making the Difference for Young People, Victims and Communities*. London: Youth Justice Board.

Youth Justice Board. (2018). *Youth Justice Statistics 2016/2017*. London: Youth Justice Board.

3

Social Impact Measurement and Youth Justice

The empowerment of young people within the Youth Justice System needs to be led through an outcomes-based approach centred on empowering young people. However, if such an approach is to be adopted it is crucial that the framework developed is grounded in theory in relation to evaluating impact. This chapter seeks to explore this prior theory in relation to social impact measurement (SIM), and relate this to criminological theory, namely 'Integrated Cognitive Antisocial Potential' (ICAP) Theory and Desistance Theory. This combined theoretical approach will be explored through an analytical lens centred upon Weberian conceptions of power, particularly in relation to how individuals within ecosystems (in this case Secure Training Centres (STC)) act with rational purpose to create value, either personally or collectively. This 'social action' by the individual or group occurs within social structures (i.e. institutional settings), which facilitates the flow of resources within the ecosystem (Weber 1978). Within the context of this book, these resource flows occur within the STC and flow in a bidirectional manner up and down a Resettlement Pyramid (outlined in Chap. 8). This way, social action and the consequent resource flows mediate both the development journey of the young people and the existent structures within the STC

C. Paterson-Young et al., *The Social Impact of Custody on Young People in the Criminal Justice System*, https://doi.org/10.1007/978-3-030-18422-3_3

and the behaviours of all stakeholders within this ecosystem. This chapter will therefore begin with an exploration of Weber's (1978) work on power, before then exploring social impact measurement, in relation to issues of definition, best practice frameworks for engaging in social impact measurement, and types of data that can be gathered. The chapter then goes on to explore ICAP theory and relate this to the SIM models presented, in order to present a case for an integrated outcomes-based focus on youth justice interventions in STCs. Throughout the chapter, the empowerment of the young people forms the central frame of analysis, as placing them at the centre of any SIM framework remains critical.

3.1 Empowerment in Youth Justice

Power remains a critical factor within any study of social structures, as it mediates the flow of resources, personal agency and the narratives that are created around issues (in this case recidivism) (Weber 1978). This leads to different stakeholder groups being able to shape discourse to differing degrees and to challenge (or prevent challenges to) dominant paradigms of thought. Within the youth justice field, power therefore acts to shape policy interventions, public perceptions of youth offending and the rules that exist within STCs (and hence how staff and young people behave within the walls), and hence ultimately the outcomes for the young people within the STC. Indeed, the discussion of the historical approach to youth justice presented in Chap. 2 provides a perfect illustration of the role that dominant discourses can have in shaping attitudes to and policy around youth justice (i.e. the Bulger case in the 1990s).

A key facet of Weberian conceptions of power relates to how power mediates (and is mediated by) social structures (Weber 1978). Furthermore, Weber also relates power within social structures to 'class structures', arguing that such structures are in part created and reinforced by access to power and resources (i.e. the disadvantaged do not have such access) (ibid). This is very pertinent in the field of youth justice, as the majority of young people accommodated in STCs are from socially and economically deprived backgrounds (or the Care system) (see Chaps. 2 and 6 for more in-depth discussions of these demographics). This lack of power means that the system does not need to respect their perspectives and/or needs, and hence young people perspectives and needs are often ignored. Indeed, as is shown throughout this book, the lack of an outcomes' focused approach centred on young people in custody that is truly concerned with reducing recidivism and enhancing life chances, only seeks to highlight this power schism.

The analysis of social impact within youth justice provides an opportunity to overcome these power deficits, by placing outcomes for young people at the centre of discourse. Indeed, by focusing on the outcomes deemed most critical by young people (mediated by other expert stakeholder groups), frameworks can be created that place young people at the centre of youth justice interventions. Such an approach surely offers the best chances of reducing recidivism and promoting positive youth transitions to adulthood for these young people. It also provides a framework from which young people can be empowered (as can frontline practitioners), as the metrics used to assess performance (and hence shape policy and practice) are centred on and embedded within the young people's experiences. SIM frameworks therefore offer a way to overcome power imbalances and shape social action in a positive fashion by acting as a tool to steer institutional behaviour, shape societal discourse, and embed social networks in ways that are positive for young people. However, as Voltan and Hervieux (2017) identify, SIM has its own inherent problems related to power, as the most powerful actors can shape the types of outcomes that they wish to see measured and/or achieved. Therefore, it is critical that those with the least power such as beneficiaries (in this case young people), are placed at the centre of SIM framework design to ensure that such power imbalances are not replicated and that the SIM frameworks produced are truly young people centred.

3.2 Defining Social Impact Measurement

One of the central problems related to SIM is the lack of definition that currently exists as to what the term constitutes (Sairinen and Kumpulainen 2006). Furthermore, Emerson (2000) argues that social value and social impact are poorly understood both as concepts and as a process. This presents problems to researchers as it is difficult to measure that which is not defined. However, in recent years there has been a greater focus on both social value and social impact measurement, both within academia and within policy and practice (Jain 2018). This increased focus has been driven by developments within the public and third sectors (i.e. increases in the numbers of social impact reports being produced); greater scrutiny of these and social impact as a concept within academia; and critically in government through the creation of policy frameworks centred on social value (the Public Services 'Social Value' Act of 2012 being a prime example). SIM is a key area for organisations to develop, as it provides legitimacy and allows for access to resources (including power) and evidence to drive organisational change (Nicholls 2009; Clifford et al. 2013). If an approach to impact measurement is adopted that is centred on the young people, this also means that the approach is beneficiary-led and that consequently policy and practice is co-developed by young people. This promotes new practice through bottom-up innovation and therefore seeks to empower young people within the Youth Justice System (i.e. it enables social action) (Weber 1978).

The increased focus on social impact has inevitably led to the development of definitions by key stakeholders in the field. These definitions are, it must be noted, contested and socially constructed themselves (Burdge and Vanclay 1996), and so are influenced by the very power structures that we sought to critique earlier in the chapter. Indeed, the organisations that are producing such definitions are themselves powerful institutional actors in the ecosystem or private sector entities with a direct profit motive (the European Commission; International Association for Impact Assessment; Inspiring Impact). Nevertheless, they provide broad overviews of what we can understand by the term 'social impact', and how it can be measured. Furthermore, whilst the frameworks are different, they contain many common elements which can be used (and have been) to develop 'common sense' approaches to social impact measurement (SIM) (Hazenberg and Clifford 2016). This allows the researcher to discern what approach works best in evaluating their specific programme (in this case STC interventions with young people), and to therefore distinguish between the numerous different methodological approaches to SIM in existence (Millar and Hall 2013; Hehenberger et al. 2013).

In providing a generic framework for the measurement of social impact, McLoughlin et al. (2009) developed the SIMPLE methodology, which focused upon the measurement of outputs, outcomes and impact. An output can be defined as the direct and easily identifiable outputs of an intervention (i.e. the number of young people engaged in an STC) (ibid). However, whilst considering whether output as a method of evaluation is useful for tracking the success of an intervention from this particular perspective, if it is employed as a singular measure, the evaluation will not include important longer-term participant benefits, i.e. outcomes. An outcome represents positive changes to participants' states of mind that will enhance their lives, their future employability and their psychological well-being (ibid). An example of this could be changes in the wellbeing of young people during their time in the STC. Impact is an even longer-term benefit and is the impact on society resulting from the intervention (e.g. the reduced criminal justice expenditure resultant from reduced recidivism) (McLoughlin et al. 2009). Impact is the most difficult area to measure, as it is focused on the wider and less tangible aspects of an intervention, where proxy financial values have to be identified and applied. However, it is important to measure this, otherwise the effectiveness of an intervention cannot be fully understood, and those with power (i.e. policy-makers, commissioners) tend to value this over beneficiary outcomes.

Perhaps the best known definition of social impact emerged out of work conducted by the European Commission's Groupe d'Experts de la Commission sur l'Entrepreneuriat Social (GECES) sub-committee on impact measurement, which built upon the work of McLoughlin et al. (2009) and provided the following definition:

> *The reflection of social outcomes as measurements, both long-term and short-term, adjusted for the effects achieved by others (alternative attribution), for effects that would have happened anyway (deadweight), for negative consequences (displacement), and for effects declining over time (drop-off).* (GECES, June 2014: 12)

What the above definition make clear, is that social impact measurement in an STC setting should be centred upon understanding: the scope of the work carried out (*outputs* of the programme); the positive and negative outcomes experienced by young people (*outcomes* for the beneficiary group); how it shapes young people's desistance over time (*impacts* on society); what roles the different stakeholders/partners have in this (alternative attribution); and what would have happened anyway in a standard intervention (deadweight/control group). However, a key theme that emerges throughout the above discussions and definitions relates to the role of different stakeholder groups and how they interact with each other, both strategically (from a power perspective) and operationally (in delivering the programme and measuring the impact). Understanding the role of multi-stakeholder approaches to programme design, delivery and evaluation is critical in SIM (Hazenberg et al. 2014), especially in the context of this study, if a holistic SIM framework is to be developed for young people in STCs. Indeed, the Resettlement Pyramid proposed in this book can only be adopted and work if all stakeholders engage with and buy-in to the process.

3.3 Multi-stakeholder Approaches to SIM

The engagement of all stakeholders in the rehabilitation process for young people is critical if a holistic approach to reducing recidivism is to be achieved, and this stakeholder group must also of course include young people as the central focus. Hazenberg et al. (2014) built upon work by Chen and Rossi (1980) centred on theory-driven approaches to evaluation, and articulated how a multi-stakeholder and multi-theory approach to intervention design and evaluation would work, with focus on three key phases: Design Phase; Implementation Phase; and Evaluation Phase (Fig. 3.1).

In the Design phase, all stakeholders are brought together to inform both the design of the intervention and its evaluation. The purpose of this phase is to ensure that all viewpoints are considered and that theoretical and practical considerations are understood. The involvement of beneficiaries here is key as whilst Hazenberg et al. (2014) argued that the fourth stakeholder group relates to 'additional stakeholders', we argue here that these additional stakeholders are the young people themselves—the beneficiaries.

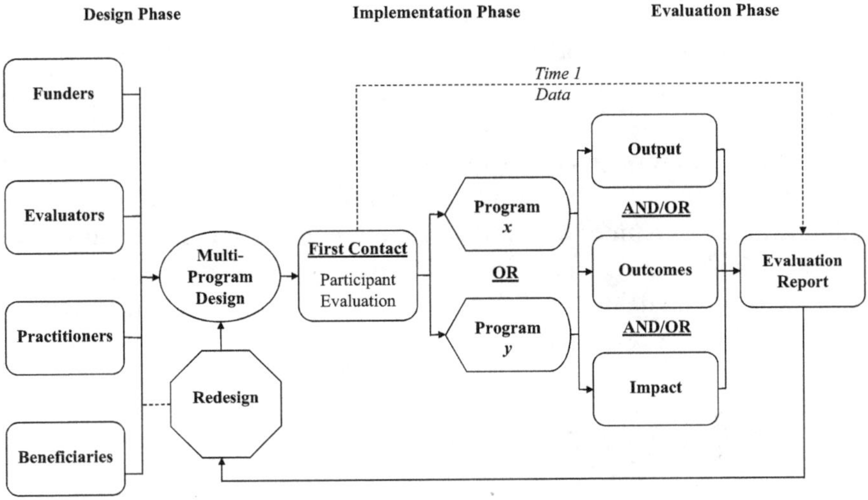

Fig. 3.1 'Multi-theory' intervention programme design and evaluation (Adapted from Hazenberg et al. 2014)

In designing the intervention and evaluation, it is key to articulate a theory of change, based in academic theory from both criminology and social science (in this case ICAP theory, desistance theory and social impact measurement theory). A Theory of Change as defined by GECES involves demonstrating a causative link between the intervention to be delivered and the outcomes to be achieved and presents a clear rationale (embedded in academic theory) that explains the change logic model (Clifford et al. 2014). In relation to this study, this relates to the embedding of ICAP and desistance theory within a social impact framework that is focused on measurable outcomes of change over time, both within the young people (internalised factors such as wellbeing) and between individuals (i.e. relationships with peers and adults). The Implementation Phase builds on this by recognising that as all young people are individuals, multiple intervention types might be required to produce the best outcomes for young people in reducing recidivism (i.e. one-size does not fit all) (Hazenberg et al. 2014). This then flows into the evaluation phase, where outputs, outcomes and impacts (as defined earlier in the chapter) are captured to assess longitudinal progress for the beneficiaries. Critically, the findings of this evaluation are then fed back into redesigns of the intervention to ensure that all programme design is evidence-led (this includes where necessary adapting the theory of change model as well) (ibid).

This provides a robust overarching approach to understanding how to develop a Theory of Change model, and then how this is applied to the whole process. However, it is also critical to understand the steps that are required within this to develop the actual SIM framework and how specific outputs, outcomes and impacts are identified. Here the European Commission's GECES framework is extremely useful in providing guidance as to how to deliver this strategically and operationally, and how this can then also be disseminated.

3.4 Building a Framework for SIM

As has been noted earlier in the chapter, a lack of definition of social impact, aligned with the plethora of methodologies that exist for measuring social impact, creates problems for organisations in understanding the 'why', 'how', and 'who' questions surrounding impact measurement evaluations. This leads to what Hazenberg and Clifford (2016) termed 'legitimacy problems' for socially orientated organisations, as the whole sector surrounding SIM is 'disjointed' and confusing. This led to the GECES sub-committee on social impact measurement identifying in their 2014 report, five key areas that should be explored in developing a SIM framework.

- *Inputs:* What resources are used in the delivery of an intervention?
- *Activity:* What is being done with the 'inputs' (i.e. the intervention)?
- *Output:* How that activity touches the intended beneficiaries?
- *Outcome:* The change arising in the lives of beneficiaries and others.
- *Impact:* The extents to which that change arise from the intervention.

(Clifford et al. 2014: 6)

As was outlined earlier, this is then combined with McLoughlin et al. (2009) SIMPLE methodology centred on the measurement of *outputs*, *outcomes* and *impacts*, and the capturing of additional data in relation to 'deadweight' (what changes would have happened anyway, regardless of the intervention?); 'alternative attribution' (deducting the effect achieved by the contribution of other organisations); and 'drop-off' (allowing for the decreasing effect of an intervention over time) (Clifford et al. 2014: 7). When also aligned with the Theory of Change, this allows the organisation to identify specific measurement tools with which to capture empirical data that can demonstrate outcomes achieved and the validity (or otherwise) of the Theory of Change model. These indicators would be in general unique, as GECES also denotes the impossibility of having one set of indicators/measures for all social impact, due to the extremely diverse nature of social missions operating across sectors (Hazenberg and Clifford 2016). Therefore, even for a framework centred upon young people and youth offending, any framework developed might only be suitable within STCs (new frameworks might be required for different settings such as Youth Offending Institutions). Nevertheless, such a framework would provide a starting point for reframing the youth justice discussion on the place of outcomes (and the young people) in the design, delivery and assessment of youth justice interventions.

In identifying a pathway towards developing a social impact measurement framework, GECES recommended five main stages (listed below). Whilst the elements of the framework outlined above are strategic in nature, these stages are operational and can act as a guide for the stakeholders as to how they can specifically approach impact measurement. The key elements here are demonstrated through the need to understand why SIM is being undertaken; identify stakeholders and a theory of change as also outlined earlier; create and/or identify measurement tools to capture and validate the theory of change (outputs, outcomes and impacts); and report the findings both externally (marketing) and internally (organisational development).

1. *Identify objectives:* What are the objectives of the impact measurement (i.e. organisation and partners)?
2. *Identify stakeholders:* Who are the beneficiaries and who provide resources?
3. *Relevant measurement:* Understand the theory of change and then utilise relevant indicators to capture this.

4. *Measure, validate and value:* Assess whether outcomes are achieved and whether they are recognised by the various stakeholders.
5. *Report, learn and improve:* Ensure the dissemination of and meaningful use of the data gathered and findings produced to internal and external stakeholders/audiences.

(Clifford et al. 2014: 7)

These five stages, when aligned with the Theory of Change, Multi-Theory Evaluation and SIMPLE models, provide a deep theoretical grounding from a SIM perspective, to be able to develop a robust SIM framework for young people in STCs. However, in order to be able to develop this further, a broader theoretical understanding of youth offending from a criminological perspective needs to be undertaken, and the following section seeks to do this through the embedding of 'Integrated Cognitive-Antisocial Potential' (ICAP) theory and desistance theory with the SIM theories already outlined, to develop a model for measuring social impact within an STC setting.

3.5 Building a SIM Framework for Youth Offending

'Integrated Cognitive-Antisocial Potential' (ICAP) theory seeks to explain offending behaviour in young people through the translation of antisocial *potential* to antisocial *behaviour* through cognitive functions that assess opportunities and victims (Farrington and Ttofi 2014). ICAP is very much centred on explaining offending behaviour in those from lower-class backgrounds (Farrington 2005) and hence is centred upon the disadvantaged young people who appeared disproportionately in the research. In ICAP this disadvantage is represented through three main areas of experience for the young people: first, economic factors such as low income/unemployment; second, relational factors such as delinquent families/peers and living in high-crime neighbourhoods; third, psychological factors/impacts such as family breakdown/poor parenting and internal functions such as low anxiety (Farrington 2007). This disadvantage leads to antisocial potential that can manifest itself into behaviours when/if the right circumstances emerge (opportunity and potential victims). These behaviours can then become crimes, and the experience of this and (potentially) punishments can lead to reinforcement/learning of behaviours that makes repeat offending more likely (ibid).

ICAP theory articulates offending in young people as being a longitudinal journey that is focused on change over time, both within the young people (internalised factors such as wellbeing) and between individuals (i.e. relationships with peers and adults). It also posits the factors that affect long-term offending behaviours and so presents the researcher with possible outcome measures that can be used to capture social impact. These outcome measures include: (low) academic ability; attention deficit; familial disruption; family criminality; hyperactivity; impulsivity; parenting problems; poverty; and (poor) school attainment (Farrington 2003, 2007). Indeed, assessing not only the risk factors, but also the protective characteristics explored by ICAP theory is critical to the development of an effective SIM framework (Paterson-Young 2018). Nevertheless, risk-factors alone do not explain offending behaviour, as motivational factors (strain; desires for material goods; status with family members or intimates; excitement; and sexual satisfaction) and the means to achieve these through legitimate (i.e. non-criminal) means also mediates behaviour (Farrington and Ttofi 2014).

Moving beyond understanding the reasons young people commit crime to understanding the process of desistance is pivotal in developing a SIM framework. The processes of desistance are explained as both natural changes (over time) and manufactured changes (influenced by activities and interventions) (Farrall and Bowling 1999; Maruna 2001; McNeill 2002). Desistance Theory describes how individuals who are regular and repeat offenders produce long-term asceticism from offending (McNeill et al. 2012). Desistance theory explores changes in behaviour as influenced by ageing, life events, social bonds and/or narrative (Maruna 2001). These changes impact on the individual's sense of self, which is influenced by the interplay between the individual and society (Farrall and Bowling 1999; Maruna 2001). Literature exploring the natural process of change builds upon early research into the influence of puberty and 'maturational reform' (Goring 1919). While conducting research into the life course of individuals in the criminal justice system,

Glueck and Glueck (1937) argued that ageing was the only significant factor in reforming behaviour. Expanding on this, Hirschi and Gottfredson (1983) noted a peak age in offending (or rather conviction) during the mid-late teenage years, with a sharp decline noted at around the mid-20s and stabilising thereafter. This 'age crime curve' was contested, Sampson and Laub (1993) arguing that the factors influencing behaviour and mediating change are more complex than simply measuring age. For example, Soothill et al. (2004) found that the peak age of conviction was dependent on the crime committed, with the peak age for burglary around 16 years-old or less, lower than the peak age of offending for motoring offences.

While research on age and desistance offers insight into the natural change that may occur in maturation, other desistance researchers focus on social bonds. Social bonds are based on four basic elements: attachment, commitment, involvement and common value systems (Hirschi 1969). Research conducted by Bersani et al. (2009) outlined the impact of prominent life experiences on desistance, arguing that strong bonds with family (for example marriage and children) and employment impact on desistance. Bersani et al. (2009) argues that marriage gives individuals a feeling of security, which strengthens social bonds. Parenthood was identified as another social bond that influences desistance (Moloney et al. 2009). Moloney et al. (2009) argued that fatherhood also emerges as a significant life event in promoting desistance. If strong social bonds impact on desistance, then separating young people from families and friends creates a strain. This strain may have a negative impact on young people, highlighting the need for improved engagement between the STC and community.

The role of self-identity and personal narrative in the desistance process is well documented in literature (Maruna 2001; and Giordano et al. 2002). Desistance from crime was explained by Maruna (2001) as a process where offenders need to develop a prosocial identity for themselves Thus, developing personal narratives helps young people reflect on experiences and find redeeming values, which encourages young people to 'make sense' of the situation (Maruna 2001). This empowers young people to own their experiences and put these experiences 'to good use' by supporting others (for example, supporting other young people in similar circumstances and/or situations).

Such processes are influenced by the individuals' motivation to change and belief that change is needed (Giordano et al. 2002). When individuals reflect on experiences and acknowledge that a change is needed, then the process of desistance can begin. This encourages individuals to develop a new sense of self, underpinned by a desire to change their behaviour (Giordano et al. 2002). Then the individual essentially utilises their environment to affect significant change in their life, meaning that changes to behaviour reflect the interplay between individual agency and social structure (ibid).

ICAP and desistance theory therefore provides SIM research with the theoretical framework from which to build a theory of change, and hence ultimately identify measurable outputs, outcomes and impacts. The exploration of SIM definitions and theory, as well as the use of ICAP to provide the theoretical basis for the SIM Theory of Change, presents us, within this chapter, with the opportunity to develop a holistic framework for assessing the social impact of STC interventions with young people. Crucially, it is imperative that such development is carried out from the young people perspective as much as possible, to ensure that the young people are empowered and embedded in the process and so are able to engage in 'social action' towards their own recidivism (Weber 1978). This is crucial to both encouraging the coproduction of the SIM framework and to prevent the discourse around youth offending (and the outcomes to be measured) being dominated by those with power within the system (Weber 1978; Voltan and Hervieux 2017). SIM when approached in this way, provides the opportunity to deliver social action through the young people, and to direct institutional behaviour and steer discourse through a young person focused, multi-stakeholder approach embedded within theory and networks.

Figure 3.2 overleaf provides an overview of the 'Young Person Centred, Theory-led SIM Framework for Youth Offending' (YP-SIM) that has been developed through this research study, and that will be utilised later in this book to identify relevant outputs, outcomes and impacts for assessing social impact in STC settings. The YP-SIM engages in the five

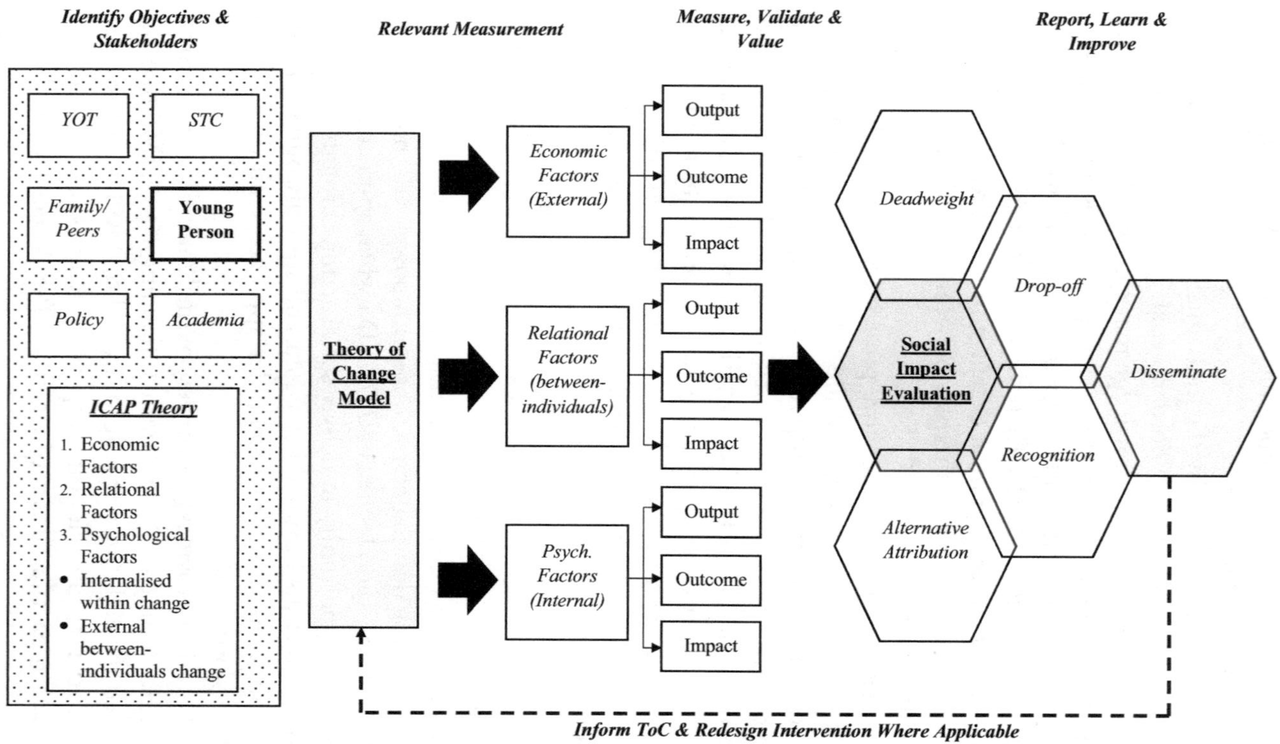

Fig. 3.2 Young person Centred, Theory-led SIM Framework for Youth Offending (Authors' Own). Nb. As was noted earlier, ICAP theory identifies three main impact areas for youth offending. 1. economic factors: such as low income/unemployment; 2. relational factors: such as delinquent families/peers and living in high-crime neighbourhoods; 3. psychological factors/impacts: such as family breakdown/poor parenting and internal functions

main stages of SIM as identified by GECES: Identify objectives; Identify stakeholders; Relevant measurement; Measure, validate and value; and Report, learn and improve (Clifford et al. 2014: 7)[1]. Embedded within these stages is multi-stakeholder engagements centred on the young people; the embedding of ICAP and desistance theory (Farrington and Ttofi 2014; Maruna 2001); the identification of a Theory of Change and the mapping of relevant outputs, outcomes and impacts (Clifford et al. 2014; McLoughlin et al. 2009) in relation to the three main elements of ICAP (economic, relational and psychological factors) (Farrington and Ttofi 2014) and three elements of desistance theory (age, social bond and personal narrative) (Maruna 2001); the inclusion of deadweight, alternative attribution and drop-off calculations (Clifford et al. 2014); and the exploration of relevance with stakeholders (and especially young people) and the dissemination of the social impact findings both externally and internally for organisational development (Clifford et al. 2014; Hazenberg and Clifford 2016; Hazenberg et al. 2014).

3.6 Summary

This chapter has explored social impact from a youth crime and offending perspective, so as to build an initial framework for measuring social impact within STCs. The chapter has recognised that young people in the Youth Justice System are disempowered (following on from the themes discussed in Chap. 2), and that SIM provides a possible means to empower young people and place them at the heart of outcomes focused programmes designed to reduce recidivism. This has been framed within a multi-theoretical lens that utilises Weberian conceptions of power (focused on how power mediates social action and behaviour), ICAP theory and desistance theory. The use of SIM frameworks to embed ICAP and desistance theory into an outcomes' focused evaluation that recognises the central role to be played by young people, acts as a mechanism

[1] For the purposes of this SIM framework however, the first two stages (identify objectives and identify stakeholders) have been merged into a single phase.

to empower young people and enable them to own their own rehabilitative work. This provides the central thrust of the arguments presented in this book, in that young people are ignored within youth justice interventions as power is concentrated in the hands of policy-makers and practitioners, and that therefore SIM provides an avenue for rebalancing power and giving young people a voice.

However, the chapter has also demonstrated that social impact is a nebulous concept, suffering from poor definition, a plethora of different methodologies and a lack of understanding around common 'gold-standard' frameworks. The research conducted by Paterson-Young (2018) sought to demonstrate that whilst these critiques are valid, it is still possible to design and deliver effective SIM frameworks for young people in STCs that focus on the outcomes relevant to their reoffending needs. The framework presented above in Fig. 3.2 provides such an approach, and one that follows SIM best-practice guidance (notably GECES) and embeds ICAP and desistance theory within this. The result is a framework and process that can provide academics and practitioners with a map for effectively evaluating the outcomes of interventions with young people. What the framework does not provide at this stage are the specific outputs, outcomes and impacts to be measured. These will be identified and developed in the following chapters, with a full framework presented in the Resettlement chapter (Chap. 8).

References

Bersani, B. E., Laub, J. H., & Nieuwbeerta, P. (2009). Marriage and Desistance from Crime in the Netherlands: Do Gender and Socio-historical Context Matter? *Journal of Quantitative Criminology, 25*, 3–24.

Burdge, R., & Vanclay, F. (1996). Social Impact Assessment: A Contribution to the State of the Art Series. *Impact Assessment, 14*, 59–86.

Chen, H., & Rossi, P. H. (1980). *The Multi-Goal Theory Driven Approach to Evaluation: A Model Linking Basic & Applied Social Science. Social Forces, 59*(1), 106–122.

Clifford, J., Markey, K., & Malpani, N. (2013). *Measuring Social Impact in Social Enterprise: The State of Thought and Practice in the UK*, London,

E3M. Retrieved from http://ec.europa.eu/internal_market/social_business/docs/expert-group/social_impact/presentation-e3m_en.pdf.

Clifford, J., Hehenberger, L., & Fantini, M. (2014). *Proposed Approaches to Social Impact Measurement in European Commission Legislation and in Practice Relating to: EuSEFs and the EaSI*, European Commission Report 140605 (June 2014). Retrieved from http://ec.europa.eu/internal_market/social_business/docs/expert-group/social_impact/140605-sub-group-report_en.pdf and http://ec.europa.eu/social/main.jsp?catId=738&langId=en&pubId=7735&type=2&furtherPubs=yes.

Emerson, J. (2000). *The Nature of Returns: A Social Capital Markets Inquiry into Elements of Investment and the Blended Value Proposition*, Harvard Working Paper Series, No. 17 Social Enterprise Series, Boston, MA. Retrieved from http://www.blendedvalue.org/wp-content/uploads/2004/02/pdf-nature-of-returns.pdf.

Farrall, S., & Bowling, B. (1999). Structuration, Human Development and Desistance from Crime. *British Journal of Criminology, 39*(2), 252–267.

Farrington, D. (2003). Key results from the First 40 Years of the Cambridge Study in Delinquent Development. In T. P. Thornberry & M. D. Krohn (Eds.), *Taking Stock of Delinquency: An Overview of Findings from Contemporary Longitudinal Studies*. New York: Kluwer.

Farrington, D. (2005). *Integrated Developmental and Life-Course Theories of Offending. Advances in Criminological Theory*. New Jersey: Transaction.

Farrington, D. (2007). Origins of Violent Behaviour Over the Life Span. In D. J. Flannery, A. T. Vazsonyi, & I. D. Waldman (Eds.), *The Cambridge Handbook of Violent Behavior and Aggression*. Cambridge: Cambridge University Press.

Farrington, D., & Ttofi, M. (2014). Developmental and Life-Course Theories of Offending. In H. Morizot & L. Kazemian (Eds.), *The Development of Criminal and Antisocial Behaviour*. New York: Springer.

Giordano, P. C., Cernkovich, S. A., & Rudolph, J. L. (2002). Gender, Crime and Desistance: Toward a Theory of Cognitive Transformation. *American Journal of Sociology, 107*, 990–1064.

Glueck, S., & Glueck, E. (1937). *Later Criminal Careers*. New York: Kraus.

Goring, C. (1919). *The English Convict*. London: His Majesty's Stationary Office.

Hazenberg, R., & Clifford, J. (2016). GECES and the Valid Measurement of Social Impact in the VCSE Sector. In R. Gunn & C. Durkin (Eds.), *Social Entrepreneurship: A Skills Approach* (2nd ed.). Bristol: Policy Press.

Hazenberg, R., Seddon, F., & Denny, S. (2014). Programme Recruitment & Evaluation: The Effect of an Employability Enhancement Programme on the General Self-efficacy Levels of Unemployed Graduates. *Journal of Education & Work, 28*(3), 273–300.

Hehenberger, L., Harling, A-M., & Scholten, P. (2013). A Practical Guide to Measuring and Managing Impact. Brussels, European Venture Philanthropy Association: 124. Retrieved from http://evpa.eu.com/publication/guide-measuring-and-managing-impact-2015/.

Hirschi, T. (1969). *The Causes of Delinquency*. Berkeley: The University of California Press.

Hirschi, T., & Gottfredson, M. (1983). Age and the Explanation of Crime. *American Journal of Sociology, 89*, 552–584.

Jain, P. (2018). *Conceptualising Social Value: Perspectives of the Public, Private and Third Sectors in the UK*. PhD Thesis, University of Northampton.

Maruna, S. (2001). *Making Good: How Ex-Convicts Reform and Rebuild their Lives*. Washington: American Psychological Association.

McLoughlin, J., Kaminski, J., Sodagar, B., Khan, S., Harris, R., Arnaudo, G., & McBrearty, S. (2009). A Strategic Approach to Social Impact Measurement of Social Enterprises: The SIMPLE Methodology. *Social Enterprise Journal, 5*(2), 154–178.

McNeill, F. (2002). *Beyond 'What Works': How and Why Do People Stop Offending?* CJSW Briefing (Paper 5).

McNeill, F., Farrall, S., Lightowler, C., & Maruna, S. (2012). *How and Why People Stop Offending: Discovering Desistance, Insights: Evidence Summaries to Support Social Services in Scotland* (Vol. 15). Glasgow: IRISS.

Millar, R., & Hall, K. (2013). Social Return on Investment (SROI) and Performance Measurement. *Public Management Review, 15*(6), 923–941.

Moloney, M., MacKenzie, K., Hunt, G., & Joe-Laidler, K. (2009). The Path and Promise of Fatherhood for Gang Member. *British Journal of Criminology, 49*(3), 305–325.

Nicholls, A. (2009). We Do Good Things Don't We? Blended Value Accounting in Social Entrepreneurship. *Accounting, Organizations and Society, 34*(6–7), 755–769.

Paterson-Young, C. (2018). *'Inspiring Futures' – How Social Impact Measurement as a Form of Organisational Performance Management Can Enhance Outcomes for Young People in Custody*, PhD Thesis, University of Northampton.

Sairinen, R., & Kumpulainen, S. (2006). Assessing the Social Impact in Urban Waterfront Regeneration. *Environmental Impact Assessment Review, 26*, 120–135.

Sampson, R., & Laub, J. (1993). *Crime in the Making: Pathways and Turning Points Through Life*. Cambridge, MA: Harvard University Press.
Soothill, K., Ackerley, E., & Francis, B. (2004). Profiles of Crime Recruitment. *British Journal of Criminology, 44*, 401–418.
Voltan, A., & Hervieux, C. (2017). Social Impact Assessment of a Community Engagement Initiative, *Paper presented at the 9th International Social Innovation Research Conference*, 12th–14th December 2017, Swinburne University of Technology, Melbourne.
Weber, M. (1978). *Economy and Society: An Outline of Interpretative Sociology*. Berkeley, CA: California University Press.

4
Health and Wellbeing

The social circumstances and experiences of children in custody are invariably marked by multiple and interconnected experiences with inequality and disadvantage. Such experiences impact on many facets of young people's lives, with health and wellbeing acknowledged as an area of significant concern (Khan 2010; Murray 2012; Hughes et al. 2012). Gunn (1999) outlined young people's experiences with health and wellbeing in prison:

> *Prisons collect [children] who find it difficult to cope, they collect excessive numbers of [children] with mental disorders, they collect [children] who have weak social supports, they collect [children] who, by an objective test, do not have rosy prospects. This collection of [children] is humiliated and stigmatised by the process of arrest, policy inquiry and court appearance. [Child] prisoners suffer the ultimate ignominy of banishment to an uncongenial institution, which is often overcrowded, where friends cannot be chosen, and the physical conditions are Spartan. Above all, they are by the process separated from everything familiar, including all their social supports and loved ones, however unsatisfactory. This is what is supposed to happen, and this is what the punishment of prison is all about.* (cited in HM Chief Inspector of Prisons 1999: 25)

C. Paterson-Young et al., *The Social Impact of Custody on Young People in the Criminal Justice System*, https://doi.org/10.1007/978-3-030-18422-3_4

Custodial environments are isolated from the outside world with services and interventions offered in a silo. The services and interventions initiated in custody inevitably cease on release, which means young people have to start the engagement process from scratch, resulting in barriers, delays and wasted resources. Khan (2010) argued that improvements to health and wellbeing achieved in custody are rarely sustained due to ineffective transitional services. The turnover rate for young people in custody creates problems for consistency and transitional care, with stability figures[1] in 2016–2017 ranging from 32% to 69%, with an average of 55%. Annually, this would equate to a turnover rate of six young people—with each placement filled roughly six times in a 12-month period. Thus, limited support is offered to address inequalities and disadvantage in custody, ensuring that the cycle of limited opportunity is repeated for young people upon release. The literature on the health and wellbeing problems experienced by young people in contact with the criminal justice system is abundant (see: Golzari, Hunt and Anoshiravani 2006; Fazel, Doll and Langstrom 2008; Kinner, Degenhardt and Coffey 2014), so to avoid repetition this chapter focuses on the mental health and wellbeing of young people in custody.

4.1 Health Inequalities for Young People Entering Custody

Health and wellbeing in the United Kingdom varies, with inequalities evident for specific groups in society (Public Health England 2017). Such inequalities exist in opposition to social justice, socially determining outcomes for individuals that they can often not control. These health and wellbeing inequalities disproportionately affect young people in custody, with research showing that young people in custody experience more problems with health and wellbeing than the general popula-

[1] The percentage of children and young people still accommodated in custody at the beginning of each month, as collected during the research study.

tion (Murray 2012; Hughes et al. 2012; Wright et al. 2016). Young people entering the STC experience health problems, including: oral health, vision, skin problems (i.e. eczema), weight (i.e. underweight or obese), respiratory illness (i.e. asthma), allergies (i.e. hay-fever, food allergies), diabetes and physical injury.

Research on the physical health needs of young people in custody is limited, with research typically focusing on mental health and wellbeing. Lader et al. (2003) found that young people commonly reported respiratory problems (10% for remand and 11% for sentenced) and musculo-skeletal problems (7% for remand and 4% for sentenced). This information was collected by Lader et al. (2003) by administering self-reported questionnaires with no evidence of physical assessment by health professionals cited. A more recent study (Chitsabesan et al. 2014) conducted in Youth Offending Institutes found physical health problems in 60% of young people, with the most common conditions related to vision (13%), oral health (12%), skin (12%), respiratory (11%), weight (11%) and genitourinary (10%). This study collected data from Youth Offending Institute physical health assessments, conducted by nurse practitioners, identifying that young people in custody commonly experience the conditions outlined above[2].

Research on the mental health and wellbeing of young people in custody, shows that they experience a higher prevalence of mental health difficulties, neurodevelopmental disorders and communication difficulties (Wright et al. 2016). Cross-sectional research (Chitsabesan et al. 2006) on the mental health, social and educational needs of young people, commissioned by the Youth Justice Board, found significant mental health needs for young people entering custody. Indeed, young people experienced depression (19%), anxiety (11%), substance use (11%), self-harm (8%) and alcohol issues (6%) (ibid.). Research with young people entering Youth Offending Institutes, found that 42% of young people experienced mental health needs (Lennox 2014). The mental health needs for young people were categorised as alcohol misuse (78%), substance misuse (73%), depression (7%) and anxiety disorders (3%). The

[2] Specific physical health needs (i.e. substance misuse) will be explored later in this chapter.

mental health and wellbeing needs of young people in custody are compounded by their backgrounds and experiences, characterised by abuse, bereavement, violence and substance misuse; with such experiences often resulting in trauma (Cohen et al. 2017). Some young people experiencing trauma will develop coping strategies that result in positive outcomes (for example, securing meaningful education); while some will develop coping strategies that result in negative outcomes (for example, involvement in offending behaviour) (Eaton and Paterson-Young 2018). The evidence of trauma for young people is difficult to ascertain due to the complexities of behaviour; however, by reading young people's accounts of their lives, the impact of childhood trauma becomes very apparent:

> *I don't have a dad though, well, I have a dad. He left years ago, before my little bro was born. He was a joke, he used to smack my mum up and stuff. He's lucky I never done him, if he came around now I would do him.* (Ethan, Young Person)

> *Dad's been in prison and mum has a ton of mental problems. When she was angry she would take her issues out on me.* (Del, Young Person)

> *I lost my mum years ago, I don't remember her much… I didn't really have a chance. I went to foster care and stuff, my brother stayed with my aunt but I was too much to handle. It's been a hard time but even my girl says I'm a strong person and I can get over it.* (Jack, Young Person)

Suffering or witnessing violence, having parents with mental health issues, or experiencing the loss of a parent can understandably negatively impact young lives. However, it is also important to note that some young people experience only limited and/or brief trauma symptoms either because of their stage of development, resilience and/or external support received (Cohen et al. 2017). Nevertheless, for children and young people experiencing prolonged exposure to abuse and/or bereavement, symptoms of trauma can endure (Cohen et al. 2017). Indeed, trauma impacts on young people's education, physical health, mental wellbeing, emotional regulation, life satisfaction and coping mechanisms (Layard 2005). The 'Beyond Youth Custody: Practitioner's guide on young offenders and trauma' (Wright et al. 2016), explains how the impact of trauma can hinder key adolescent developments; for example, being able to anticipate and consider consequences of behaviour. These are impacts that are easily linked to anti-social behaviour, such as impulsive aggression or emotional avoidance, which can contribute to criminal activity.

Experiences of trauma, coupled with social inequality, create challenges for coping with emotions and other aspects of daily life. Many young people (68%) entering the STC reported experiencing difficulties understanding and regulating emotions, and these difficulties are compounded in custodial environments (Zamble and Quinsey 2001). Zamble and Quinsey's (2001) research reported that over 300 individuals in custody described times of emotional challenges and difficulties preceding criminal activity. They found that recidivists were more likely to describe such feelings than non-recidivists, with 65% of recidivists describing times of emotional challenge and difficulty in the 48 hours preceding criminal activity (compared to just 11% of non-recidivists) (ibid.). These findings are consistent with findings from Hanson and Harris (2000), who found that recidivists were more likely to describe experiencing negative emotions in the time preceding criminal activity.

The isolation in secure environments and the intensity of confinement, rules and boundaries can hinder emotional regulation (Planalp 1999; Laws and Crewe 2016), compounded by the fact that many of the young people in custody have had adverse childhood experiences. Dealing with emotions is challenging for young people with adverse experiences, but for young people in custody, the challenges are vast. Research by Eaton and Paterson-Young (2018) found that young people use both positive mechanisms (such as problem-solving) and negative mechanisms (such as substance use) to manage such situations. Substance use is higher for individuals experiencing traumatic events (Lawson et al. 2013), illustrating the role substance use plays in helping young people to cope with traumatic experiences. Research exploring substance use as a coping mechanism is limited, with the available research exploring substance use in relation to sexual abuse (Harrison, Fulkerson, and Beebe 1997). The findings from research conducted by Harrison et al. (1997) show that young people experiencing abuse in childhood may start using substances earlier than non-abused peers, as a method of coping with the physical and emotional pain of abuse and they argue that substance use provides young people with an escape from their traumatic experience. This was evident from the research conducted in the STC, with young people referring to substance use as a coping mechanism, not only for coping with emotions and/or trauma, but also for coping with physical health problems:

> *Smoking calms me, I have smoked since I was... I don't know... young like. It helps me cope with stuff, like I have ADHD, it helps me cope with it. I can't have weed in here so I have meds... but... that makes me want to sleep all the time.* (Del, Young Person)

> *You know I smoke drugs, not like the drugs you are thinking off though, just weed. It's the only things I have ever done and I won't stop doing that ever. It helps me cope with all the bad in life. It keeps me cool.* (Liam, Young Person)

> *Well, mostly weed but I have smoked other stuff too. I like weed, it relaxes me but they don't let you have it here. I think it should be legal'cause some people need it, like me.* (Michael, Young Person)

Substance use for young people entering custody was high, with 87% of young people reporting substance use[3]. Participant responses (above) indicate both the "normalisation" of substance use (Parker et al. 1998) and the view of substance use as a coping mechanism. Parker et al.'s (1998) research showed that despite engagement with substance misuse professionals on arrival in custody, around half of young people (49.7%) were uncertain of how to access substance use services in custody, illustrating young people's confusion over the services available in the STC. This confusion could arguably relate to information overload on arrival and/or relate to young people's view of substance use as 'normal' (Parker et al. 1998). The self-reported questionnaire administered as part of the research project found that young people rarely recognised their substance use as problematic. Many young people (63%) did not view substance use as a problem, despite information in case files suggesting

---

[3] 100% reported using cannabis and 37% reported polydrug use. Polydrug use refers to the use of more than one drug.

otherwise. For those young people using substances as a coping mechanism, the STC have a responsibility to help young people find alternative coping mechanisms. This raises questions related to whether young people in STCs are receiving the correct support, and whether the support services available are offering trauma-informed approaches?

4.2 Health and Wellbeing for Young People in Custody

Reports of suicidal thoughts, attempted suicides and self-harm were higher in custodial environments than in the general population (Lader et al. 1997; Jacobson et al. 2010). In Jacobson et al.'s (2010) study, 20% of young people in custody reportedly self-harmed in comparison with only 7% of the general population. The research underpinning this book explored this issue in STCs, finding that 55% of young people reported incidences of self-harm or suicidal thoughts (Paterson-Young 2018). This number is higher than the number presented by Jacobson et al. (2010), which arguably reflects the vulnerabilities of young people in STCs and the increase in self-harm incidents generally (from 5.1% in 2012 to 12.5% in 2018) (Youth Justice Board and Ministry of Justice 2019). Indeed, figures show an overall increase in self-harm related incidents of 40% to nearly 1800 incidents, 535 of which required medical treatment; whilst the biggest increase during the last year has been in STCs, with a rise from 29 to 160 incidents requiring medical treatment (ibid.). Responses to incidents of self-harm and suicide attempts in secure environments revolve around managing the immediate concern, with limited exploration of the underlying trauma; trauma that is evident from the background and experiences of young people in custody.

Custodial environments play a central role in supporting young people to deal with their mental health problems (i.e. self-harm and suicide); and their past (traumatic) experiences to promote good mental health and wellbeing. The Health Survey for England (2015) utilises health and wellbeing measures with young people aged 13–15 years-old (NHS 2016), with such measures using questions such as "How satisfied are you with your life right now?" and "To what extent do you feel the things you do in your

Table 4.1 Descriptive statistics on life satisfaction ($n = 68$) [Scale 1–7]

	Mean
My life is just right	2.21 (32%)
I would like to change many things in my life	1.85 (26%)
I wish I had a different kind of life	1.90 (27%)
I have a good life	2.06 (29%)
I have what I want in life	1.85 (26%)
My life is better than most kids	1.94 (28%)
My life is going well	1.88 (27%)

life are worthwhile?". These questions measure life satisfaction, defined as the reflective appraisal of life experiences based on how well all aspects of life are and/or have been going (Argyle 2001). The Health Survey for England (2015) demonstrated that young people generally rated their life satisfaction as high. Indeed, the life satisfaction rates for young people ranged from 75% to 88%, with variations depending on age and gender (NHS 2016). Measures used in The Health Survey for England (2015) were adapted for our research in STCs to create a health and wellbeing measure for young people in custody. The mean of the overall satisfaction for young people participating in the research was 1.96 (7-point Likert scale)[4], indicating that young people in custody experience low-levels of satisfaction. Table 4.1 illustrates a breakdown of responses to life satisfaction statements for young people participating in the research.

Life satisfaction is influenced by a multitude of internal and external factors, such as relationships and social networks, secure accommodation, education or employment and mental and physical health (Argyle 2001; Layard 2005). The combinations of adverse experiences and low life satisfaction levels for young people in custody highlight the role of custodial environments in promoting health and wellbeing; not only in offering access to health services, but in supporting young people to achieve the positive outcomes that contribute to life satisfaction (e.g. the ability to cope with problems and difficult situations). Factors contributing to life satisfaction such as optimism, usefulness and managing problems were measured for young people in the STC in our research (see Fig. 4.1), with higher levels of optimism, usefulness and problem management associated with fewer health and wellbeing problems.

[4] Equivalent to a wellbeing score of 28%.

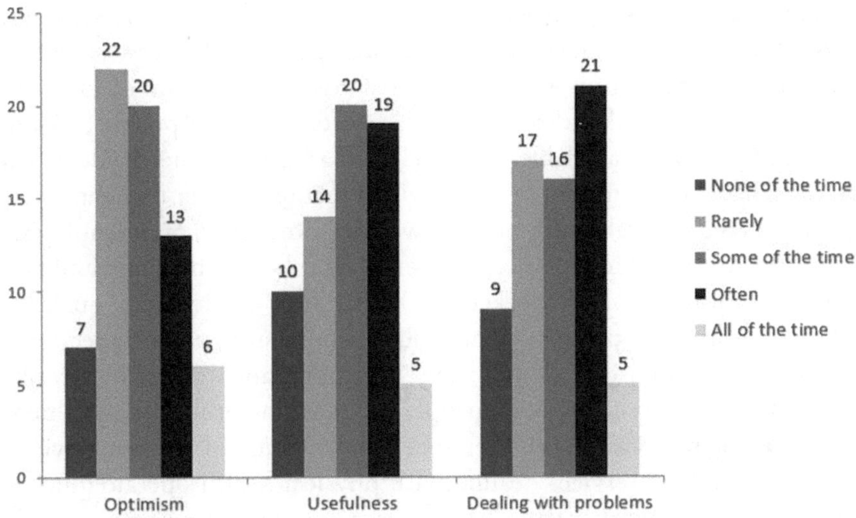

Fig. 4.1 Responses to factors associated with mental well-being (N)

When it comes to experiences of young people in relation to optimism and usefulness, those reporting positive relationships (non-criminal family and a home life free of abuse or violence) reported higher levels of optimism and usefulness ($p < 0.05$). This supports the claim that positive relationships impact affirmatively on life satisfaction. Similar results were noted for optimism and usefulness in relation to young people's satisfaction with education ($p < 0.05$) and their desire to continue with education ($p < 0.05$). The impact of trauma and arguably life experiences in general on young people, should be explored by practitioners to support young people to have life satisfaction and achieve positive outcomes.

4.3 Approaches to Health and Wellbeing in Custody

The health and wellbeing of young people in custody, compounded by social inequality and experiences of trauma, mean that custodial environments have a central role in developing trauma-informed practices for supporting young people. On entering custody, a qualified health care professional engages young people in a Comprehensive Health Assessment Tool (CHAT) (University of Manchester 2013). This assessment is reviewed in conjunction with medical records, with the aim of identifying both the physical and mental health needs of young people arriving in custody. Services available in the STC to address the needs identified by the CHAT were limited in 2017, with a locum psychiatrist employed, two registered mental health nurses, two part-time assistant psychologists and three substance misuse practitioners (one full-time manager and two 2.5 full-time equivalent workers) (Ofsted 2007). Although qualified mental health practitioners (and substance misuse practitioners) are employed, role-division limited the services available for young people. Furthermore, with many young people experiencing problems with mental wellbeing in STCs, there is therefore a higher demand on these services.

Conversely, the services dealing with physical health operate quickly, with the most recent Ofsted (2018: 1) showing that *"The dentist and GP offer a responsive flexible service which is symbolic of the good working relationship between the primary care partners…. needs are assessed promptly"*. Staff offering health care in custodial environments vary, with the STC researched here employing a core team consisting of: one Healthcare Manager, two Deputy Healthcare Managers, four Registered Mental Health nurses (RMNs) and two Registered General Nurses (RGNs). The Psychology and Substance Misuse provisions are offered separately to core Healthcare Services. Young people are able to self-refer for access to healthcare services, if required, receiving an initial consultation with the nurse. Staff and other professionals are also able to refer young people to healthcare services. The Ofsted (2018) report for the STC acknowledges improvements in the healthcare services offered, but with waiting lists demonstrating the requirement for additional psychology services. Overall, young people in the STC viewed healthcare provisions negatively, with only 39% of reporting that the provisions were good (Ofsted 2018).

Concerns over the health and wellbeing of young people in custody in England and Wales highlights the secure estate's responsibility for providing appropriate health and wellbeing services in custody. A recent Ofsted (2018) report commented on the delays young people have experienced in accessing services, which could be disastrous given the adverse experiences of young people. Staff working in the STC discussed the issues with healthcare and support provisions in custody, with one staff member arguing that:

> *…we are really tight on resources for psychology… I think if we had more people on the team then there would be a lot more that we could do with the young people. I mean I had a young person that was getting psychology support and it wasn't frequent support. And that's one thing, because we have to cut things and we have young people that are on shorter sentences, we have to prioritise them and he missed out.* (Sam, Staff Member)

Vulnerable young people in custody need help if they are to benefit from their time in the STC, the lack of psychological support mentioned by this member of staff is a hindrance to them and does nothing for their wellbeing. Staff recognised that shortages were damaging the young people in their care:

> *I don't think our service is big enough for the young people that require it, in short. I mean we have 80 young people and we have 1.2 psychologist or assistant psychologists if you like. And they are expected to do everything for everyone and their waiting list is as long as their bloody arm. So unfortunately for a lot of our young people who require interventions, our most complex kids that require the most in depth intervention can't get it.* (Naz, Staff Member)

> *I don't feel like we have enough in terms of resources in terms of staff. Because I think the psychology and substance misuse team is quite a small team in terms of the substance misuse issues and the psychology, kind of issues if you like, that we have in the centre.* (Pat, Staff Member)

This illustrates the concerns STC staff had about the available services, interventions and resources available for young people in custody. Centre staff outlined the challenges of providing support in practice, especially with the contractual obligations placed on secure providers:

> *…That's what these centres were set up for, the focus was on education. I mean if you have a young person who has horrendous drug issues, no amount of education, whether they are engaging here or not, will tick the boxes for them when*

> *they are outside because they still have the same issues, in the same environment with the same people tempting them with drugs. That's the problem, it's still focused on that education being the priority. And that's, I think, all of that, is why the STCs are completely failing.* (Jane, Staff Member)

> *We have like 80 or 90 kids in here and there is no way that the workers can see them all outside education. I think we need to give intervention staff the opportunity to take them out of education and do work with them. For some of these kids, interventions are more important than education—especially for the young people that have substance misuse issues or psychological issues.* (Val, Staff Member)

The adequacy of current provisions in the STC are questionable; however, there were plans to enhance the available provisions by employing additional staff members to deal with the complexities and/or vulnerabilities experienced by young people. Only time will tell if this additional recruitment positively impacts young people's custodial experiences and hence outcomes post-transition.

4.4 Summary

A plethora of literature on the health and wellbeing problems experienced by young people exists (Khan 2010; Murray 2012; Hughes et al. 2012), although literature on health and wellbeing with reference to trauma is limited. This chapter explored health and wellbeing with reference to trauma, offering new insights into the experiences of young people in custody. The health inequalities and experiences of young people prior to entering custody impact on the development of emotional regulation, coping mechanisms and life satisfaction. Custodial environments play a pivotal role in developing interventions and services to support young people to understand and address their health and wellbeing issues and how these impact on their future. Young peoples' experience of trauma in STCs, with restraint procedures mimicking experiences (both direct and indirect) of domestic violence, are explored in Chap. 6, but it is worth acknowledging that the STC environment, in some cases, plays a role in exacerbating trauma. In the event that custodial environments did offer services and interventions to support young people, transitional care would be required to ensure these were available on release.

Currently, services and interventions offered to young people in custody are withdrawn on release, essentially leaving young people to start the process again from scratch. Introducing appropriate services and interventions, with transitional care, would allow custodial environments to use a SIM framework to identify any outcomes and impact. Health and wellbeing inequalities, coupled with experiences of trauma, contribute to recidivism and desistance. Thus, offering appropriate services for young people is pivotal. Measuring the impact of health and wellbeing inequality is essential for developing effective and sustainable services. It would allow custodial environments, and other stakeholders (for example, the Ministry of Justice and the Youth Justice Board), to measure young people's experiences at arrival, release and post-release, to identify whether the services offered in custody result in any change. Understanding effectiveness in this area is critical to supporting young people to make positive transitions and to reduce recidivism.

References

Argyle, M. (2001). *The Psychology of Happiness* (2nd ed.). Hove: Methuen and Co.

Chitsabesan, P., Kroll, L., Bailey, S., Kenning, C., Sneider, S., MacDonald, W., Theodosiou, L., et al. (2006). Mental Health Needs of Young Offenders in Custody and in the Community. *British Journal of Psychiatry, 188*, 534–540.

Chitsabesan, P., Lennox, C., Theodosiou, L., Law, H., Bailey, S., & Shaw, J. (2014). The Development of the Comprehensive Health Assessment Tool for Young Offenders within the Secure Estate. *Journal of Forensic Psychiatry and Psychology, 25*, 1–25.

Cohen, J. A., Mannarino, A. P., & Deblinger, E. (2017). *Treating Trauma and Traumatic Grief in Children and Adolescents* (2nd ed.). London: The Guildford Press.

Eaton, J., & Paterson-Young, C. (2018). *The Little Orange Book*. Derby: Victim Focus.

Golzari, M., Hunt, S. J., & Anoshiravani, A. (2006). The Health Status of Youth in Juvenile Detention Facilities. *Journal of Adolescent Health, 38*(6), 776–782.

Hanson, R. K., & Harris, A. J. R. (2000). Where Should We Intervene? Dynamic Predictors of Sexual Offense Recidivism. *Criminal Justice and Behavior, 27*, 6–35.

Harrison, P. A., Fulkerson, J. A., & Beebe, T. J. (1997). Multiple Substance Use Among Adolescent Physical and Sexual Abuse Victims. *Child Abuse and Neglect, 21*, 529–539.

HM Chief Inspector of Prisons. (1999). *Suicide Is Everyone's Concern: A Thematic Review by HM Chief Inspector of Prisons for England and Wales*. London: Home Office.

Hughes, N., Williams, H., Chitsabesan, P., Davies, R., & Mounce, L. (2012). *Nobody Made the Connection: The Prevalence of Neuro-disability in Children and Young People Who Offend*. London: Children's commissioner.

Jacobson, J., Bhardwa, B., Gyateng, T., Hunter, G., & Hough, M. (2010). *Punishing Disadvantage: A Profile of Children in Custody*. London: Prison Reform Trust.

Khan, L. (2010). *Reaching Out, Reaching in: Promoting Mental Health and Emotional Well-Being in Secure Settings*. Centre for Mental Health. Retrieved September 28, 2017, from http://www.ohrn.nhs.uk/resource/policy/Reachingoutreachingin.pdf.

Kinner, S. A., Degenhardt, L., & Coffey, C. (2014). Complex Health Needs in the Youth Justice System: A Survey of Community-Based and Custodial Offenders. *Journal of Adolescent Health, 54*, 521–526.

Lader, D., Singleton, N., & Meltzer, H. (1997). *Psychiatric Morbidity Among Young Offenders in England and Wales*. London: Office for National Statistics.

Lader, D., Singleton, N., & Meltzer, H. (2003). Psychiatric Morbidity Among Young Offenders in England and Wales. *International Review of Psychiatry, 15*, 144–147.

Laws, B., & Crewe, B. (2016). Emotional Regulation Among Male Prisoners. *Theoretical Criminology, 20*(4), 529–547.

Lawson, K. M., Back, S. E., Hartwell, K. J., Maria, M. M., & Brady, K. T. (2013). A Comparison of Trauma Profiles Among Individuals with Prescription Opioid, Nicotine, or Cocaine Dependence. *American Journal on Addictions, 22*(2), 127–131.

Layard, R. (2005). *Happiness: Lessons from a New Science*. London: Penguin.

Lennox, C. (2014). The Health Needs of Young People in Prison. *British Medical Bulletin, 112*(1), 17–25.

Murray, R. (2012). *Children and Young People in Custody 2011/12: An Analysis of the Experiences of 15–18 Year Olds in Prisons*. London: HMIP/the Youth Justice Board.

NHS. (2016). *Health Survey for England 2015: Health, Social Care and Lifestyles*. NHS Digital and Office for National Statistics.
Ofsted. (2007). Establishing Successful Practice in Pupil Referral Units and Local Authorities. Retrieved from http://dera.ioe.ac.uk/6542/1/Pupil%20referral%20units%20establishing%20successful%20practice%20in%20pupil%20referral%20units%20and%20local%20authorities%20PDF%20format%29.doc.pdf.
Ofsted. (2018). *Inspection of Secure Training Centres – Inspection of Oakhill Secure Training Centre*. Retrieved October 1, 2018, from https://reports.ofsted.gov.uk/sites/default/files/documents/secure-training-centre-reports/oakhill/Oakhill%20STC%20June%202018%20report.pdf.
Parker, H., Aldridge, J., & Measham, F. (1998). *Illegal Leisure. The Normalization of Adolescent Recreational Drug Use*. London: Routledge.
Paterson-Young, C. (2018). *'Inspiring Futures' – How Social Impact Measurement as a Form of Organisational Performance Management Can Enhance Outcomes for Young People in Custody*. PhD Thesis, University of Northampton.
Planalp, S. (1999). *Communicating Emotion: Social, Moral, and Cultural Processes*. Cambridge: Cambridge University Press.
Public Health England. (2017). Health Inequalities: Reducing Inequalities in Local Areas.
University of Manchester. (2013). The Comprehensive Health Assessment Tool. Retrieved September 23, 2018, from http://www.ohrn.nhs.uk/OHRNResearch/CHATManualV32013.pdf.
Wright, S., Liddle, M., & Goodfellow, P. (2016). Young Offenders and Trauma: Experience and Impact: A Practitioner's Guide. Beyond Youth Custody. Retrieved from http://www.beyondyouthcustody.net/wp-content/uploads/BYC-Trauma-experience-and-impact-practitioners-guide.pdf.
Youth Justice Board & Ministry of Justice. (2019). Youth Justice Statistics 2017/18. England and Wales. Retrieved from https://assets.publishing.service.gov.uk/government/uploads/system/uploads/attachment_data/file/774866/youth_justice_statistics_bulletin_2017_2018.pdf.
Zamble, E., & Quinsey, V. L. (2001). *The Criminal Recidivism Process*. London: Cambridge University Press.

5

Relationships

One of the rungs on the ladder to successful resettlement is relationships; these can be positive or negative and include family, institutional staff and peer relations. The nature and quality of relationships can motivate young people to desist, successfully survive custody and positively transition upon release (Clancy et al. 2006; Maguire and Raynor 2006; Bateman and Hazel 2014). A lack of positive role models can be damaging to individuals, especially vulnerable and disadvantaged young people leading chaotic lives. Peer influence is a significant factor in decisions made by young people in relation to joining groups or offending (Young et al. 2007). Indeed, the importance of relationships is highlighted by research that demonstrates how young people in care want professionals who show genuine interest and concern, who listen, have open and honest dialogue and spend quality time with them (Fletcher 1993; Baldry and Kemmis 1998; Bell 2002; Morgan 2006; McLeod 2008).

Phoenix and Kelly (2013) completed research exploring the importance of relationships for young people in the Criminal Justice System, finding that young people wanted workers that 'care'. Research by HMI Probation (May 2016) on desistance highlighted the importance of several factors when it came to moving young people away from offending

C. Paterson-Young et al., *The Social Impact of Custody on Young People in the Criminal Justice System*, https://doi.org/10.1007/978-3-030-18422-3_5

behaviours, including 'professional relationships'. The research called for balanced, trusting and consistent working relationships with at least one case worker; as well as 'meaningful personal relationships' and a 'sense of belonging to a family' (ibid.). Research by NHS England (2017) with young people involved in the Youth Justice System reiterates this need for stable relations, illustrating how young people require practitioners who empathise with them and have the requisite skills to build trusting relationships with them.

Poverty also affects young people in a range of ways that can influence, both directly and indirectly, their peer relationships and offending. For example, they may live in deprived areas with poorer quality housing and schooling and be exposed to more anti-social behaviour, with crime being normalised (Young et al. 2007). Families living in poverty may suffer from increased stress, which can adversely affect health, schooling and relationships. In addition, a lack of positive male role models for boys has been linked to an increased prevalence of criminal behaviour (House of Commons 2007). Conversely, young people with positive relationships with their schooling and teaching staff are less likely to undertake criminal behaviour or carry a weapon (Aspy et al. 2004).

Family relationships are central to resettlement and require inclusion in young people's transition plans to education, training and employment (Hazel et al. 2016). This chapter will explore how relationships shape recidivistic behaviour, both prior to incarceration in an STC and the period residing in the STC. The discussion seeks to highlight the importance of relationship building, trust and reciprocity in assisting young people to navigate the transition to adulthood post-STC. The building of such relationships helps to empower young people and involve them in coproducing their own rehabilitation strategies and environments.

5.1 Relationships Prior to the STC

Relationships are critical to the development of offending behaviour in young people and are also critical in promoting desistance and reduced recidivism. Indeed, prior research has identified that poor familial relationships, delinquent influences (amongst peers) and negative educational experiences all contribute to increased risks of offending behaviour (Sampson and Laub 1993; Farrington 2005; Farrington and Ttofi 2014). The importance of these relationships in both promoting offending behaviour and in assisting offenders to desist, creates a tension in effectively supporting young people to reduce recidivistic behaviour. For instance, where pro-criminal family members have been a critical cause of offending behaviour in young people previously, it may not be appropriate to engage them in young people's rehabilitation, even though in the long-term strong and stable familial relationships could be a good thing for the young people (Hazel et al. 2016). This may be particularly difficult when seeking to empower young people in their own desistance programmes, as a young person may not recognise the negative effect that these relationships have on their behaviour [i.e. there is a power imbalance between the young person and the family member(s)].

This has been recognised by prior research including ICAP and Differential Association Theory, both of which recognise the impact that negative relationships, particularly with family members, can have on young people's recidivistic behaviour (Matsueda 1988; Farrington and Ttofi 2014). Within this research study young people within the STC were surveyed to understand the extent of their pro-criminal relationships prior to incarceration. The data demonstrates that pro-criminal relationships, particularly amongst peers, but also within family environments, contributed to offending behaviour. Furthermore, the data also revealed a statistically significant inverse relationship ($p < .05$) between pro-criminal relationships amongst young people and being sorry for the harm caused to their victim. Fig. 5.1 below outlines this:

Familial relationships are also critical in relation to exposure to negative experiences, such as domestic violence. These can be traumatic for young people and lead to reduced psycho-social functioning and a tendency towards higher tolerances as adults to violence (and ultimately violent behaviour) (Kitzmann et al. 2003; Holt et al. 2006). This can also have the knock-on effect of reducing wellbeing in young people, a critical factor in enabling them to envisage positive/optimistic futures and transitions to adulthood (Umberson and Montez 2010). Indeed, experiences of domestic violence, exposure to pro-criminal attitudes, or even just a lack of emotional and financial support from family members, can place

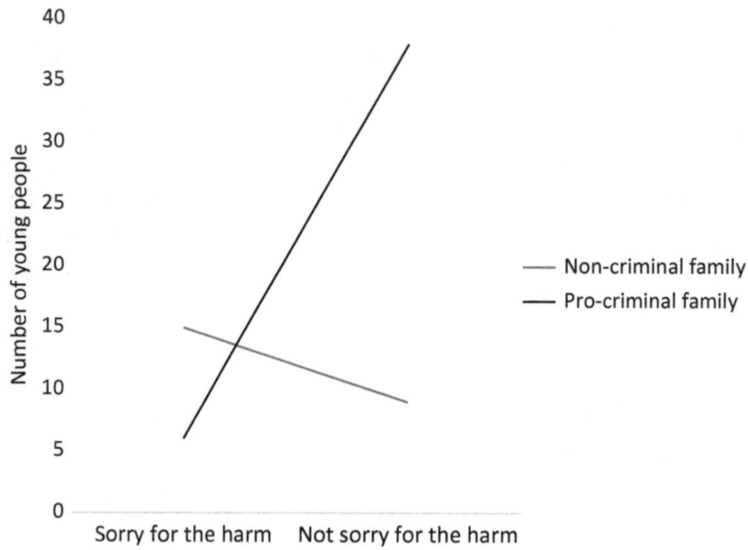

Fig. 5.1 Pro-criminal relationships and desire to apologise to their victim

young people in what Rogers (2011) states as a position of 'instant adulthood', where the gradual process of youth transition does not occur. This places pressures on young people that can manifest themselves in youth offending behaviours, or anti-social behaviours (i.e. exclusion from school). Given that in the STC, young people's experiences of significant relationships prior to incarceration are negative, it is critical to ensure that positive, stable and trusting relationships are developed during incarceration if reduced recidivism is to be achieved upon release.

Young people spoke about their familial and peer relationships in the interviews, with many of them having lived at home with their immediate families prior to incarceration:

> *My step mum, my dad, younger brother and step sister. I have a good relationship with my family, well, with my brother and step-sister.* (Faisal, Young Person)

> *I lived with my three brothers, sister and my mum. There are a lot of us at home, we have a small house. I got on with all my brothers and sisters, they are my family like.* (Zak, Young Person)

> *I lived with my mum, sisters and little brother before I came here. I got on with my family until this stuff happened.* (Liam, Young Person)

> *I used to live with my mum, I have three brothers and three sisters. There are a lot of us. I only lived with my little brother and sister before I come here. My other brothers and sisters are all older and own their own houses. We had a good relationship.* (Cam, Young Person)

> *I lived with my grandparents, it was fine there. They are strict though. I don't want to talk about my parents but I have brothers and sisters. I got one older one, my sister, then me, then my brother, then my sister and then my brother. There are a lot of us.* (Michael, Young Person)

The participants came from a range of family types, the vast majority reported living with single parent families, whilst others had lived with step-parent(s) or grandparents. All of the participants had larger than average families, with the smallest being three siblings and the largest seven siblings. Larger families have been linked in some studies (Ellis 1988; West and Farrington 1973; Farrington 1993) to increased criminal behaviour, with explanation for this including a lack of parental attention per child and/or household overcrowding. Some of the participants mentioned the positive nature of these relationships, *'I got on with all my brothers and sisters, they are my family'*, or *'I have a good relationship with my family'*. However, others were less positive, *'I had a dad…he was a joke…'*. Most of these relationships will have impacted the young people either positively or negatively and continuing relationships may also impact them upon their release. One of the young people interviewed had lived in a hostel due to bereavement:

> *I lived in a hostel, I think I should be going back there now. They haven't closed my hostel down and I should be going back to there. Which is brilliant…I lost my mum years ago, I don't remember her much and then I lost my dad… I didn't really have a chance. I went to foster care and stuff, my brother stayed with my Aunt, but I was too much to handle.* (Jack, Young Person)

Whilst the familial relationships for this young person had been lost due to bereavement, others had broken down due to their behaviour.

What is striking about the above account is the strong bond that the young person had made with the hostel, perhaps as it was the only constant variable in their home life prior to incarceration. Another participant had been disowned by his family because of his offending and hoped to live with foster parents on his release:

> *My mum and dad don't talk to me anymore because of the offending and other stuff. Mum just wanted to disown me anyway, she hated me. It's difficult at times 'cos my family hate me… I need foster care; I need parents to help me.* (Del, Young Person)

The desire for caring relationships and the feeling that this was needed came across very strongly. Clearly, for these young people, their connections/relationships (as part of their mesosystem[1]); whether with a hostel, their family or a foster family, were significant and would undoubtedly play a role in their successful resettlement. However, for those who had them, the relationships with biological family were also of great importance:

> *Mum visits me sometimes but my brother and sister can't get here so I never see them. I do wish I could see them more though, I miss them.* (Ethan, Young Person)

> *Mum visits me but it's hard cause of the kids and stuff. She tries. I don't really have anyone else in my life now. I wish I had people visiting all the times but life is life. It's difficult in here, I want to see the kids more, they are cool man and we are close but it's hard. I miss them.* (Neal, Young Person)

> *I miss them being in here, they come and visit me every 2 weeks but they can't come all the time. I don't want my younger brother to know I'm here so he never visits, he doesn't know what happened.* (Faisal, Young Person)

> *My family, cause like my mum's upset, it upset my mum and dad. They don't get to see me so much. I lived with my mum, my dad and my brothers and sisters.*

[1] This relates to Bronfenbrenner's (1979) theory that children develop not just by their familial environment, but due to wider environmental factors also.

There are a lot of us at home. I miss them cos I don't get to see them and stuff. It's hard because I'm in here now but I still speak to my family on the phone and they will visit me too. (Joe, Young Person)

Mum visits me but it's hard 'cause she works hard. It's hard, I don't see my brother though… my brother is locked up too… I wish I saw my brother 'cause we are close like, never apart. Now I never see my bro, he writes me letters but I hate writing letters. (P8)

The value of positive familial relationships and the sense of sadness from missing relatives was evident throughout the interviews. With many young people in custody having significant mental health needs and being some of the most vulnerable members of society, it is regrettable that they are unable to have more regular visits from family whilst incarcerated. The Beyond Youth Custody (2017) research has shown that resettlement plans need to help young people, by providing support to allow them to move forward and change the way they think about themselves. Family, wherever this is possible, can be an important resource, providing personal support to change within the home environment (Mulvey et al. 2004; Cid and Martí 2012).

When it came to friends, the relationships described varied, with many young people having friends that were also offenders and/or victims of crime and therefore unable to visit them:

I used to have a lot of friends, but some are no longer friends. One was killed by stabbing, he was a good friend…My gang friends are actually family, I mean some are my real family, like blood. I never see my friends though, they can't visit me here because of crimes. Some call me and write to me…It makes me feel wanted, makes me feel like I'm not rotten. (Mo, Young Person)

I have friends that come visit me here too, they need to be approved and my Youth Offending Team worker just approves them for me like. It's good to see my friends and family. (Zak, Young Person)

I have gang mates and other mates. Some are in for the same shit as me but some are free. I like my mates 'cos they know me, they understand me. If I do stuff they get me. (Neal, Young Person)

The desire to be liked and accepted, despite their crimes, makes friends a powerful influence. Research (BYC 2017) suggests that interacting with friends associated with their offending can help to reinforce the identity associated with crime, which may make desistance more challenging and recidivism likely. Some young people didn't see their friends because of their links to crime either through their own choice:

> *I had a good relationship with some of my friends, but some of them commit crime and stuff. Some I commit crime with and others I didn't. When I get out, I'm not gonna hang around with none of my friends.* (Cam, Young Person)

Or because of the intervention of the Criminal Justice System:

> *Most of my friends are involved in offending too, the same stuff as me. They can't visit me though, because they haven't been approved. They can't visit but it's not like I don't have criminal friends here, new friends that I made here. I still have a good relationship with my friends…I only have friends that get into shit too so they don't judge me for being here, it's cool with them like, honour man.* (Liam, Young Person)

> *I don't see friends much though or speak to them because you need them approved. They won't approve my friends, well my Youth Offending Team worker won't, and they don't approve people that have offended.* (Faisal, Young Person)

Research (Moore et al. 2013; Abrams 2007) shows that after release when young people return to their former environments, even if they are planning to desist, they can be vulnerable if they do not have a support network that extends beyond their former friendship groups. Romantic relationships were also mentioned by some young people as either a source of support:

> *I miss my girl and stuff. It's been a hard time but even my girl says I'm a strong person and I can get over it. I have just done that; I haven't cried or nothing. I have bettered myself, this, this has taught me so much. This experience has made me think I need to change my ways big time init. I have been with her (girl-*

friend) for a long time. I was 14 and she was 13. She messaged me in here and calls me. I used all my credit on her. (Jack, Young Person)

or the opposite:

I had a good relationship with my girlfriend, until it ended. I have hate for her like; she didn't support me so I'm done with her. (Mo, Young Person)

Weak social relationships and relationships with peers engaging in criminal activities are predictors for both serious and violent offending (Lipsey and Derzon 1998). If young people are to be supported to not offend or reoffend then developing and maintaining positive relationships, whether with family members or peers, must be part of the solution. For those young people in custody in the STC successful relationships with staff members are also vital.

5.2 Relationships in the STC

Creating positive and trustful relationships in custody is pivotal in supporting young people to desist from offending and to develop healthy relationships with family and friends upon release (Clancy et al. 2006; Maguire and Raynor 2006). The value of positive and trusting relationships cannot be underestimated, with research suggesting that it contributes to motivation and self-reflection (Partridge 2004). A key issue in custodial environments is the isolation from the outside world, which leads young people to lose links with family and friends outside. Creating opportunities for young people to maintain links with family and friends, helps to develop positive healthy relationships, which are pivotal for transition and effective resettlement (Hazel et al. 2016). Developing relationships in custody and upon release helps the family to support young people by promoting strengths and goals, stable foundations, personal identity, emotional support, and relapse recovery (Hazel et al. 2016).

Existing research on the role staff play in supporting young people to develop positive outcomes is limited. The majority of young people, participating in the research, reported positive relationships with staff (96%); however, these relationships were dependent on staff members' attitudes, as evident from the interviews:

> *Some staff I have good relationships with, but others I don't. Some don't believe in me, I speak slang and they are laughing at me. They think I have no chance of changing, it's obvious. I am different now but they don't notice, well some do but most don't. I listen to them and I want them to believe I will change. I'm not sure what to do, I end up asking myself questions. One day at a time. It's like, you don't know me and they don't pay you to care about me but you are listening and you are nice. They aren't nice sometimes, some are, but most, they just come and go and ignore us. They don't actually listen; they never really listen. They just judge me.* (Ethan, Young Person)

> *The staff are alright, they are friendly and nice and stuff…some are like, well, they come here and they go home and we are just a job. But some care… some speak to us and ask us what we want. It's nice to be asked what we want, feels like we aren't just criminals like.* (Joe, Young Person)

> *My relationship with the staff here is standard. We talk, no need to argue with them or anything. It's not like I'm going to trust them though, be honest like, they are here to do a job. It's only a job to them here and we all know it.* (Zak, Young Person)

> *Some of the staff are cool, like (name of staff member), she gets to know us and treats us like people. But some treat us like shit, like a job, I mean we are a job for them but they don't have to tell us that… But most staff don't trust you, even if you do nothing.* (Michael, Young Person)

The comments about staff being paid to be there and it being 'just a job' clearly highlight the insecurities and vulnerabilities of young people in the STC. Custody as has been acknowledged by many, including the Local Government Association's Young People Board (2017), as an environment that is unsafe for young people. One reason for this is that young people are being asked to trust and rely on a group of adults, who receive 12 weeks' training, with limited experience working with young people. After this training they are being asked to manage and care for, what one STC staff member described as young people who *'are dangerous and… scary at times'* (Karen, Staff Member). Clearly the training staff receive and the YJ system are not the most effective for rehabilitation if this is how staff and young people within it feel about one another. Perhaps more effective training, along the lines of Bjorgvin Prison (Kidson 2013), where staff are trained on the needs and rights of young people and are highly motivated to help them, would be more appropriate? Data from interviews with young people reveal that their relationships with some staff are more positive than others:

> *Some are cool man; they treat you like you're alright. But some treat you shit like, they just want to restrain and control you. If they don't respect me, I don't respect them. Like my dad man, some treat me like I don't matter, I matter. The ones that treat me nice, I respect them like, I don't give them shit. The ones that are cunts, I just give them shit until they leave. I like making them leave. We control the staff man; they think they control us but we control them. It's easy here.* (Neal, Young Person)

> *I like most of the staff but not all of them. I like the staff that are good man, but some treat you like you're bad. The staff that are nice, they speak to you like they like you, treat you like a man. I like those staff. Those staff help you stay out of trouble here like, some don't help you though, some expect you to fuck up. I hate it man. I have had stuff happen here sometimes, and the staff fucking grab you and treat you like a thug. They act like thugs too. They twist your arm up your back and restrain you. I hate it. I hate them. Some staff just talk to you and calm you down and it's fine. They don't restrain you. Other staff don't do that, they piss you off like and then restrain you. It's like they want to restrain you.* (Chase, Young Person)

> *I get on with some staff here, like staff on the unit. Some I get along with and some I don't. If they get alone with me then they will have a good shift, if they don't then I will make it hell for them. I have been restrained lots of times, for fighting, play fighting, and assaulting staff. Oh and for criminal damage and stuff. It hurts when you get restrained but you get used to it.* (Liam, Young Person)

Although young people report positive relationships, analysis of information available in STC case files shows that key staff members assigned to support young people change regularly. Indeed, young people receive support and interventions from an average of 4.1 members of staff, excluding the staff members assigned to units. This is the result of a revolving door of staff members, with case managers assigned to young people changing regularly. It is important to note that this cohort of young people have already had negative interactions with professionals in the Criminal Justice System (for example, police and courts), with experiences in the STC serving to strengthen these negative interactions. This creates a negative view of the Criminal Justice System which impacts on attitudes to offending.

Developing positive and trusting relationships in custody therefore, is pivotal in helping to change young people's attitudes to offending, thus promoting desistence. So, how can STCs develop these positive and trusting relationships? First, organisations need to establish the reasons for high staff turnover rates and deal with the problems to reduce disruption for young people (Whitebook and Sakai 2003; Ofsted 2017). Once the organisation has dealt with the problems, Hart (2015) recommends developing small living units, with holistic support offered to young people. Data from interviews with STC staff revealed some of their views on the young people and their relationships:

> *I think we should do a lot more work with families. And I say that because, if I am saying part of the issue is when they leave we are sending them back to the same environments, then the only way to try and tackle that a little bit is to bring some of the environment into the centre and try and unpick it. And support, not just the young person, but the parents or the carer or whoever…young people…don't understand the parent/carer view, it's that the parent/carer doesn't understand the young person's view. Sometimes we need to do that mediation to ensure that some of those relationships and understanding is clearer. I don't think we do enough of that work.* (Jan, Staff Member)

The value of positive and functional family relationships was highlighted by the above member of staff as being important to reducing reoffending. Another member of staff felt that there was little that the STC could do when it came to young people to going back out into the community and picking up with old connections/friendships:

> *Some obviously don't re-offend while others do re-offend. It depends on the person and depends if the person moves away from the area and starts again and others just go back to the area and fall straight back into the way they were. If they were in a gang, they might fall back into that and with friends that commit crime. Then, nothing can be done, if they are out there then there is nothing we can really do.* (Abi, Staff Member)

One member of staff described the impact of some of the interventions on their relationship with a young person and how the use of language and how staff interact with young people being pivotal:

> *I went to a conference not long ago…an ex-care kid did a speech…He advises people about language and interaction from his experiences of care. And I use it …I said to a YP, do you know who I am and he said, "yes you are the one that always tells me not to swear". Then I explained a bit more, and then he got very animated during his bit and telling me what was what. He said "fucking" and then he said, "I'm really sorry for swearing". To me, that's a very big thing, that he has associated me with that. I say we don't actually, in terms of nationally what people say we should be achieving, probably not. But there are those little things that are positive, and kids have formed really positive relationships with staff…for him, he had all that structure and relationships, probably huge amounts have been achieved for him but not things that people out there would say. In terms of his offending, have we stopped his offending behaviour, probably not, but I don't know if that's our faulty or the length of time he was here.* (Jane, Staff Member)

The importance of such small, but significant steps cannot be underestimated when it comes to building relationships that can have positive impacts on young people. Whilst such steps may not necessarily lead to reductions in reoffending, they can help reduce violence in the STC and help with staff motivation and retention; both of which are the key to developing a positive environment for young people.

5.3 Relationships Beyond the STC

The resettlement of young offenders is and has always remained a significant challenge when seeking to reduce recidivism, with the need to help shift the young people's identity away from one that is focused on offending to one that is more prosocial (Hazel et al. 2017). As was highlighted earlier in this chapter, the creation of prosocial identity is in part dependent on young people's relationships, and prior research has identified the role that 'supportive others' can have in leveraging positive outcomes post-custody (ibid.). These 'supportive others' should empower the young people to make better decisions in their lives, especially in relationships, and be part of a supportive environment that is critical to successful engagement and resettlement (ibid.).

The establishment of these supportive relationships occurs when the young people are first introduced to the STC, but continuity of relationships post-release and ensuring buy-in from the family of the young person are critical to ensuring that resettlement is successful and the young people desist from reoffending (Beyond Youth Custody, April 2017). When considering this alongside the social impact delivered by youth justice interventions, such relationships are critical to ensuring positive outcomes for the young people and hence fiscal savings to the state. Indeed, research into the costs and benefits of youth custody interventions demonstrates that positive social value is not created for society (at least in financial terms) until the young person is a significant length of time post-release (sometimes as much as 12 months). Data also shows that these can only occur if young people are empowered and supported through individualised resettlement plans (Liddle 2016).

Earlier in the book there was an exploration of how young people are disempowered in the Youth Justice System (Chap. 2), and how social impact measurement frameworks can be utilised to empower young people in their own rehabilitation (Chap. 3). The arguments presented in these chapters were focused around ensuring that young people were empowered and enabled to undertake social action within their own rehabilitative framework. This remains the central thrust of the arguments presented here, albeit there has to be acknowledgement that such empowerment can only occur through positive and supportive relationships. Indeed, fostering possible futures and opportunity amongst young offenders, especially in young women (Goodfellow et al. 2015), is essential to this process of empowerment through the 'relational factors' discussed within ICAP theory (Farrington and Ttofi 2014). Meaningful and long-term change in young people, and the decision to engage in 'social action' towards their own rehabilitation, must come from within (internalised change) (Farrington and Ttofi 2014), and this is enabled precisely by external factors such as positive relationships. Indeed, as Vaughan (2007) identified, the self-reflexivity required to desist from offending behaviours, occurs through an internal moral conversation that is mediated by relationships with others. This is part of the development of a prosocial identity that therefore empowers the young people (Hazel et al. 2017) and enables them to engage in Weber's (1978) positive social action.

When developing a social impact measurement framework for the evaluation of youth offending interventions, particularly those developed in STCs, it is therefore essential to embed the development of strong, stable and trusting relationships within the support offered. The creation of a rehabilitative environment therefore has to include relationships as the next level of need after health and wellbeing (see Chap. 8 for further discussion of our Resettlement Pyramid). Earlier in this chapter the role of negative relationships prior to incarceration (most notably pro-criminal family members and peers) was identified as a key enabler of offending behaviour (Sampson and Laub 1993; Farrington 2005; Farrington and Ttofi 2014), reflective of the young people's lack of empowerment in their home/community environments. Both ICAP and Differential Association theory identify the role that negative relationships have on young people's ability to engage in internalised change (Matsueda 1988; Farrington and Ttofi 2014; Maruna 1997, 2001). The development of positive, stable and trusting relationships within the STC and beyond custody during resettlement are therefore critical to reducing recidivism. Such relationships can help to mitigate the effects of negative relationships that the young people may reengage in after release. Indeed, earlier in the chapter the powerful effect of a young person's desire to 'fit-in' with friends and family who may be associated with their past offending behaviours was identified (Moore et al. 2013; Abrams 2007). The research and data reviewed in this chapter reinforces this message and demonstrates that only through the development of positive relationships can young people be empowered to take charge of their own rehabilitation. These positive relationships can provide the bulwark internally that allows the internal moral conversations identified by Vaughan (2007) to take place and endure, ensuring that young people can sustain their desistance from offending. This then provides the underpinnings required to allow further support around education and training (see Chap. 6) and independent living (see Chap. 7) to positively impact the young people's rehabilitation into society.

5.4 Summary

This chapter has identified how relationships are a critical enabler of reduced recidivism in young people that provide the next element of need within the Resettlement Pyramid beyond health and wellbeing. Developing and maintaining trusting relationships helps motivate and support young people to desist from offending, which in turn helps them achieve positive outcomes and effectively transition from custody (Partridge 2004; Clancy et al. 2006; Maguire and Raynor 2006; Hart 2015). These relationships are influenced by the development of pro-social relationships, addressing early childhood experiences such as exposure to domestic abuse, staff continuity and consistency and the identification of stable accommodation on release. Research shows that strong and supportive relationships aid desistance from offending, with Sampson and Laub (1993) suggesting that offending behaviour is influenced by poor family relationships, negative school experiences and delinquent influences.

A focus on young people's relationships within a holistic SIM framework that places the young people at the centre, acts as a powerful enabler of change, both within the STC (or other custodial environment) and beyond custody during resettlement. Positive relationships allow the young people to engage in internalised change (Farrington and Ttofi 2014) and to enable the self-reflexivity that is required to be able to resist negative influences and sustain desistance (Vaughan 2007; Maruna 1997, 2001). Only then can more context-specific support be offered (such as education, employment and training) and this will be discussed in the next chapter.

References

Abrams, L. S. (2007). From Corrections to Community: Youth Offenders' Perceptions of the Challenges of Transition. *Journal of Offender Rehabilitation, 44*, 31–53.

Aspy, C. B., Oman, R. F., Vesely, S. K., McLeroy, K., Rodine, S., & Marshall, L. (2004). Adolescent Violence: The Protective Effects of Youth Assets. *Journal of Counseling and Development, 82*(3), 268–276.

Baldry, S., & Kemmis, J. (1998). What Is It Like to Be Looked After by a Local Authority? *British Journal of Social Work, 28*, 129–136.

Bateman, T., & Hazel, N. (2014). *Youth Justice Timeline*. Retrieved from http://www.beyondyouthcustody.net/wp-content/uploads/youth-justice-timeline.pdf.

Bell, M. (2002). Promoting Children's Rights Through the Use of Relationship. *Child and Family Social Work, 7*, 1–11.

Beyond Youth Custody. (2017, April). *Lessons from Youth in Focus: Research Report*, Big Lottery Fund. Retrieved from http://www.beyondyouthcustody.net/wp-content/uploads/Lessons-from-Youth-in-Focus-Research-Report.pdf.

Bronfenbrenner, U. (1979). *The Ecology of Human Development*. Cambridge, MA: Harvard University Press.

Cid, J., & Martí, J. (2012). Turning Points and Returning Points: Understanding the Role of Family Ties in the Process of Desistance. *European Journal of Criminology, 9*(6), 603–620. https://doi.org/10.1177/1477370812453102.

Clancy, A., Hudson, K., Maguire, M., Peake, R., Raynor, P., Vanstone, M., & Kynch, J. (2006). *Getting Out and Staying Out: Results of the Prisoner Resettlement Pathfinders*. Bristol: Policy Press.

Ellis, L. (1988). The Victimful-victimless Crime Distinction, and Seven Universal Demographic Correlates of Victim Criminal Behaviour. *Personality & Individual Difference*.

Farrington, D. P. (1993). Childhood Origins of Teenage Antisocial Behaviour and Adult Social Dysfunction. *Journal of the Royal Society of Medicine*. 86.

Farrington, D. (2005). *Integrated Developmental and Life-Course Theories of Offending. – Advances in Criminological Theory*. New Jersey: Transaction.

Farrington, D., & Ttofi, M. (2014). Developmental and Life-Course Theories of Offending. In H. Morizot & L. Kazemian (Eds.), *The Development of Criminal and Antisocial Behaviour*. New York: Springer.

Fletcher, B. (1993). Not Just a Name: The Views of Young People in Residential and Foster Care. Who Cares? National Consumer Council, London.

Goodfellow, P., Wilkinson, S., Hazel, N., Bateman, T., Liddle, M., Wright, S., & Factor, F. (2015). *Effective Resettlement of Young People*. London: Nacro/Beyond Youth Custody.

Hart, D. (2015). Correction or Care? The Use of Custody for Children in Trouble. *Prison Reform Trust.*

Hazel, N., Goodfellow, P., Liddle, M., Wright, S., Lockwood, K., McAteer, L., Francis, V., & Wilkinson, S. (2016). *The Role of Family Support in Resettlement.* Beyond Youth Custody. Retrieved from http://www.beyondyouthcustody.net/wp-content/uploads/The-role-of-family-support-in-resettlement-a-practitioners-guide.pdf.

Hazel, N., Goodfellow, P., Liddle, M., Bateman, T., & Pitts, J. (2017). *"Now All I Care About Is My Future": Supporting the Shift – Framework for the Effective Resettlement of Young People Leaving Custody*, Beyond Youth Custody. Retrieved from http://www.beyondyouthcustody.net/wp-content/uploads/Now-all-I-care-about-is-my-future-Supporting-the-shift-full-research-report.pdf.

Holt, S., Buckley, H., & Whelan, S. (2006). The Impact of Exposure to Domestic Violence on Young People: A Review of the Literature. *Journal of Child Abuse and Neglect, 32*, 797–810.

House of Commons. (2007). Young Black People and the Criminal Justice System, House of Commons Home Affairs Committee, Second Report of Session 2006–07 Volume I. Retrieved from https://publications.parliament.uk/pa/cm200607/cmselect/cmhaff/181/181i.pdf.

Kidson, H. (2013). Reducing Recidivism Amongst Young People in Custody Through Welfare Lead Rehabilitation. Winston Churchill Memorial Trust. Retrieved from https://www.wcmt.org.uk/sites/default/files/migrated-reports/1189_1.pdf.

Kitzmann, K., Gaylord, N., Holt, A., & Kenney, E. (2003). Child Witnesses to Domestic Violence: A Meta-Analytic Review. *Journal of Consulting and Clinical Psychology., 71*(2), 229–235.

Liddle, M. (2016). *Resettlement Work with Young People: Using Individual Case-Studies to Assess Costs and Benefits*, Beyond Youth Custody. Retrieved from http://www.beyondyouthcustody.net/wp-content/uploads/Resettlement-work-with-young-people-using-individual-case-studies-to-assess-costs-and-benefits.pdf.

Lipsey, M. W., & Derzon, J. H. (1998). Predictors of Violent or Serious Delinquency in Adolescence and Early Adulthood, A Synthesis of Longitudinal Research. In R. Loeber & D. P. Farrington (Eds.), *Serious and Violent Juvenile Offenders: Risk Factors and Successful Interventions*. Thousand Oaks, CA: Sage.

Local Government Association. (2017). *Councils Call for Urgent Action to Improve Safety in Youth Offending Institutions*. Retrieved January 10, 2019, from http://www.beyondyouthcustody.net/wp-content/uploads/The-role-of-family-support-in-resettlement-a-practitioners-guide.pdf.

Maguire, M., & Raynor, P. (2006). How the Resettlement of Prisoners Promotes Desistence from Crime: Or Does It? *Criminology and Criminal Justice, 6*(1), 19–38.

Maruna, S. (1997). Going Straight: Desistance from Crime and Life Narratives of Reform. *The Narrative Study of Lives, 5*, 59–93.

Maruna, S. (2001). *Making Good: How Ex-Convicts Reform and Rebuild Their Lives*. Washington, DC: American Psychological Association Books.

Matsueda, R. L. (1988). The Current State of Differential Association Theory. Crime and Delinquency. Retrieved from http://cad.sagepub.com/cgi/content/abstract/34/3/277.

McLeod, A. (2008). 'A friend and An Equal': Do Young People in Care Seek the Impossible from Their Social Workers? British Journal Social Work, Advance Access, 1–17.

Moore, T., McArthur, M., & Saunders, V. (2013). Young People Talk About Transitioning from Youth Detention to the Community: Making Good. *Australian Social Work, 66*, 328–343.

Morgan, R. (2006). Young People and Offending (Foreword). In M. Stephenson (Ed.), *Young People and Offending – Education, Youth Justice and Social Inclusion*. London: Routledge.

Mulvey, E. P., et al. (2004). Theory and Research on Desistance from Antisocial Activity Among Serious Adolescent Offenders. *Youth Violence and Juvenile Justice, 2*(3), 213–236. https://doi.org/10.1177/1541204004265864.

NHS England. (2017). Just Health: An Enquiry into the Emotional Health and Wellbeing of Young People in the Youth Justice System, Peer Power Research. Retrieved from http://www.peerpower.org.uk/wp-content/uploads/2017/01/Just%20Health%20Report%20(for%20Web).pdf.

Ofsted. (2017). Inspection of Secure Training Centres – Inspection of Oakhill Secure Training Centre. Retrieved February 12, 2018, from https://reports.ofsted.gov.uk/sites/default/files/documents/secure-training-centre-reports/oakhill/OakhillSTC_January2017.pdf.

Partridge, S. (2004). *Examining Case Management Models for Community Sentences*. Home Office Online Report 17/04. London: Home Office.

Phoenix, J., & Kelly, L. (2013). 'You Have to Do it for Yourself' – Responsibilization in Youth Justice and Young People's Situated Knowledge of Youth Justice Practice. *British Journal of Criminology, 53*, 419–437.

Rogers, R. (2011). 'Instant Adulthood' and the Transition of Young People Out of State Care. *Journal of Sociology, 47*(4), 411–426.

Sampson, R., & Laub, J. (1993). *Crime in the Making: Pathways and Turning Points Through Life*. Cambridge, MA: Harvard University Press.

Umberson, D., & Montez, J. (2010). Social Relationships and Health: A Flashpoint for Health Policy. *Journal of Health and Social Behavior, 51*, S54–S66.

Vaughan, B. (2007). The Internal Narrative of Desistance. *British Journal of Criminology, 47*, 390–404.

Weber, M. (1978). *Economy and Society: An Outline of Interpretative Sociology*. Berkeley, CA: California University Press.

West, D. J., & Farrington, D. P. (1973). *Who Becomes Delinquent?* London: Heinemann.

Whitebook, M., & Sakai, L. (2003). Turnover Begets Turnover: An Examination of Job and Occupational Instability Among Child Care Center Staff. *Early Childhood Research Quarterly, 18*(3), 273–293.

Young, T., Fitzgerald, M., Hallsworth, S., & Joseph, I. (2007). *Groups, Gangs and Weapons*. London: Youth Justice Board.

6

Education

Recent government policy on youth custody places education at the centre. Currently however, outcome measures for youth custody focus solely on reoffending rates with limited data available on achievements or qualification gained through education. Education in custody is provided by several organisations, including: schools, academies, colleges, commercial companies and charities. The Youth Justice Board are responsible for commissioning education in custody and the Department for Education are responsible for the education of children leaving custody. Young people in the Youth Justice System have often been excluded from school or have missed time through truancy as a result of this lack of engagement, and because many of them also have learning difficulties and come from disadvantaged backgrounds, the literacy and numeracy levels of many of those in youth custody are far below average. Educational establishments (including nurseries) are a crucial element in solving youth recidivism. In this chapter, the responsibilities of schools and the Youth Justice Board in relation to young people are reviewed, alongside an examination of the educational backgrounds of young people in custody. The chapter concludes by making recommendations for improvements, alongside a

C. Paterson-Young et al., *The Social Impact of Custody on Young People in the Criminal Justice System*, https://doi.org/10.1007/978-3-030-18422-3_6

framework for educational provision in STCs that could lead to more positive outcomes for young people.

6.1 What Responsibilities Do Schools Have in Relation to Young People and Exclusions?

Schools have a statutory duty (DfE 2017b; DfE 2018a) not to discriminate against students on the basis of characteristics such as race or gender and are asked to give particular consideration to students who are vulnerable to exclusion, such as those with SEND or LAC. However, government statistics (DfE 2018b) demonstrate that school exclusions disproportionately affect boys, young people with SEND, those receiving FSM and BAME groups. The guidance stipulates that *'disruptive behaviour can be an indication of unmet needs'* (DfE 2017b: 6) and schools should consider a multi-agency assessment. The figures for Permanent and Fixed Period Exclusions in England 2016–2017 showed that the number of permanent exclusions had increased from 6685 to 7720, with 83%, of these being in secondary schools. In the same period the number of fixed-term exclusions also increased in secondary schools increased (270,135 to 302,890) and in primary schools (55,740 to 64,340) (DfE 2018b). There were several demographic characteristics linked with these exclusions including:

- **Age:** over half of all exclusions were for those in Year Nine and above.
- **Gender:** boys were over three times more likely to receive a permanent exclusion.
- **Socio-economic status:** students eligible for FSM were four-times more likely to be excluded
- **SEND:** students with identified SEND made up almost 50% of all excluded students and were seven times more likely to be excluded than those without a SEND
  - those with an Education, Health and Care Plan were six-times more likely to receive a fixed-term exclusion.

- **Ethnicity:** Black Caribbean students were nearly three times more likely to be permanently excluded than the school population as a whole[1].

Date gathered from (DfE 2018b)

It can be argued that the above differences are related to the marketisation of the English school system that has occurred from 1988 onwards (Education Reform Act), which has seen parents increasingly treat schooling as a commodity. Indeed, Evans and Vincent (1997) suggested that social class differentials affect how parents are positioned within the market as 'competent/incompetent' consumers, which then translates into children being 'desirable/undesirable' customers for schools. Children can be seen as commodities with varying market value, and children with certain SEND, such as behavioural, emotional and social difficulties, could be seen as less desirable.

This marketization has created fundamental tensions in education, with schools and teachers trying to meet the conflicting demands of the 'standards agenda' (Barton 1998; Gewirtz et al. 1995) and educational inclusion. This leaves the families of children with SEND struggling to find schools that fit their child's needs, which becomes increasingly difficult in secondary school, where many parents of children with SEND are unhappy with provision (Bajwa-Patel and Devecchi 2014). Harris and Ranson (2005) asserted that this marketization of education was very likely to increase inequality and decrease social mobility for young people from disadvantaged communities, as schools showed preference to those students who they believe are more likely to improve their performance in the league tables (Gorard et al. 2003). This view is supported by Runswick-Cole (2011) who found that schools were falling short in their efforts to include children whose achievement/behaviour does not meet the standards that schools require in order to meet academic attainment targets. This raises the question as to whether young people from low socio-economic backgrounds, poorer academic attainment levels and/or

[1] Gypsy, Roma and Irish Traveller pupils have the highest exclusion rates of all pupils, but are not included here as the DfE report states that the sample-size for these populations is too small and therefore potentially not reliable.

SEND are being failed by the education system and therefore disproportionately over-represented in our youth custody system?

6.2 What Place Education?

The risk factors for youth offending and wider issues of anti-social behaviour are similar to those for educational under-achievement (Rutter et al. 1979; Farrington 1996). Research has shown that the quality of teaching and organisation within a primary school is more significant as an explanation of differences in the educational progress of young people than characteristics such as social background (Mortimore et al. 1988; Sutherland et al. 2005). Research commissioned by the Youth Justice Board (2005) highlighted that educational achievement was the second most prevalent risk factor identified for youth crime. The report (ibid) reflects on the fact that educational under attainment is much more common in disadvantaged areas. Another factor that can increase offending risk are school changes and moves; indeed, even moving between schools at normal transition points can have a negative impact (Youth Justice Board 2005).

Research shows that children from disadvantaged backgrounds show the greatest benefits from having high-quality pre-schooling (Lazar et al. 1982; Rutter 1985; Sylva et al. 1999) and investment in high-quality early years' education has positive effects for children from across the socio-economic spectrum (Dodge et al. 2016). Mixing with and learning to play with other children at pre-school age helps develop communication and social skills that last into adolescence and beyond. The impact of education policies on crime rates has been researched by many (see: Lochner and Moretti 2004; Machin et al. 2010; Gallipoli and Fella 2007; Meghir et al. 2011).

Heckman's work (2006) on early childhood development shows that high-quality (birth to five years) educational provisions for disadvantaged children, can deliver a significant return on investment through positive impacts on a range of areas including drug use, crime, years spent in education and income. The 2006 Youth Justice Board report (Engagement in Education, Training and Employment), lists a range of specific programmes, which can reduce risk factors, including pre-school education, family literacy and reading schemes. The evidence on risk factors is considerable and suggests that young people offend for a variety of often complex reasons. For this reason, society can only meet the needs of these young people and hope to reduce reoffending through a complex response, which must always include education. McNeil (2006) focused on a desistance-based approach to advocate that effective engagement in education and training as a key factor in reducing recidivism, a point supported by the Taylor (2016) review. The review highlights the fact that many young people in the Youth Justice System have missed a great deal of schooling through truancy and exclusion, which means the literacy and numeracy levels of many of those in youth custody are at the levels of a 7–11-year-old (Ministry of Justice 2013). Indeed, the Youth Justice Board (2006) report found that many of the young people in custody were struggling to access full-time education and training.

Social exclusion and crime often have their roots in exclusion from school. Indeed, BAME, LAC and FSM students are more likely to be excluded from education and to be over-represented in the Youth Justice System. Clearly, the link between youth justice and education is not straightforward, with some researchers (Watt et al. 2004; Rutter et al., 1998) arguing that disengaging with education is a significant factor when it comes to anti-social behaviour and recidivism. The Taylor Report (2016: 3) stated categorically that *'schools and colleges are crucial in preventing offending'*, whilst Morgan (2006), argued that educational policy was more important than sentencing in preventing crime. Nevertheless, the relationships are complicated (Utting 1996), with Moffitt (1993) arguing that offending behaviour can interrupt learning.

What cannot be disputed however, is the overwhelming evidence that young people in the Youth Justice System in England and Wales deprived in society and educationally (Lanskey 2011). Indeed, statistics (MoJ and DfE 2016) on the levels of under-achievement of young people in custody aged 10–17 years and at Key Stages Two and Four, are both concerning and inexcusable. However, achievement is not the only area where young people fare poorly in our schools; the figures on persistent absence (absent from more than 10% of total available school sessions) from school or permanent exclusions are equally poor. The numbers of young people sentenced to less than 12 months in custody who were looked after (i.e. in the care of the local authority) was 27% (MoJ and DfE 2016). Finally, young people eligible for Free School Meals (FSM) are three-times more likely to have SEND (for young people sentenced to less than 12 months) (44%), when compared with the overall school pupil population at the end of Key Stage 4 (15% have SEND) (MoJ and DfE 2016).

6.3 Exploring the Current Youth Justice Board/Ministry of Justice 2016/17 Statistics

In 2016/2017 there were 74,800 arrests of young people (aged 10–17 years) by police in England and Wales, with a total of 870 young people in custody at any one time (Youth Justice Board and MoJ 2018). Whilst the number of young people who receive a caution or sentence has dropped dramatically over the last ten years, the proportion of young people in custody for more serious offences (e.g. murder, sexual assault, possession of a weapon) has continued to increase. Furthermore, young people from a BAME background made up 28% of the arrests, compared to the same group making up only 18% of the 10–17-year-old population; whilst BAME young people in custody accounted for 45% of the custodial population. Males were over-represented in the number of arrests of young people, accounting for 84% of arrests (Youth Justice Board and MoJ 2018).

The following section uses data from young people sentenced in 2014 (Youth Justice Board and MoJ 2018). When it comes to different types of sentences, those young people sentenced to custody rather than given Youth Rehabilitation Orders (YRO), Referral Orders (ROs) or Cautions had lower Key Stage 2 (KS2) attainment levels. Figure 6.1 highlights KS2 attainment for those young people with shorter custodial sentences (i.e. less than 12 months), with 47% achieving this in maths, 56% in reading and 28% in writing. Those young people with sentences longer than 12 months had slightly better achievement, with attainment levels of 52% for maths, 58% for reading and 33% for writing.

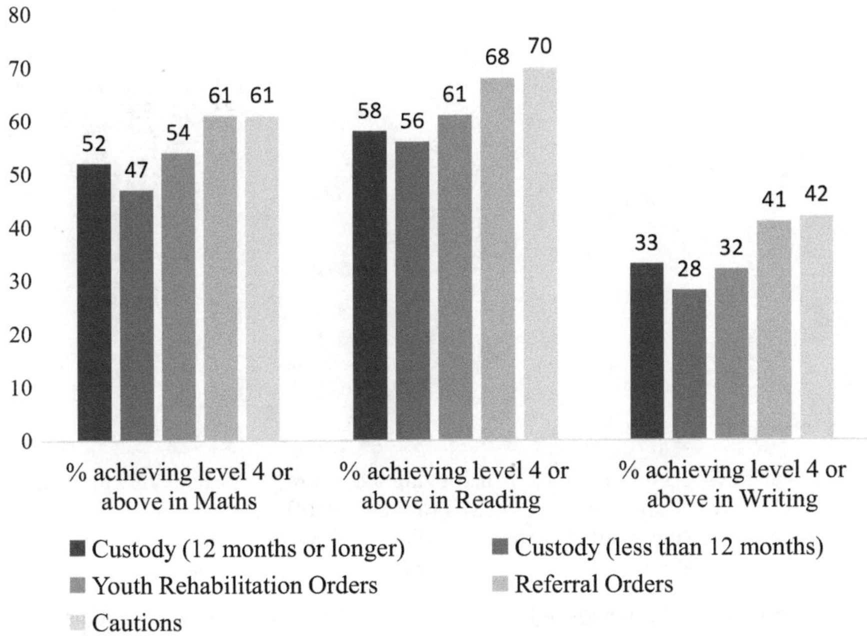

Fig. 6.1 KS2 attainment of matched young offender cohort sentenced in 2014, based on data from the Youth Justice Board and MoJ (2018)

6.4 Why Do Young People in Custody Score So Much Lower at KS2?

For those young people sentenced in 2014, whom were at the end of Key Stage 4 (KS4) in the academic year 2012/13, they were also less likely to have attained the KS4 performance measures than the overall pupil population. Those given custodial sentences had lower attainment at KS4 than those who were given community sentences or cautions. Only 1% of those sentenced to less than 12 months in custody achieved 5 or more GCSEs (or equivalent) graded A∗-C (including English and Maths). For those given Referral Orders the equivalent figure was 14%; whilst for Cautions it was 17%. Figure 6.2 shows that at the end of KS4, across all three measures ('Any Pass', 5+ GCSE A∗-G and 5+ GCSE A∗-C), those receiving custodial sentences of less than 12 months had the lowest

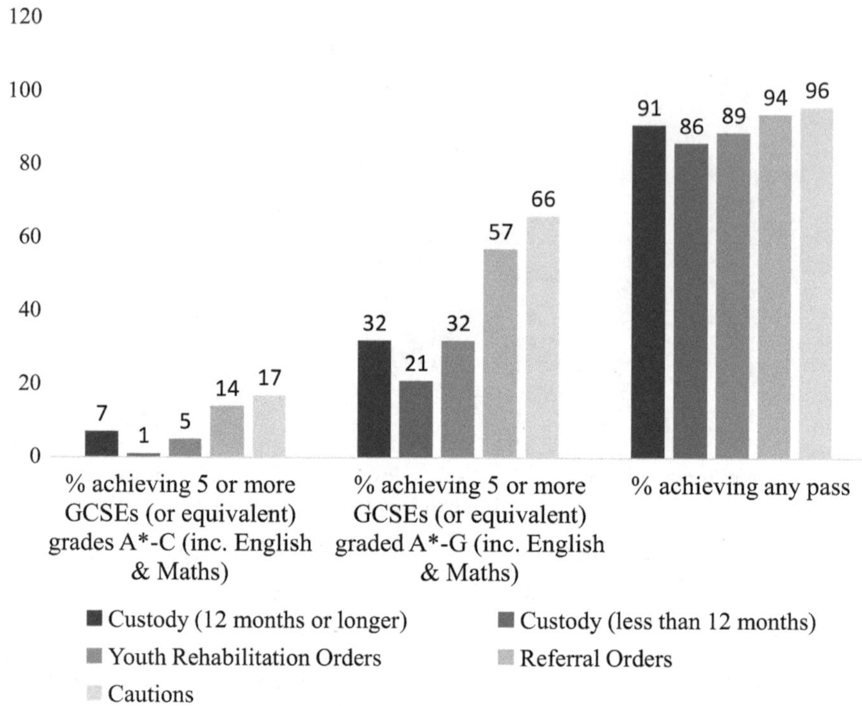

Fig. 6.2 Key Stage 4 Attainment for 2014 matched young offender cohort by youth justice disposal type at the end of Key Stage 4 in academic year 2012/13

attainment. In the 'Any Pass' category the difference between the custodial group and the general pupil population is 13.7%, in the 5+GCSE A∗-G category the difference is 70%, and in the 5+ GCSE A∗-C the difference is 58%.

Table 6.1 below summarises the statistics on young people given custodial sentences or YROs in 2014 (YJB and MoJ 2018). The aim of the project was to improve understanding of the educational background and demographics of young people sentenced in England and Wales. The results reveal that young people have below average attainment, are from a deprived socio-economic background, have special educational needs (often undiagnosed), and that they may have been excluded from school. This reveals a group of young people who have fallen through the social care/education net and ended up in trouble or in custody.

Table 6.1 A summary of the educational backgrounds and characteristics of young people sentenced across England and Wales in 2014

Demographic Variable	Overall proportion of 16–17-year-olds in general population[1] (%)	Young people sentenced to <12 months in 2014 (end of KS4 in 2012/13) (%)	Young people sentenced to >12 months in 2014 (end of KS4 in 2012/13) (%)	Those sentenced, to YROs in 2014 (end of KS4 in 2012/13) (%)
Free school meals	No comparison data	44	44	40
SEN (without a statement)	17	45%	46	46
SEN (with a statement)	4	28	21	22
School exclusion—Permanent	No comparison data	23	16	19
Looked after children (LAC)	1	27	31	19

Based upon ONS (2014) data

Whilst the figures above provide the broad background to young people in the youth estate, the education and backgrounds of the young people in the STC in this research are also relevant. Analysis of the case file information revealed that a high proportion of those young people participating in the STC research (83%), had ceased attending their specific educational establishments prior to their arrival in custody, with over 36% having left education 12 months beforehand. Those young people in the STC who would be seen as NEET (not in education, employment or training) was nearly 34% versus an overall NEET level of 11% (ONS 2017). Of those young people who did attend education before their arrival at the STC, nearly 34% attended full-time education and the remaining 66% attended part-time. Case file analysis of the young people in the STC, revealed that just under 43% of the young people at the STC had a documented SEN statement or EHCPs, compared to 4% of the population with a statement or EHCP at the end of KS4. There is therefore little doubt that the statistics on the young people in the STC show a complete failure of our educational systems to nurture and educate some of the most vulnerable young people in our society.

The interview data gathered from participants in the STC, provides further insights into the views of young people in the STC towards education. Unsurprisingly, many of those interviewed were negative about their previous mainstream and alternative provision educational experiences:

> *I have been out of education for about 2 years. I was permanently excluded when I was 14 years. I have been excluded from education, college and the PRU. The PRU is like a college thing with lots of idiots. I think education is boring, I don't like education at all.* (Mo, Young Person)

> *No education for like 3 years, I chose to leave but I have been kicked out of 4 different schools and the PRU*[2] *and stuff.* (Liam, Young Person)

> *I never really went to education before man, I was kicked out. The first time I was kicked out for fighting man, smacking people up like. They sent me to a PRU but I hate it so never went. I have been sent to loads of different things like, waste of time. None of them are good. Teach you rubbish man.* (Neal, Young Person)

Participants had missed years of schooling and had low opinions of the schooling that they had received, especially in the Pupil Referral Unit. Government statistics show that 35 students are permanently excluded from school each day (DfE 2017a). Persistent disruptive behaviour is the most common reason for such exclusions, followed by physical assaults. Many of the young people excluded from schools have complex needs and/or they may face additional barriers in their lives, such as family problems, being in a gang, risk of abuse or harm, and mental ill health or poverty. Alongside official exclusions, which are recorded, many young people are also 'unofficially excluded' each day, some as 'managed moves' (where a student is moved to another school), others through alternative provisions or 'off-rolling' (where parents are encouraged to home educate their children). When official exclusion figures (DfE 2018) are compared to local authorities' census data on alternative provisions there is a huge discrepancy, with five-times the number of students in alternative provision than recorded as officially excluded. The quotes from the young

[2] Pupil Referral Unit.

people above indicate that the alternative provision, in their cases PRUs, were clearly unable to meet their needs and resulted in further exclusions and eventually youth custody.

> *I got kicked out of secondary school and two units (PRU), I was home schooled in the end. It's all a circle you know, you get kicked out of school and have nothing to do. You end up committing crime because you have nothing to do, you get bored, and then you end up here…* (Faisal, Young Person)

Faisal ended up being home-schooled, which is often 'elected' as the only route left to desperate parents. The Association of Directors of Children's Services estimated that the total number of home educated children in England in 2017 was 45,500, an increase of 21% on the previous 18 months (House of Lords 2018). The reasons behind this increase are complicated, but the marketization of education along with cuts to support staff can both be seen as contributory factors. There is very little regulation of Elective Home Education and consequently no data on educational attainment or socio-economic progress of those young people (Casey 2016). Clearly for Faisal, home-schooling did not engage him sufficiently and consequently he ended up 'committing crime'.

Another alternative for some young people when it comes to education (either after or as an alternative to exclusion), is attending a special school. Indeed, with 43% of the young people having SEN statements or EHCPs, it is not surprising to find some attended special schools. Statistics from the Department for Education (2018c) show that from 2010 onwards there has been a year-on-year increase in young people with a statement or EHCP attending special schools (4.2% in 2010 to 6.3% in 2018). The types of special schools vary and for some young people they do not fit very well. Indeed, research by Bajwa-Patel (2014) shows that many families face the dilemma that the school that will fit their child's needs best, simply does not exist. As the quote below indicates, this young person did not feel that the special school they were in suited them:

> *I went before, a long time ago and it was boring, you never did anything interesting. I went to a special school with all these stupid kids, I ain't stupid, I just don't like school. So I left.* (Michael, Young Person)

Being excluded from educational establishments, often several times, is clear evidence of a young person in crisis and the consecutive failures of a range of educational facilities. As Ofsted (2007: 7) reported, PRU staff, *'frequently saw an educational 'fresh start' or 'second chance' as a core part of their purpose…PRU leaders saw as vital an appropriate curriculum that emphasised the necessary basic skills to help pupils overcome barriers to learning'*. The comments above highlight that for these young people the PRU was not a second chance and failed to provide them with an education that they felt was relevant. However, despite many of the young people interviewed having such negative experiences in education, some of them were positive about learning and wanted more vocational and relevant education in the STC:

> *I would like to learn how to work with cars here but they don't do it. I do learn English and maths, it's alright.* (Neal, Young Person)

> *In Hair and Beauty, we learned how to do plaits, which is cool 'cause I never knew how to do plaits before that. Its good cause they teach you in this class, I like it learning the Hair and Beauty stuff…I have done some stuff here though have a painting and decoration qualification, oh and food tech and functional skills too. But other than that, I haven't done any qualifications yet. I do like learning though.* (Ethan, Young Person)

> *I do the vocational stuff like wallpapering and hair and beauty. I like those, they are more practical and stuff.* (Cam, Young Person)

> *I want a qualification for working with cars but we don't have these here. That would help me the most.* (Chase, Young Person)

Such comments suggest that if education was made more relevant, less young people would disengage whilst achieving better outcomes, and there would be less persistent absences, fewer exclusions and reduced underachievement. For some young people, their views on education had changed because of the education they received in the STC:

> *I never went to education, mum used to try and force me to go but I would just leave. I think education is pointless man, I tried but the teachers are stupid…I*

like hair and beauty…We learn stuff and it's not all about maths and shit. I want more vocation stuff, I like practical stuff. I have done good since being here, I have passed exams and have maths and food qualifications like. (Chase, Young Person)

Education is good in here; I am doing my exams at the moment. They are going ok like I hate exams though. The art exam was 5 hours, 5 hours of drawing. I'm good at art but 5 hours is a long time for an exam. (Del, Young Person)

Getting back into education, it's shown me how much I missed education. (Jack, Young Person)

Some of the participants were making the most of the opportunities they had in the STC, as they felt that education, even when it was difficult, was worth trying at. Indeed, subjects such as maths, food and art were mentioned positively in many interviews. Research by McCrone and Morris (2004) suggests that vocational qualifications are important for young people aged 16–17 years-old, as they also help build their self-esteem and identity. However, not all the participants' comments were as positive about the education in the STC:

You do more work on the unit that you do in education. You don't do anything here, you colour man, what's the point in that, I don't learn nothing doing that, nothing at all. I'm not a fan of education. (Zak, Young Person)

I like education, the education here isn't very good. Because it's just, I wouldn't even count it as education really, it's like, you go to a lesson and the teacher will turn up like 20 minutes late and you're just there colouring. I am expecting to go into A-levels now and I'm sitting here colouring in, I'm not even revising. My GCSEs were alright until I got here, because I never had my glasses for three weeks. I couldn't see without my glasses. I finished my GCSEs just as I got my glasses. I was struggling, and I couldn't read what I was looking at. (Cian, Young Person)

The negativity of these comments about education in the STC gives an indication of the uphill battle that can epitomise education in custody. Young people who have had poor experiences and outcomes, often in mainstream schooling and alternative provision, are unlikely to suddenly switch on to the educational opportunities that may be available to them (especially when incarcerated). Those young people with the literacy and numeracy levels of a child 7–11 years old (Ministry of Justice 2013), who make up most young people in custody, will have built up walls of distraction techniques and defences against teachers and education. Getting past these barriers remains a significant challenge for educators and social workers. This was an area that was recognised by the STC staff:

> *I don't think that they learn enough, if I'm perfectly honest. I don't think that they learn what they need to be learning. I mean you got young people doing GCSEs but these young people aren't being pushed. You have young people that could do so much more and they just don't have the facilities to push those 8 individuals (one classroom) to their limits. I feel that sometimes, you walk into a classroom and they are just colouring for an hour or 45 minutes… The LSAs and teachers do a fantastic job with the young people of lower abilities. But the staff can't really help in the classrooms, they have no training to teach. They come here to behaviour manage and that is the role in education.* (Karen, Staff Member)

The logistical difficulties of managing a group of young people of varying ages, many of whom cannot mix with others and who have different educational backgrounds and emotional needs, are undoubtedly challenging in the STC environment:

> *The kids must do 25 hours' education. We have had numerous criticisms from the Youth Justice Board because we can't take kids out of school to do psychology work. We have one full time psychologist …and a part-time psychologist trying to see 80 potentially, I mean they all should be seen, really vulnerable kids and really damaged kids outside the school day. It's physically impossible. But that's what these centres were set up, the focus was on education, I mean if you have a YP, who has horrendous drug issues, no amount of education whether they are engaging here or not will tick the boxes for them when they are outside because they still have the same issues, in the same environment with the same people tempting them with drugs. That's the problem, it's still focused on that education being the priority. And that's, I think, all of that, is why the STCs are completely failing… The kids coming in seem to be a lot more damaged than the 12–14 years olds back in 1999.* (Jane, Staff Member)

Jane explained how the contractual obligation to provide 25 hours of education was not the most helpful for the cohort of young people they were currently dealing with. This obligation, alongside the worry of being criticised by the Youth Justice Board, seemed to be the guiding principles rather than perhaps the needs of each individual young person. Whilst being accountable to the Youth Justice Board and having contractual obligations are both necessary to ensure the wellbeing of the young people in custody, the inflexibility they create can mean that some of the young people in the STC are not receiving the help they need to ensure desistance on transition. The frustration of being unable to provide young people with the help that they actually need and the pressure this puts on staff, could go some way towards explaining the significant staff rotation and high-levels of violence within the STC.

> *I do think education is the department that doesn't work that well for the young people. It's difficult because you have boys with really, really low literacy and numeracy skills and boys that are ready to do their GCSEs. I think it is difficult to educate right across the board because these boys are all in one class…there will be a number of boys that leave the centre that haven't actually gained anything in education. And the boys that aren't willing to learn and take part in education still, they are almost forced to go, and I feel that perhaps takes away from some of the boys that do gain from it. They aren't separated by ability and I don't… I think that education is one of the biggest areas that could be improved…The young people need to do 25 hours a week and I'm not sure it's what all young people need—not as a priority anyway.* (Harry, Staff Member)

Harry was unequivocal about the issues with education in the STC, as in his view the current system does not work and fails a number of young people who leave without gaining anything from the experience. Psychological needs combined with drugs and low-levels of literacy and numeracy, alongside previous school exclusion and SEND (16–23% based upon STC data), make the work of the education department as it currently stands a challenge.

> *Most of the kids, if you can call them kids that we have here now are like 16 and 17. The older kids are intense because they are set in their ways and don't want to listen to the rules. They will go to education but they constantly com-*

plain about the work in education and the fact they don't think it benefits them, well most of them. I think the need to change the values and principles to reflect our current kids, the focus on education is good but it needs to be appropriate education (Val, Staff Member)

The use of more qualitative data would allow for more effective monitoring and improvements. The contractual obligation to provide 25 hours of education is too inflexible to meet the needs of such a diverse and vulnerable population as the young people in a STC and needs to be urgently reviewed for the wellbeing of those in STCs. The Edinburgh Study of Youth Transitions and Crime[3] demonstrated that young people who become involved in serious offending (i.e. those in STCs), were some of the most impoverished, vulnerable and damaged in society (McAra and McVie 2010). Clearly, the one-size-fits-all response within this STC is not going to meet their needs in any meaningful way.

However, our data shows that the bigger failure occurs not once young people are in the STC, but many years before:

I haven't been in education for years, since I was in Year 7, so I must have been like 11–12, not sure but I was young (Zak, Young person)

Being unable to provide an education for an eleven-year-old child and excluding them from an educational establishment where they should be nurtured and encouraged to succeed is nothing short of a total failure. Schools and colleges need to provide an education that meets the needs of, and can manage the behaviour of all young people in the UK regardless of their family and socio-economic background. Such an education would ensure that the social and economic needs of the country are met and, more importantly, young people are empowered. As outlined in Chap. 3, placing young people at the centre of youth justice interventions is vital to reducing recidivism and promoting positive transitions. Empowering young people so that they never even become involved in the Youth Justice System in central to decreasing crime and anti-social

[3] This was a longitudinal programme of research on pathways into and out of offending, based on a group of 4,300 young people who began secondary school in Edinburgh in 1998.

behaviour in our society and reducing disengagement and underachievement in our education system.

Education in the twenty first century is changing, there is an increased focus on behaviour (Bailey 2009), linked to emotional wellbeing, intelligence, interpersonal skills, more use of technology, a focus on resilience (Evans and Hardaker 2015) and self-efficacy. However, what has not changed is the inequality that is embedded within the system (judged by Ofsted based on examination results), which does little to support the needs of all the young people it is supposed to serve. A study by Daniels et al. (2003) that tracked the careers of 193 young people after permanent school exclusion found that different forms of provision appealed to and had success with different young people. Most pertinently, young people who had been permanently excluded cannot be forced down routes that they resist. Provision therefore, must take account of what motivates them and what they believe they are capable of achieving. Indeed, where staff with adequate skills and resources worked with excluded young people, many of them then experienced positive outcomes.

6.5 What Are the Responsibilities of the Youth Justice Board?

The Youth Justice Board are responsible for the commissioning and monitoring of education provision within youth custody, which is often contracted out to private providers. It is also responsible for gathering data in relation to the hours of education provided and the progression and achievement of each young person. Education contracts last for five years and are administered by the Skills Funding Agency, who specify how the provider must assess and manage the education of each young person, from their entry into the system until their release. The exception to this is for looked after children, whose care and education remain the responsibility of the Local Authority as laid out in Annex 2 of the latest Government guidance (Promoting the education of looked after children) (DfE 2018a). Although a report by Her Majesty's Inspectorate of Prisons (2011) found that even though Local Authorities have a statutory

Table 6.2 Current provision in youth justice

Type of establishment	Young people in custody (%)	Mandatory hours of education	Recidivism rate (%)	Cost per bed per year
Youth offending institution	68.5	30	73	£65,000
Secure training Centres	21	25	70	£178,000
Secure Children's homes	10.5	30	76	£212,000

responsibility to young people in custody, the reality is that their involvement is often dependent upon the commitment or otherwise of individual social workers, some of whom try to end their involvement whilst the young people are in custody. This view of Local Authority care is also substantiated by the Howard League (2010), and a National Children's Bureau report (Hart 2006). The structure of current provision is summarised below in Table 6.2 (House of Parliament 2016).

When young people enter custody, information on their educational past should be available through the information given to magistrates from schools. Assessments, such as CHAT and ASSET, completed when young people are taken into their respective youth custody establishment, can provide information on developmental, mental health and education needs, which are then used to compile individual learning plans and timetables.

Education staff in Youth Offending Institutions and STCs are employed by the private sector contractors that run education. For example, Manchester College is the education contractor for Cookham Wood Youth Offending Institution; whilst Prospects is the provider for Feltham Youth Offending Institution[4]. An Institute for Learning paper (2013), in response to the Ministry of Justice consultation 'Transforming youth custody, putting education at the heart of the detention' (2013), gathered data from their members who are specialist teaching and training practitioners working with young people in youth custody. The paper made several recommendations relating to three main areas: relationships and

[4] In Secure Children's Homes they are employed by the local authority.

training; structural issues such as payments and funding; and the role of businesses and employers.

This chapter has highlighted the many links between education and youth justice and it is impossible to deny that the overrepresentation of disadvantaged groups amongst incarcerated young people and those excluded from schools. Back in 2004, the Home Office released a report stating that education *"plays a central role in measures to prevent actual or potential offending amongst their pupils as well as improve their 'life chances'"* (Home Office 2004: 5). Over ten years later, the Government's response to Taylor's (2016) review of the Youth Justice System reiterated the aim of punishment, albeit framed as facing *'the consequences of their actions'* and claimed that they would *'put education and health at the heart of youth custody and ensure that all young people are in education, training and employment on release'* (2016: 22). The Government responded to the Taylor (2016) review by setting out their vision to introduce Secure Schools, placing education and health at the centre of the secure estate. Secure schools aim to implement Taylor's (2016) vision of a child focussed therapeutic environment with strong leader, specialised practitioners and bespoke provision for individual young people.

In 2018, the Government released plans to replace Medway STC with a Secure School (HM Government 2018). The plan aims to refurbish the current site, with three main zones: Education/Training and Healthcare, Residential and Accommodation; and Administration and Operation (HM Government 2018). Providers delivering secure schools will be expected to have a child focussed ethos, demonstrating knowledge of the complexities of engaging young people in custody and the skills to deliver positive outcomes. Perhaps the Taylor review has already had some impact, as data from a recent Ofsted report (2018) of a STC showed 60% of respondents felt they had been given advice about training or jobs in the future; 78% reported that they had learnt new skills for jobs that they might like to do in the future; and 60% felt that their education/training in the STC would help them when they left. Although with the Chief Inspector of Prisons (HMIP 2017) declaring in 2017 that not one establishment in England and Wales was a safe environment to hold young people, it is difficult to be optimistic about the educational experiences for young people in STCs. Indeed, it is difficult to learn when one does not feel safe. The structural barriers to successful learning such as disadvantage, mental health issues and special educational needs must be addressed alongside improving education in custody.

6.6 Summary

This chapter has identified the role of the Youth Justice Board when it comes to educating young people in custody, the majority of whom have the literacy and numeracy levels of a 7–11-year-old child. Inspection of the statistics on school exclusion rates clearly show that many of the young people from disadvantaged areas are being failed by the current school system, which often fails to deal with their needs or help them gain a high-quality education. The roots of both social exclusion and crime can be found in the school exclusion rates, with many disadvantaged young people being educationally marginalised from a young age, with low reading and numeracy levels leading to underachievement at Key Stage 2. High quality teaching and learning, especially in the early years, can protect young people at risk from turning to crime. Many of the young people in the STC felt let down by the school system, as they had missed school through exclusion or truancy and for most of them education in the STC also failed to meet their needs. STC staff felt that the limitations of the Youth Justice Board contract and 25 hours of (often traditional) academic schooling, was failing to meet the complex needs of the young people they worked with.

The Prisoner Reform Trust review (2017) of looked after children, chaired by Lord Lamey, recommended that Local Authorities should ensure that young people are effectively supported to do well in school and that Initial Teacher Training (ITT) and Continuing Professional Development (CPD) should make teachers aware of the additional needs that looked after children can have. This additional training, alongside more effective behaviour management in schools should follow the Taylor checklists for behaviour (DfE 2011). All initial training (i.e. ITT and CPD courses) must prepare teachers for supporting young people with SEND (i.e. ASD and ADHD) in mainstream classrooms. This combination could lead to decreasing exclusion rates that should effectively lead to desistance. Figure 6.3 presents a framework based upon our discussion in this chapter for educational provision in STCs.

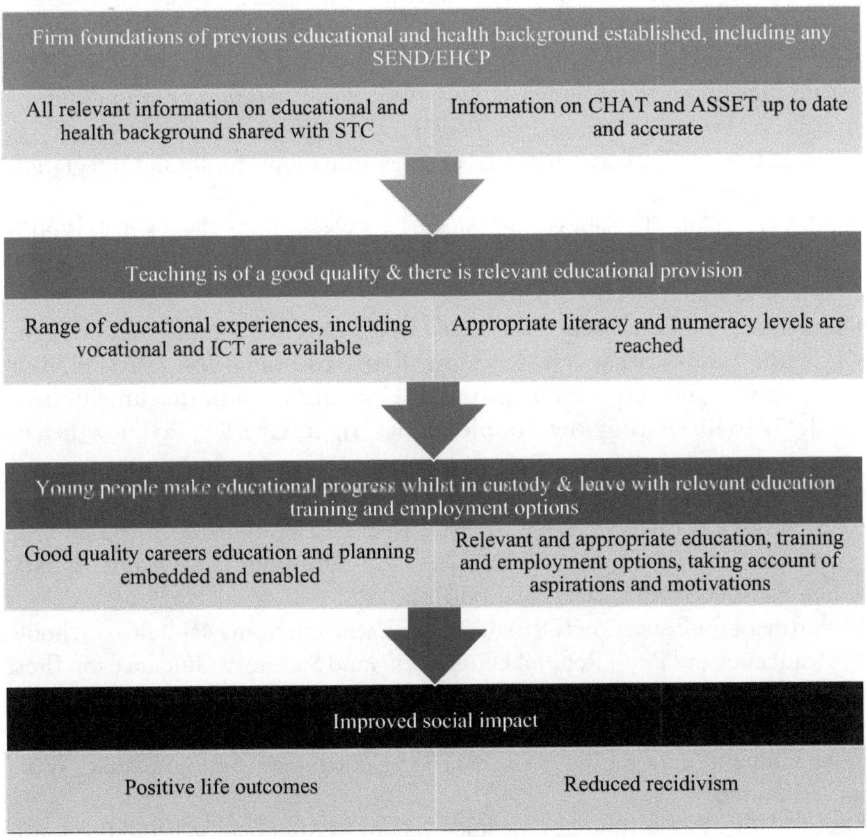

Fig. 6.3 Framework of improved educational provision in STC

References

Bailey, R. (2009). Well-being, Happiness and Education. *British Journal of the Sociology of Education, 30*(6), 795–802.

Bajwa, M. (2014). Parental Choice and School Placement – Issues for Parents of Children with Statements of Special Educational Needs. Doctoral thesis. University of Northampton. Retrieved from http://nectar.northampton.ac.uk/8847/.

Bajwa-Patel, M., & Devecchi, C. (2014). 'Nowhere That Fits': The Dilemma of School Choice for Children with Statements of Special Educational Needs in England. *SFL, 29*(2), 117–135.

Barton, L. (1998). Developing an Emancipatory Research Agenda: Possibilities and Dilemmas. In P. Clough & L. Barton (Eds.), *Articulating with Difficulty: Research Voices in Inclusive Education*. London: Paul Chapman.

Casey, L. (2016). The Casey Review: A Review into Opportunity and Integration, December 2016.

Daniels, H., Cole, T., Sellman, E., Sutton, J., Visser, J., & Bedward, J. (2003). Study of Young People Permanently Excluded from School. London: DfES. Research Report No 405.

Department for Education (DfE). (2011). Getting the Simple Things Right: Charlie Taylor's Behaviour Checklists. Retrieved from https://assets.publishing.service.gov.uk/government/uploads/system/uploads/attachment_data/file/571640/Getting_the_simple_things_right_Charlie_Taylor_s_behaviour_checklists.pdf.

Department for Education (DfE). (2017a). Permanent and Fixed-Period Exclusions in England: 2015 to 2016. Retrieved from https://assets.publishing.service.gov.uk/government/uploads/system/uploads/attachment_data/file/645075/SFR35_2017_text.pdf.

Department for Education (DfE). (2017b). Exclusion from Maintained Schools, Academies and Pupil Referral Units in England Statutory Guidance for Those with Legal Responsibilities in Relation to Exclusion. Retrieved from https://assets.publishing.service.gov.uk/government/uploads/system/uploads/attachment_data/file/641418/20170831_Exclusion_Stat_guidance_Web_version.pdf.

DfE. (2018a). Promoting the Guidance of Looked After Children and Previously Looked After Children. Statutory Guidance for Local Authorities. Retrieved from https://assets.publishing.service.gov.uk/government/uploads/system/uploads/attachment_data/file/683556/Promoting_the_education_of_looked-after_children_and_previously_looked-after_children.pdf.

DfE. (2018b). Permanent and Fixed Period Exclusions in England: 2016 to 2017. Retrieved from https://assets.publishing.service.gov.uk/government/uploads/system/uploads/attachment_data/file/726741/text_exc1617.pdf.

DfE. (2018c). Special Educational Needs in England: January 2018. https://assets.publishing.service.gov.uk/government/uploads/system/uploads/attachment_data/file/729208/SEN_2018_Text.pdf.

Dodge, K. A., Bai, Y., Ladd, H. F., Muschkin, C. G. (2016). Impact of North Carolina's Early Childhood Development Programmes and Policies on Educational Outcomes in Elementary School. https://doi.org/10.1111/cdev.12645.

Evans, C., & Hardaker, G. (2015). Understandings and Applications of Resilience. *Journal for Multicultural Education, 9*(3), 1.

Evans, J., & Vincent, C. (1997). Parental Choice and Special Education. In G. Glatter, P. A. Woods, & C. Bagley (Eds.), *Choice and Diversity in Schooling: Perspectives and Prospects*. London: Routledge.

Farrington, D. (1996). Understanding and Preventing Youth Crime. Report retrieved from https://www.jrf.org.uk/report/understanding-and-preventing-youth-crime.

Gallipoli, G., & Fella, G. (2007). Education and Crime Over the Life Cycle. Rimini Centre for Economic Analysis, Working Paper Series. 81. https://doi.org/10.1093/restud/rdu014.

Gewirtz, S., Ball, S. J., & Bowe, R. (1995). *Markets, Choice and Equity in Education*. Buckingham: Open University Press.

Gorard, S., Taylor, C., & Fitz, J. (2003). *Schools, Markets and Choice Policies*. London: Routledge Falmer.

Harris, A., & Ranson, S. (2005). The Contradictions of Education Policy: Disadvantage and Achievement. *British Educational Research Journal, 31*(2), 571–587.

Hart, D. (2006). *Tell Them Not to Forget About Us*. London: National Children's Bureau.

Heckman, J. J. (2006). Skill Formation and the Economics of Investing in Disadvantaged Children. *Science, 312*(5782), 1900–1902. https://doi.org/10.1126/science.1128898.

HM Chief Inspector of Prisons for England and Wales. (2017). *Annual Report 2016–17*. London: HMIP.

HM Government. (2018). The Site for the First Secure School. Retrieved from https://assets.publishing.service.gov.uk/government/uploads/system/uploads/attachment_data/file/752377/site-brochure.pdf.

Home Office Research, Development and Statistics Directorate. (2004). The Role of Education in Enhancing Life Chances and Preventing Offending. London: Home Office. Retrieved from https://webarchive.nationalarchives.gov.uk/20081107201453/http://www.crimereduction.homeoffice.gov.uk/youth/youth55.htm.

House of Lords. (2018). Written Answers. https://www.parliament.uk/written-questions-answers-statements/written-question/lords/2018-04-26/HL7326.

Houses of Parliament. (2016). POSTNOTE: Education in Youth Custody. Number 524. May 2016.

Howard League for Penal Reform. (2010). *Access to Justice Denied*. London: Howard League for Penal Reform.

IfL. (2013). Retrieved from https://set.et-foundation.co.uk/media/796985/2013_05_IfL_Transforming-Education-in-Youth-Custody.pdf.

Lanskey, C. (2011). Promise or Compromise? Education for Young People in Secure Institutions in England. *Youth Justice Journal, 11*(1), 47–60.

Lazar, I., Darlington, R., Murray, H., Royce, J., & Snipper, A. (1982). The Lasting Effects of Early Education: A Report from the Consortium for Longitudinal Studies, Monographs of the Society for Research in Child Development, 47 (2–3), serial no. 195.

Lochner, L., & Moretti, E. (2004). The Effect of Education on Crime: Evidence from Prison Inmates, Arrests, and Self-Reports. *The American Economic Review, 94*(1), 155–189.

Machin, S., Marie, O., & Vuji¢, S. (2010). The Crime Reducing Effects of Education, CEP Discussion Paper No 979.

McAra, L., & McVie, S. (2010). Youth Crime and Justice: Key Messages from the Edinburgh Study of Youth Transitions and Crime. *Criminology and Criminal Justice, 10*(*2*), 179–209. https://doi.org/10.1177/174889580936097.

McCrone, T., & Morris, M. (2004). Research into the Impact of Pre-16 Vocational Education. Report published by NFER, July 2004. Retrieved from http://cep.lse.ac.uk/research/skills/Skills_Publications/McCrone_Morris_2004.pdf.

McNeil, F. (2006). A Desistance Paradigm for Offender Management. *Criminology and Criminal Justice, 6*(1), 37–60.

Meghir, C., Palme, M., & Schnabel, M. (2011). The Effect of Education Policy on Crime: An Intergenerational Perspective. Institute for Fiscal Studies Working Paper W11/11. Retrieved from, https://doi.org/10.1111/cdev.12645.

Ministry of Justice. (2013). Analysis of Education Funding Agency Administrative Data, published in Transforming Youth Custody. Retrieved from https://www.gov.uk/government/consultations/transforming-youth-custodyputting-education-at-the-heart-of-detention.

Ministry of Justice and DfE. (2016). Understanding Educational Background of Young Offenders. Full report. Retrieved from https://assets.publishing.service.gov.uk/government/uploads/system/uploads/attachment_data/file/577542/understanding-educational-background-of-young-offenders-full-report.pdf.

Moffitt, T. E. (1993). Adolescence-Limited and Life-Course-Persistent Antisocial Behaviour: A Developmental Taxonomy. *Psychological Review, 100*(4), 674–701.

Morgan, R. (2006). *Stephenson, M. (2011). Young People and Offending: Education, Youth Justice and Social Inclusion*. Oxon: Routledge.

Mortimore, P., Sammons, P., Stoll, L., Lewis, D., & Ecob, R. (1988). *School Matters: The Junior Years*. Wells: Open Books.

OFSTED. (2007). Establishing Successful Practice in Pupil Referral Units and Local Authorities. Retrieved from http://dera.ioe.ac.uk/6542/1/Pupil%20referral%20units%20establishing%20successful%20practice%20in%20pupil%20referral%20units%20and%20local%20authorities%20PDF%20format%29.doc.pdf.

OFSTED report. (2018). Inspection of Oakhill STC. Retrieved from https://files.api.ofsted.gov.uk/v1/file/50010313.

ONS. (2014). Estimates of the population for the UK, England and Wales, Scotland and Northern Ireland. Available online at: https://www.ons.gov.uk/peoplepopulationandcommunity/populationandmigration/populationestimates/datasets/populationestimatesforukenglandandwalesscotlandandnorthernireland/mid2014

ONS. (2017). Young People Not in Education, Employment or Training (NEET), UK: March 2018. Retrieved from https://www.ons.gov.uk/employmentandlabourmarket/peoplenotinwork/unemployment/bulletins/youngpeoplenotineducationemploymentortrainingneet/march2018.

Prison Reform Trust. (2017). In Care, Out of Trouble. How the Life Chances of Children in Care Can Be Transformed by Protecting Them from Unnecessary Involvement in the Criminal Justice System—Impact Report, London: PRT. Retrieved from http://www.prisonreformtrust.org.uk/Portals/0/Documents/Care%20review%20impact%20report%20Jan%202017%20UPDATE%20FINAL.pdf.

Runswick- Cole, K. (2011). Time to End the Bias Towards Inclusive Education? *British Journal of Special Education, 38*(3), 112–119.

Rutter, M. (1985). Family and School Influences on Cognitive Development. *Journal of Child Psychology and Psychiatry, 26*(5), 683–704.

Rutter, M., Maughan, B., Mortimore, P., & Ouston, J. (1979). *Fifteen Thousand Hours: Secondary Schools and Their Effects on Children*. London: Open Books.

Sutherland, A., Merrington, S., Jones, S., & Baker, K. (2005). *The Role of Risk and Protective Factors*. London: Youth Justice Board for England and Wales.

Sylva, K. (1994). The Impact of Early Learning on Children's Later Development. In C. Ball (Ed.), *Start Right: The Importance of Early Learning*. London: The Royal Society for the Encouragement of Arts, Manufacturers and Commerce.

Taylor, C. (2016). *An Interim Report of Emerging Findings from the Review of the Youth Justice System*. London: Ministry of Justice. Retrieved July 1, 2016, from https://www.gov.uk/government/news/review-of-the-youth-justice-system.

Utting, D. (1996). *Reducing Criminality Among Young People: A Sample of Relevant Programmes in the United Kingdom*. Home Office Research Study 161. London: Home Office

Watt, B., Howells, K., & Delfabbro, P. (2004). Juvenile Recidivism: Criminal Propensity, Social Control and Social Learning Theories. *Psychiatry, Psychology and Law, 11*(1), 141–153.

Youth Justice Board. (2005). Risk and Protective Factors. Retrieved from http://mws-73973.mws3.csx.cam.ac.uk/people/academic_research/david_farrington/riskprot.pdf

Youth Justice Board. (2006). Engagement in Education, Training and Employment. Retrieved from http://dera.ioe.ac.uk/7999/1/Barriers%20to%20ETE%20report%20FINAL.pdf.

Youth Justice Board. (2016). Youth Custody Report January 2016. Ministry of Justice.

Youth Justice Board and Ministry of Justice. (2018). Youth Justice Statistics 2016/17. England and Wales. Statistics Bulletin. Retrieved from https://assets.publishing.service.gov.uk/government/uploads/system/uploads/attachment_data/file/676072/youth_justice_statistics_2016-17.pdf.

7

Independence and Attitudes

7.1 Independence

Independence relates to the personal and social skills that support individuals to transition from adolescence to adulthood. The independence skills individuals need for transition to adulthood include communication, emotional management, employment, financial management, securing accommodation and accessing services (Montgomery, Donkoh and Underhill 2006). The factors influencing recidivism are rooted in socialisation, intelligence, cognitive ability and motivation; thus, developing independence is pivotal for helping young people to overcome the factors hindering desistance. Research on the experiences of young people in custody suggests that custodial sentences decrease emotional stability, interrupting both engagement in education and relationships with families and peers (Beal 2014). Research on transitions from the secure estate outlines the role of independence in the empowerment and resilience of young people.

Resilience is the process of adapting to experiences in life, with an emphasis on dealing with adversity, trauma, threats, stress and tragedy (Masten 2001). Masten (ibid) explored the concept of resilience,

C. Paterson-Young et al., *The Social Impact of Custody on Young People in the Criminal Justice System*, https://doi.org/10.1007/978-3-030-18422-3_7

describing it as the development of positive outcomes despite serious threats or challenges to development. For young people accommodated in secure estates, good outcomes are dependent on developing effective services for addressing key areas, including: empowering young people to develop positive relationships, secure education placements, and dealing with health and wellbeing problems. Masten (2001) explored the notions of resilience, focusing on the environment in fostering and how it can hinder the individual's ability to thrive. Resilience then, exists as a dynamic process with the interactions between the environment and individuals central to developing positive outcomes. These interactions are influenced by the existence of effective interventions, which are central to helping children cope with emotions and develop resilience (Rutter 1985; Pinkerton et al. 2004; Ungar 2005).

The factors associated with resilience vary in research, with Rutter (1985) outlining factors such as self-esteem, confidence and self-efficacy. This can also be linked to General Self-efficacy (Schwarzer 1992; Schwarzer and Jerusalem 1995), which has been shown to consist of confidence, motivation and self-esteem (Judge et al. 1997) and has been linked to youth transitions and employability (Hazenberg et al. 2014). However, for the purposes of this discussion we will use resilience for the remainder of this chapter to refer to these broad psychometric constructs[1]. What is missing from the prior research, is the role independence skills have in developing self-esteem, confidence, self-efficacy and overall therefore, resilience. Despite research outlining the importance of independence and resilience, young people in custody are (generally at least) expected to adapt to a specific environment and culture.

In the case of STCs, this environment and culture fails to promote independence or resilience. For example, in STCs young people receive daily support in cooking, cleaning, attending education, arranging healthcare, regulating emotions and developing relationships; however, this level of support significantly reduces upon leaving the STC. From this perspective, developing independence in young people has a central

[1] These distinctions do have implications for social impact measurement research in this area however, as different scales have been developed and validated for general self-efficacy and resilience, in addition to the self-regulative efficacy and proactive coping inventory scales discussed in Chap. 4.

role in ensuring positive outcomes in the future. The STCs statement of purpose (2015) No. 12 states *"Centre staff are committed to helping sentenced young persons as they move into the community, supporting them to have appropriate accommodation and education and training on release"*. This shows the commitment to support young people in terms of accommodation and education/training; however, there are no provisions and/or resources to support the development of independence and resilience. The STC should be preparing young people for release from prison by supporting them to develop independence and resilience skills in custody; skills that are essential for release and are linked to positive outcomes.

Any approach that decides to place the empowerment of young people at the centre of an outcomes based intervention designed to reduce recidivism, has to include resilience provision as part of this empowerment. Indeed, the building of independence and resilience in custody would begin the process that would enable the young people in the STC to take positive 'social action' upon their release (Weber 1978), as was discussed in Chap. 3. The converse scenario is that this support is not provided and young people leave custody unsure of their role in and their ability to shape their transition into the community and adulthood. The question is therefore posited, as to whether young people learn independence and resilience when in custody?

7.1.1 Where Will I Go? What Will I Have?

It is unsurprising that accommodation is a feature in the transition and resettlement of young people. Stable accommodation gives individuals a feeling of safety and security, a factor that empowers and motivates change. It has been argued that stable accommodation influences (directly and indirectly) desistance on release from prison (Niven and Stewart 2005; Lewis et al. 2007; Schofield, Thoburn, Howell and Dicken 2005) by maintaining the gains achieved in prison during release and resettlement (Harper and Chitty 2005). This research found that 63% of young people in the STC were uncertain about future accommodation, which creates insecurity and impacts negatively on emotional wellbeing and motivation (Paterson-Young et al. 2017). Research by Dickens et al. (2007) found that secure and stable accommodation reduced the emotional turmoil resulting from heightened expectation with the potential for serial losses. The emotional wellbeing of young people in STCs has already been explored, with this research finding that 68% of young people had emotional regulation difficulties. Our research has also shown a higher rate of uncertainty for young people with pro-criminal family members. This uncertainty was evident in interviews, with young people citing uncertainty in relation to parents moving area and the availability of social care placements:

> *Mum and dad are moving to a new area, its rubbish. I can live on my own but might stay with my parents. I don't know though. I want to go back to my area. My heart's there.* (Mo, Young Person)

> *To be honest with you, I don't really have hopes and fears. I just don't care. It's hard, I had plans, but then I came here and my foster placements closed. I don't know where they will send me after I leave here so I can't really make plans for the future.* (Del, Young Person)

Both Mo and Del use emotive language in describing their situations, but both display uncertainty and a lack of hope, which is not conducive to desistance. This total lack of autonomy and security again makes it unsurprising that recidivism levels are so high, as the young people are not being empowered to take charge (with support) of their own transitions. Further, there is often not a desire (or ability) within the young person's family to re-accommodate them on release:

> *I used to live with my mum. I have three brothers and three sisters. There are a lot of us. But my mum has moved to a new area, the house is smaller so she told the social worker to find some other place.* (Cam, Young Person)

Cam must face a life without his family as they have simply moved to a new place that cannot accommodate him, and so have asked for him to be found 'some other place'. Such rejection and uncertainty would shake most young people; effectively, their horizons for action are being limited (Hodkinson et al. 1996). Another young person experiencing uncertainty was Jack:

I lived in a hostel; I think I should be going back there. I hope they haven't closed my hostel down. I should be going back to there. Yesterday I spoke to my social worker and she told me the hostel was closing, I told her I ain't moving.

Jack was hopeful that a hostel he previously lived in would still be available, so when he found out that it had been closed and that he faced release to unknown accommodation, it was unsurprising that he was reluctant and unhappy. This uncertainty impacts on young people's security, motivation and emotional wellbeing, which inevitably disempowers them. It is perhaps unsurprising then that the recidivism rate for young people leaving custody between October 2015 and December 2015 was 42% (Ministry of Justice 2017). The disempowerment and demotivation resulting from uncertainty was most evident in Jack's journey, as on the day of the interview he had received confirmation that his early release was approved, and he was leaving later that day. After hearing about his early release, Jack was positive and agreed to participate in an interview (earlier than planned). Jack's positive attitude remained visible after the interview and he invited the researcher to experience his journey to release. This positive attitude ended when Jack discovered his original hostel placement was closed and another hostel placement had been secured for him in another Borough. Jack expressed anger to staff and threated to harm his social worker if she failed to secure his original hostel placement. He spoke to his social worker, but the situation remained unresolved. It is unsurprising, based upon his story and other examples from the literature, that Jack received another custodial sentence within 4 weeks of his release.

7.1.2 Does Custody Equip Young People with Independence?

Secure environments operate in isolation, for the most part, with provisions and resources operating in silos—detached from community involvement. Young people receive daily support in the STC to cook (breakfast), clean, attend education, access healthcare, regulate emotions and form relationships; however, this level of support ceases upon release from custody. Lewis et al. (2007) argue that to develop and sustain motivation to change, young people need links to resources upon release. Research also suggests that custodial environments play a role in fostering or hindering an individual's ability to thrive on release (Masten 2001). The removal of the connected arrangements available in secure environments results in a dislocation for young people, a dislocation that occurs at a pivotal point in the transition period when the young person is at greater risk of involvement in criminal behaviour. This dislocation reduces the available protective factors for young people, impacting on security and motivation (Farrington and Ttofi 2014; Paterson-Young et al. 2017).

So what support do young people receive in STCs and does this help with transitions back to the community? This research found that 59% of young people believed that no support was offered in STCs that would allow them to develop independence or secure accommodation, employment and relationships (Taxman 2004). Young people expressed dissatisfaction at the lack of opportunity for learning independence, with 'cooking' the only independence (or survival) skill cited:

> *I learned how to cook here actually. Nothing else though. I don't know anything about finance etc. They don't teach use that here. It's pointless here, we don't learn the stuff we need to know.* (Mo, Young Person)

Mo had learned to cook, he showed understanding of the fact that he would need to understand something about finances, but also recognised that the STC had done nothing to equip him with such skills.

> *Ummm…I don't know really. I learned how to do a plait in Hair and Beauty. So I can do my own hair and stuff. But nothing else. That's why I need foster care, I need parents to help me.* (Del, Young Person)

Del had learnt to plait hair but 'nothing else', he felt that he needed parents to support him, support that most young people have (many well into their twenties):

> *No, don't learn anything like that in here; like no budgeting. They are supposed to be changing the incentives and stuff, so maybe we will learn this stuff. Like they will make you budget and buy your own stuff, like shower gel and soap. We don't do that now; they buy it for us.* (Faisal, Young Person)

I don't think so, we learn maths but that's like sums and shit. We don't learn anything else. I don't know about paying bills, except that they are fucking expensive. I want to help my mum with that but I don't know how much bills are like. (Neal, Young Person)

I know how to cook and stuff but I will get to do other stuff here. I know we have to cook and clean but I know this already. Don't think I will learn anything else here to be honest. (Joe, Young Person)

Several of the participants understood that they needed to know more and had not been equipped with these skills in the STC. Indeed, not 'learning anything' was a constant refrain from some young people, many of whom will be living independently and require a lot of knowledge and skills if they are to cope successfully upon their release.

I don't think I learned anything about independent living but that's cool because I will just live with mum. (Liam, Young Person)

Participants like Liam were unusual in knowing that they had a parent who would look after them; indeed, he was very fortunate as he too had learned nothing whilst in the STC. The lack of opportunities available for young people to learn independence points to the inadequacy of STC provision. Overall, young people learn some general household skills, such as cooking and cleaning; however, other independence skills, such as financial management and budgeting remain elusive (see Table 7.1).

Young people's views directly contradict STC Purpose 12 that states that *"Centre staff are committed to helping sentenced young persons as they move into the community, supporting them to have appropriate accommodation and education and training on release"* (STC Statement of Purpose 2015). The perceptions of the young people were also supported by staff participating in the research:

…they don't learn anything, like you wouldn't expect a young person to have a set amount of money to go and do a food shop. To make that last them for a week. For them to know that this has to last them a whole week. You don't get

Table 7.1 Young people's understanding of factors for independence ($n = 65$)

Knowledge type	Disagree (%)	Neither (%)	Agree (%)
Knowledge of applying for education, training and employment opportunities	69	3	28
Confidence filling out forms (for example bank and job application)	74	2	25
Knowledge of accessing alcohol and substance misuse services	41	16	43
Knowledge of accessing housing benefit and jobseekers allowance	75	6	19
Knowledge of accommodation on leaving custody	54	15	31

> *that here… Not ever should a young person be able to manage being homeless and not manage to live independently… I had a young person say 'I'll manage being homeless, but if I have a home, I don't know what bills to pay, I don't know that I have to make this money last for this long'.* (Karen, Staff Member)

The lack of knowledge displayed by young people in the STC is hardly unusual for young people of their age, although of course there are exceptions e.g. with young people who are young carers. However, the fact that centre staff recognise this, but are not teaching them the required skills, shows a failing in terms of practice within the STC.

> *But I think the biggest thing about being independent is actually the level of independence. Here, they know they are safe and fed and clean but I'm not sure that continues when they are on their own. It must be scary when they go to semi-independent living and stuff… we spend a huge amount of money replacing expensive clothing that the boys shrink in the washing machine or damage play fighting—we are not teaching them anything when we do this… I don't think they learn skills to manage money and finances.* (Harry, Staff Member)

> *No. I will tell the kids do their own laundry and then five minutes a member of staff is collecting it all up and doing it. We are supposed to support the young people to do laundry not do it for them. But we do it for them. I mean we give young people food, money, soap, TV and we take them to and from appointments and education. We spoon feed the boys here and then we wonder why they can't survive in the community. I think we need to teach them about money,*

shopping, rent, bills, arranging appointments, attending appointments etc. not just how to cook. (Val, Staff Member)

Statement of Purpose 12 relates to moving into the community, accommodation, education and training, but skills such as financial awareness and independence are not explicitly mentioned. They can be seen as part of the 'moving into the community' remit, but the focus is most definitely on somewhere to live (accommodation) and something to occupy the young people (education and training), which whilst more expensive, are both more tangible and easily achievable. Timetabling and staffing the teaching of independence skills is perhaps less straightforward and therefore falls by the wayside, although staff comments made it clear that they knew there was a need for such skills.

But unfortunately, there is not enough of focus on independent learning skills given to them. I think there should be a role created in which people should work with young people prior to release where they can go and deliver independent learning. Like how to go to a bank to get some money out, know how to do simply things like putting a duvet sheet on. Normal things like that. (Sam, Staff Member)

I remember I had a young person that was so frustrated going to education, kicking doors, saying "I don't want to go to school. I don't want to go to school". I said come and tell me why it is that you don't want to go to school. And after a while I managed to get it out of him, he didn't know how to tie his shoelace; something as simple as that. He was with us for quite a long time. He was a very complex young person, by the end he learned to tie his shoe laces. It took about a week for him to do, but then he knows how to do it. So we literally don't think of it, just an everyday thing to us. But for him, it was a massive thing and then he didn't want to wear shoes because they were loose because he couldn't tie the shoe laces. (Sam, Staff Member)

You know we have platinum rooms that should be made into cooking rooms. We have a cooking room over on Maple that is just not used how it should be… We can get a lot better. I think some aspects we do in the daily routine, for instance, clean your room, and make your bed… I think we do teach them minimal stuff, but not again, not as effectively. (Abi, Staff Member)

Centre staff showed a desire to help young people learn independence skills; however, this is hindered by limited resources and inconsistent approaches from other staff members. Several staff members reflected on the fact that other staff contradict the decisions of others, which results in young people being 'spoon fed'. Another area of frustration surrounds the inadequate use of resources, with opportunities for learning independence skills (i.e. young people staying in platinum rooms[2]) missed. Indeed, the platinum rooms were often used, not to support young people to learn independence skills, but rather to accommodate difficult or challenging young people.

So why is there a limited priority placed upon independence training? Speaking in relation to secure environments, Morris and Morris (1963) and Dixey and Woodall (2011) found that staff employed in such environments prioritised punishment, with release preparation viewed as a secondary role. The prioritisation of punishment is still prevalent today, despite the apparent focus on education and resettlement, practically demonstrating the conceptual clash between the welfare and punitive approaches discussed in Chap. 2. It also demonstrates that empowerment has institutional antecedents (Weber 1978), with the culture inside the STC having a direct influence on how support is provided. Where the culture is one focused on punitive measures and isolation, this fails to deal with the underlying causes of negative behaviours amongst young people (i.e. trauma, poor emotional regulation and limited independence/resilience). This then fails to prepare the young people for their release and leads to a limiting of both their ability to engage in positive social action and their opportunities to desist back in the community.

7.1.3 What Do Young People Need?

Secure environments offer limited provisions for young people in developing independence skills. Despite these limited provisions, young people positively commented on the routine provided in the STC. This structure is a starting point in supporting and empowering young people:

---

[2] Platinum rooms offer young people the opportunity to spend time in a separate area with cooking facilities attached.

You know what I learn, the structure. The structure was brilliant for me. So the wake up, the shower, because I used to skip some things—I would wake up, skip brushing my teeth and the shower and just go out with my mates. Now, I wake up, brush my teeth, have a shower, do push ups.... I love that structure... (Jack, Young Person)

Young people in custody experience this structure and routine for the length of their sentences, but unfortunately this ceases completely on release. Structure and routine are important for helping young people thrive in the community (Bortner and Williams 1997); however, young people and families receive limited support to continue structure and routine on release from the custodial environment. Indeed, young people have to deal with a "never-ending series" of transitions (Liptak 2008: 4). Dealing with the transition from custody, in addition to the usual transitions experienced in childhood and adolescence, may discourage participation in positive activities, hence impacting on recidivism. The Department of Education outlines the regulations and guidance for supporting young people's Transition to Adulthood, based on recommendations in the Childrens' Act 1989. The regulations and guidance encourage practitioners to view young people holistically, supporting individual needs. This is reiterated in 'The Child Placement Handbook', which outlines the need for regular assessments that cover young people's accommodation, practical life skills, education and training, employment, financial support, specific support needs and contingency plans if independent living breaks down (Schofield and Simmonds 2009). This research, alongside the body of prior literature outlined in this book, suggests that young people are not getting this support in STCs or post-release. Indeed, one could argue that by not providing these skills and development opportunities in custody, young people are being set up to fail by the Criminal Justice System.

Transition for young people relies on the development of effective life skills. These skills are generally associated with managing daily life and accomplishing personal goals (Liptak 2007, 2008; Leider 1994). Researchers (Leider 1994; Leutenberg and Liptak 2009) argue that developing effective life skills allow young people to develop skills for:

- Effective human development
- Dealing with personal challenges
- Understanding negative patterns
- Performing better in education and employment
- Understanding the change process
- Managing and creating change
- Coping with adversity
- Managing feelings, motivation and life satisfaction
- Improving time and self-management skills

Developing a life skills inventory for young people is essential for assessing the skills learned. Table 7.2 outlines the independent life skills required for young people in custody, by combining research from Leider (1994) and Leutenberg and Liptak (2009), with our research conducted in the STC.

These essential skills should be learned in stages (basic, intermediate and advanced) with young people encouraged to advance through each stage. Support to advance through each stage is required in custody and on transition to the community. Developing effective and sustainable services that support young people to develop life skills is therefore essential in supporting young people to achieve positive outcomes.

7.2 Attitudes and Regulating 'The Self'

Personal narrative plays a crucial role in developing independence and resilience, as well as understanding recidivism and desistance (Maruna 2001). It is also a key feature of youth transitions more generally (Hodkinson et al. 1996). Research places individuals involved in offending into two distinct categories, desisters and recidivists (Maruna 2001). Recidivists tend to view their personal circumstances, environment and background as uncontrollable variables that influence and justify offending behaviour; whilst desisters acknowledge their responsibility for decisions and accept control over their life (Maruna 2001). Indeed, research has also demonstrated how an individual's locus of control, that is their belief in their ability to shape outcomes through their own actions, is

Table 7.2 Independent life skills for young people in custody

Life Skills	Basic	Intermediate	Advance
Dealing with money	• Understands value of money • Can complete purchases and count change • Understands 'necessity' and 'luxury' • Understands how to save money	• Can open a bank account • Can make withdrawals/ deposits. • Can use a calculator to add, subtract, divide and multiply • Understands how to save • Understands tax/national insurance	• Understands monthly budgeting • Can read monthly bank statements • Can comparison shop (unit pricing) • Has regular savings program • Understands buying on credit, loans etc.
Food management	• Washes hands before preparing and eating food • Understands the food pyramid • Can use cooking utensils • Can prepare breakfast • Can prepare lunch • Can prepare dinner	• Can write/follow a shopping list • Can use cooking utensils effectively and safely (knives, can opener etc.) • Can use kitchen appliances effectively and safely • Understands how to use dates on food packages to prevent spoilage	• Recognises signs of food spoilage • Can follow the instructions for preparing food • Can plan nutritious weekly menu • Can shop for weekly meals and stay on food budget • Can complete a weekly grocery shop • Can stay on food budget

(*continued*)

Table 7.2 (continued)

Life Skills	Basic	Intermediate	Advance
Appearance and hygiene	• Can bathe self • Knows how to use soap, shampoo, deodorant etc. • Can dress self in a reasonably acceptable fashion (underwear, socks and fastened shoes) • Understands oral health (brushing teeth, flossing)	• Showers or bathes regularly • Keeps hair clean and neat • Dresses in clean clothing • Knows appropriate clothing to wear • Understands the cost (and can budget) for hygiene products	• Can read clothing labels and determine washing/drying instructions • Can sort and machine-wash clothes using appropriate temperatures and washing liquid • Can dry clothes in a dryer using appropriate settings • Can iron clothes
Health problems	• Knows how and where to get emergency health care • Knows not to take someone else's medication • Knows parts of the body and sexual functioning • Understands pregnancy prevention techniques • Has selected a doctor, dentist or clinic for regular health care	• Can recognise and describe symptoms of common health problems (i.e. cold) • Understands what to do for minor injuries (i.e. cut or burn) • Understands the risks of pregnancy and sexually transmitted diseases • Understands the risks of drug and alcohol abuse • Can call a doctor or dentist and schedule an appointment	• Can nurse self through cold or flu • Can take own temperature using an oral thermometer • Understands the correct use of 'over the counter' drugs (i.e. paracetamol) • Can read a prescription label correctly and follow the instructions • Can take medication without supervision • Knows how to dispose of drugs in a safe manner

(continued)

Table 7.2 (continued)

Life Skills	Basic	Intermediate	Advance
Chores and housekeeping	• Can wash dishes adequately using soap and hot water • Can change a light bulb • Can make/change a bed • Knows how to dispose of garbage • Knows how to recycle • Perform routine house-cleaning	• Can use and empty vacuum cleaner • Knows how to prevent sinks and toilets from clogging • Knows how to wash surfaces, floors and windows • Knows how to clean bathtub, shower, sink and toilet • Understands the appropriate cleaning products to use for different tasks	• Can defrost the refrigerator if necessary. • Knows how to stop a toilet from running • Knows how to use a plunger to unstop a toilet or sink • Understands how to conserve energy and water • Uses drawers and closets appropriately for storage.
Transportation	• Understands and uses seat belts • Familiar with local public transportation • Knows how much money is required for public transport • Knows route to the nearest town with public transport • Can ride a bicycle safely	• Aware of consequences of driving without a license and insurance • Has successfully navigated public transport (with changes) • Knows how to call a taxi and provide information needed • Knows the approximate cost of taking a taxi. • Can give directions	• Can arrange routine transportation • Understands requirements for driving • Has provisional/full driving license • Can repair a puncture • Can read a map / satellite navigation • Can estimate cost of owning and operating a car (i.e. insurance, tax, monthly repayments)

(continued)

Table 7.2 (continued)

Life Skills	Basic	Intermediate	Advance
Accessing services/ resources	• Knows how to get emergency information by telephone • Knows how to travel to the nearest supermarket or shop • Knows how to access emergency food and shelter • Knows how to access emergency help lines (i.e. Samaritans)	• Knows where local bank is located • Can use the Yellow Pages or online directory to obtain information. • Knows location of nearest post office • Knows location of nearest emergency services (i.e. police station, hospital)	• Knows who to contact if utilities disconnected (i.e. gas company) • Knows where the nearest job centre is located • Can obtain a copy of birth certificate • Knows where to access specialised resources (i.e. mental health, counselling)
Secure Accommodation	• Understands the concept of renting (public and private) • Knows how to access emergency shelter • Knows the role of a landlord	• Knows how to search for accommodation • Understands basic terms (i.e. short-term tenancy, deposit, references) • Understands the costs associated with different types of housing • Understands the pros and cons of living with a roommate • Can complete a rental application	• Can identify housing that is within budget • Understands the initial costs association with renting (i.e. deposit, utility, connection fees) • Shows some concern for the rights of other residents (i.e. noise) • Understands the landlords obligation for repairs

(continued)

Table 7.2 (continued)

Life Skills	Basic	Intermediate	Advance
Education	• Understands their current qualifications and educational achievement • Understands the importance of education in securing a job • Can fill out forms to enrol in an educational program.	• Can discuss educational/ vocational plans with teachers (and professionals) • Is aware of educational resources available in the community • Knows how to obtain school transcripts	• Has an appropriate educational plan for the job selected • Understands the cost of higher education/vocational training (if any) • Understands the difference between a loan and a grant • Can identify the connection between education and employment
Employment	• Understands the types of jobs available • Understands minimum wage • Can read the want ads and find appropriate leads	• Can fill out a standard job application form • Can give appropriate answers to potential interview questions (i.e. mock interview) • Knows appropriate clothing to wear for the interview • Can write a C.V.	• Has completed a job application • Knows to prepare for a job interview • Knows the function of the job centre • Can contact temporary employment services (i.e. Office Temps) • Understands the general terms of employment (i.e. part-time, full-time)

(continued)

Table 7.2 (continued)

Life Skills	Basic	Intermediate	Advance
Understanding legal matters	• Knows who to call if arrested • Understands what actions are against the law • Understands the consequences of breaking the law • Understands who to contact if they are the victim of crime	• Knows personal rights if arrested • Understands the function of a lawyer • Understands the legal age for certain activities (i.e. buying alcohol, sexual activity) • Knows how to read a contract • Understands substance dependency • Knows how and where to register to vote	• Understands the availability of free legal services • Understands the consequences of signing a contract or a lease • Understands the specific, legal penalty for various crimes • Understands the highway code
Parenting and child care	• Understands options for birth control • Understands the dangers of substance misuse during pregnancy • Understands how to access pre-natal care • Knows how to access emergency services if child is injured/sick	• Can provide appropriate supervision for a child • Knows how to bathe child and change diapers • Knows how to engage child in appropriate play (i.e. reading) • Knows the available options for regular childcare	• Can select toys appropriate for the child's age and developmental level • Can discipline without using extreme measures. • Keeps to childcare drop-off and pick-up times • Spends "quality" time with child each day (i.e. listening to the child). • Knows how to access parenting support

(*continued*)

Table 7.2 (continued)

Life Skills	Basic	Intermediate	Advance
Emergency, health and safety	• Understands the functions of police, ambulance and fire departments (and emergency numbers) • Knows proper way of disposing of cigarettes • Knows how to lock and unlock doors and windows • Knows how to check smoke alarm/carbon monoxide detector and how to replace battery	• Understands basic fire prevention (i.e. not smoking in bed) • Knows how to use a fire extinguisher • Understands that improperly used appliances can cause fires • Can recognise if there is a gas leak • Knows who to call if there is a gas leak	•Understands the different methods for putting out different kinds of fires • Knows how to properly store cleaning materials • Knows basic first aid

shaped by personal experiences (Goldsmith et al. 1996). Research exploring desistance and recidivism found that projects addressing attitudes to offending, with links to resources upon release, have higher rates of desistance and lower rates of recidivism (Lewis et al. 2007). Thus, addressing young people's attitudes to offending and internalising their locus of control, is central in developing and sustaining their motivation to change.

There are a multitude of factors contributing to young people's attitudes to offending, such as relationships (discussed in Chap. 5), impulsivity, uncertainty and hopelessness. Impulsivity has been explored in relation to criminal and antisocial behaviour for decades (Defoe et al. 2013; Farrington 1990, 1992; Higgins et al. 2013), with impulsivity noted as a factor with young people in custody in the STC:

> *I was angry then, I swung at some of the staff and they grabbed me. I just kept swinging and swinging but I never hit anyone. Well, I might have hit someone in the chest but I don't actually know if I did or not. I'm allowed to be angry you know, I'm human and I can be angry if I want.* (Del, Young Person)

> *It's hard. I think about stopping offending but it's difficult. I mean, sometimes stuff happens and I just go crazy. I don't care who I hurt. It's like I can't control something inside me and I go crazy.* (Neal, Young Person)

This illustrates the impact of impulsivity on offending behaviour, particularly in relation to control and violence. Research conducted by Jolliffe and Farrington (2004) explored concentration and impulsivity in relation to violence, finding that violent and aggressive behaviour was related to early impulsiveness. Supporting young people to manage impulsiveness (and regulate emotions), empowers young people to manage difficult situations. This is linked to self-regulation and the theme of resilience that runs through this chapter. The need for young people to cope proactively with difficult situations is paramount if they are to desist post-release.

Beyond Youth Custody (BYC) aims to challenge, advance and promote the effective resettlement of young people by recommending changes to policy and practice (Hazel et al. 2017). One such recommendation refers to the key characteristics for effective and sustainable resettlement support: constructive (focused on identify shift, strength-based approaches and empowerment); co-created (focused on inclusion of children, young people and supporters); customised (focused on individual and diverse support); consistent (focused on designing a seamless process from admission); and co-ordinated (focus on widespread partnership). These characteristics, when combined with the resettlement approach outlined in this book, illustrate best practice for supporting young people to develop emotional stability, educational achievements, healthy relationships, independence and resilience. This returns to our central argument that interventions need to focus on empowering young people and making them the central focus for outcome-based performance (and hence reduced recidivism and wider positive social impact for society).

7.2.1 Sense of Hopelessness and Uncertainty

A factor in supporting young people to regulate the self-surrounds the management of expectations and uncertainty for the future. Sentencing young people to custody results in challenges and obstacles, not only in the isolation from family and friends, but with the added obstacles of isolation from the outside world. Entering custody creates a sense of anger and despair, which results in decreased motivation for some young people (Paterson-Young 2018). In STCs, young people's view of future offending varies, with a number reporting uncertainty. This uncertainty is compounded by young people's view that the future is hopeless:

> *I want to stop, but I don't want to stop. It's hard like. I have nothing except for my parents outside here. I don't want to come back in here though. I have goals but I don't know if I can make it.* (Mo, Young Person)

The complete lack of direction and hope expressed here by Mo is difficult to comprehend, with so little to hope or aim for, the lure of the certainty and security of a return to the STC is understandable. This provides a strong example of how the young people's horizons for action, that is their perceptions of the opportunities ahead of them, are limited by custody (Hodkinson et al. 1996). While hopelessness is a factor for some young people, others express concerns over factors such as environmental and gang involvement:

> *I really don't know it depends on my frame of mind at the time. There are loads of gangs in my area and I'm part of a gang, you can't just leave. If you need to do something, then you need to do it like.* (Faisal, Young Person)

Another factor commonly reported by young people related to views that certain offences are not harmful:

> *I don't know, mostly no. I don't want to come here again, but I won't get caught. I have nothing outside here except my mum and my little bro/sis. Why would I stop offending? It's hardly like I hurt people man. All I do is take the stuff I want, loads of people take stuff they want. I don't have money to pay for it so I take it from the people that have money. Like Robin Hood man.* (Neal, Young Person)

It is evident that uncertainty is compounded by factors relating to finance, environment, gang participation, hopelessness and views of offending as harmless. Young people participating in this research may express a desire to stop offending, but this desire is overshadowed by uncertainty. For some of these young people, gang participation and gang politics were explicitly mentioned as a factor in uncertainty, with statements such as *'I'm part of a gang, you can't just leave'*, *'Once you are in the gang, you are in the gang'* and *'The gang are my family, my blood'* all demonstrating the strength of gang associations. These responses illustrate not only young people's fear associated with exiting the gang, but also their desire to maintain gang status, factors that influence anti-social potential (Farrington and West 1995; Farrington, Loeber, Yanming and Anderson 2002; Farrington 2005). For example, some young people express belief that they have 'no-one' except for close family, leading them to view their gang (and other offending peers) as gains; gains ranging from financial to belonging. Gang participation, then, fills the void created by a lack of education, employment, meaningful activity and secure family attachments (Pitts 2007). These issues, highlighted by young people, were also reiterated by centre staff during interviews:

> *Sometimes the young people don't actually want to change. We try as much as possible and I have worked with young people on a one to one basis and at the end they will say "I'm really sorry K, thanks for all your help, but I'm going back to what I know and where I have come from". As much as you have those*

conversations and as much as you do the consequences of behaviour work, you can't change everyone. I sort of learnt that after I started. (Ella, Staff Member)

Ok, you can come here and put all the interventions into the world and they could reap the most amounts from this centre, but if this stuff isn't continued in the community then they haven't got a hope in hell. Because if they come here, for example, on a 12 do 6, they spend 6 months getting all this support and stuff then go out and they don't have anything, and the community aren't putting that in (social services, Youth Offending Team services), then literally all the work that has been done can potentially be undone in half the amount of time. And then in a few months they are committing. (Pat, Staff Member)

The views from staff illustrate the issues with sending young people back to communities plagued with social inequality, poverty, gangs and violence. This demonstrates society's responsibility for recidivism and desistance, removing responsibility from young people who are often victims of circumstance. Much of the existing literature places the responsibility for reducing recidivism on young people, rather than exploring the wider issues impacting on offending and re-offending, such as neighbourhood, gang involvement, social deprivation, health inequalities and challenging family situations (Case and Haines 2009). Young people are effectively treated as if institutional and class-based power imbalances do not exist in society, when in reality they shape/limit social action (Weber 1978). Research has shown that the majority of young people in custody have experienced adverse circumstances, which contribute to their involvement in offending behaviour (Beal 2014; Muncie 2014; Paterson-Young et al. 2017), circumstances that society has shaped and should bear responsibility for. If all children were treated equally and provided for in a socially just society, institutions like STCs would perhaps not be necessary (or at least their provision would be better).

7.2.2 Remorse: "Shame and Guilt"

Remorse refers to the individuals' guilt-related reflection and/or response to their situation (for example, regret and sorrow). Research conducted by Paterson-Young (2018) explored remorse, finding that around two-thirds of young people in the STC (62%) had no desire to apologise or make amends to victims. The research found a statistically significant correlation between young people's desire to apologise and desire to make amends. This was explored in relation to young people's exposure to pro-criminal relationships, finding that young people with pro-criminal relationships were significantly less likely to show a desire to apologise or make amends. Jolliffe and Farrington (2004) explored the role of empathy in recidivism and desistance, finding strong relationships between offending and low cognitive empathy. Research on restorative practices found that recidivism was lower for young people that participate in restorative justice programs in comparison to young people in comparison groups (Umbreit and Zehr 1996; Braithwaite 2002). These programmes are guided by the principles that crimes impact on individuals and communities; thus, restorative justice programs are designed to rebuild relationships. Delivering effective and sustainable restorative justice interventions impacts on recidivism and supports young people to understand the impact of offending on the victims. Despite the importance of developing restorative attitudes, young people rarely participate in meaningful restorative interventions, with existing restorative interventions delivered by untrained staff[3]. This again highlights institutional barriers to effective rehabilitation in the Criminal Justice System.

Hosser et al. (2008) completed a longitudinal analysis of event-history, finding an association between desistance and remorse. This research found lower levels of recidivism for individuals expressing remorse for past behaviour. Research conducted by Tangney et al. (2014) found similar results, with guilt-proneness related to recidivism and desistance. While guilt/remorse is linked to desistance, the work completed with young people in STCs to address such factors is limited. For the majority of young people in STCs, understanding of the impact on victims was limited, with young people often expressing a lack of remorse:

[3] Staff members delivering restorative practices, mediation services and offence-based work, require appropriate training (for example, staff require restorative practices training before facilitating restorative justice conferences, restorative meetings or victim awareness packages).

> *Yeah, it affected the victim. Well actually, I'm just saying that cause that's what people want us to say; that we are sorry for the victim. I don't actually feel emotions like that really.* (Del, Young Person)

> *It doesn't bother me being in here really. This isn't a prison, it's just low man. It's a joke…I suppose what I did might have caused problems for the victims like they might feel bad about what happened. Don't really know, but they might. I don't really care though.* (Zak, Young Person)

The first factor that related to remorse was young people's view of themselves as victims of circumstance:

> *I don't care…why should I? I mean no one cares about me so why would I care what happens to them. No one was hurt because I was robbing, hardly like it hurts them. (*Neal, Young Person)

The second factor that related to remorse was young people's view of the victim as deserving:

> *He deserved it like, I told you, he run his mouth. He won't do that again. I suppose he was hurt, but he deserved it, so…* (Chase, Young Person)

The background and experiences of young people entering custody are often adverse, with experiences and/or exposure to abuse, domestic violence, parental separation, substance use and pro-criminal family and/or peers. This relates back to the theme of trauma that was explored in-depth in Chap. 5. Thus, many young people have experiences, both direct and indirect, of victimisation. Research outlining the powerlessness of young people has argued that young people are at risk of victimisation, especially at times when youth is subjugated with 'threat' (Muncie 2014). For example, high-levels of regulation of young people means much of their movement is secret and/or hidden, leaving them at increased risk of victimisation.

The fifth statement of purpose in STCs is *"preventing re-offending and preparing young people for their return to the community"*. But how effective is the STC in preventing re-offending? Only 49% of young people in STCs believed they would not offend in the future, with a further 24% expressing uncertainty. This research found that young people accepting responsibility for crimes and/or expressing remorse were more likely to indicate a desire to stop offending. This raises questions over the effectiveness of STCs in promoting desistance and reducing recidivism, questions that are strengthened by staff's views. A significant number of staff members (73%) participating in this research, argued that young people would offend in the future, with staff reporting that recidivism was related to a number of factors; the first being length of sentence:

> *In terms of his offending, have we stopped his offending behaviour, probably not, but I don't know if that's our fault or the length of time he was here.* (Jane, Staff Member)

The second factor was related to the services/interventions available for young people in the centre, with one staff member commenting that:

> *We don't provide offending intervention so the kids just leave with the same attitude. The only time we make a difference is with the kids that have only offended once, but honestly, I don't think those kids would offend again. For the ones that have multiple offences, they just laugh it off.* (Val, Staff Member)

The final factor was rewarding bad behaviour, which was expressed by several staff members as both a problem for managing young people in custody and a problem for recidivism.

> *I think we teach young people here the worse you behave, the more you get… We had one young person… he destroyed his room completely, I mean completely… and he lived on a corridor where the louder he shouted, the more he got.* (Rich, Staff Member)

The misalignment between staff member's views and the strategic goals of STCs creates questions over the effectiveness of such custodial environments. If staff members do not believe the environment can prevent re-offending, then how can we change attitudes to offending and reduce youth recidivism?

7.3 Summary

The isolation experienced by young people impacts on their transition from custody to the community, and more generally, the transition to adulthood (Farrington et al. 2002; Farrington 2005, 2007; Montgomery et al. 2006). Independence relates to the personal and social skills that young people need to transition from adolescence to adulthood, including communication, emotional management, employment, financial management, securing accommodation and accessing services (Montgomery et al. 2006). Developing interventions and services that support young people to develop independence is pivotal for supporting young people to transition from custody to the community. It also helps young people to develop resilience that helps promote good outcomes, in spite of challenging situations.

Young people in custody receive limited opportunities to learn independence skills and develop resilience in custody, which are central elements to reducing recidivism. Both of these areas are easily taught, and alongside increased literacy and numeracy training, would allow young people to live more successful and inclusive lives in their communities. Prior research has shown that the positive social impact of custody, is for a significant number of young people is minimal (Paterson-Young et al. 2017). In measuring the impact of custody on the development of independence, developing an impact measurement approach is crucial as it allows professionals to identify young people's understanding and development of independence skills. One element of such a framework must include a focus on independence and resilience, as this is central to successful transitions, reduced offending and the empowerment of young people. Indeed, this empowerment and internalised locus of control (Goldsmith et al. 1996), has been shown in this chapter to be central to young people believing that their 'horizons for action' and ability to engage in 'social action' will reap positive outcomes for their future (Hodkinson et al. 1996; Weber 1978).

References

Beal, C. (2014). Insider Accounts of the Move to the Outside: Two Young People Talk About Their Transitions from Secure Institutions. *Journal of Youth Justice, 13*(1), 63–75.

Bortner, M. A., & Williams, L. M. (1997). *Youth in Prison*. New York: Routledge.
Braithwaite, J. (2002). *Restorative Justice and Response Regulation*. New York: Oxford University Press.
Case, S., & Haines, K. (2009). *Understanding Youth Offending: Risk Factor Research, Policy and Practice*. Cullompton: Willan.
Defoe, I. N., Farrington, D. P., & Loeber, R. (2013). Disentangling the Relationship Between Delinquency and Hyperactivity, Low Achievement, Depression, and Low Socio-economic Status: Analysis of Repeated Longitudinal Data. *Journal of Criminal Justice, 41*, 100–107.
Dickens, J., Howell, D., Thoburn, J., & Schofield, G. (2007). Children Starting to Be Looked After by Local Authorities in England: An Analysis of Inter-authority Variation and Case-centred Decision-making. *British Journal of Social Work, 37*, 597–617.
Dixey, R., & Woodall, J. (2011). Prison Staff and the Health Promoting Prison. *International Journal of Prisoner Health, 7*, 8–16.
Farrington, D. (1990). Implications of Criminal Career Research for the Prevention of Offending. *Journal of Adolescence, 13*(2), 93–113.
Farrington, D. (1992). Juvenile Delinquency. In J. C. Coleman (Ed.), *The School Years* (2nd ed., pp. 123–116). London: Routledge.
Farrington, D. (2005). *Integrated Developmental and Life-Course Theories of Offending. Advances in Criminological Theory*. New Jersey: Transaction.
Farrington, D. (2007). Origins of Violent Behaviour over the Life Span. In D. J. Flannery, A. T. Vazsonyi, & I. D. Waldman (Eds.), *The Cambridge handbook of Violent Behavior and Aggression*. Cambridge: Cambridge University Press.
Farrington, D., & Ttofi, M. (2014). Developmental and Life-Course Theories of Offending. In H. Morizot & L. Kazemian (Eds.), *The Development of Criminal and Antisocial Behaviour*. New York: Springer.
Farrington, D., & West, D. (1995). Effects of Marriage, Separation, and Children on Offending by Adult Males. In Z. Blau & J. Hagan (Eds.), *Current Perspectives on Aging and the Life Cycle*. Greenwich: JAI Press.
Farrington, D., Loeber, R., Yanming, Y., & Anderson, S. (2002). Are Within-Individual Causes of Delinquency the Same as Between-Individual Causes? *Criminal Behaviour and Mental Health, 12*(1), 53–68.
Goldsmith, A. H., Veum, J. R., & Darity, W., Jr. (1996). The Psychological Impact of Unemployment & Joblessness. *Journal of Socio-Economics, 25*(3), 333–358.
Harper, G., & Chitty, C. (2005). The Impact of Correction on Re-offending: A Review of 'what works'. *Home Office Research Study* 291.
Hazel, N., Goodfellow, P., Liddle, M., Bateman, T., & Pitts, J. (2017). *"Now All I Care About Is My Future" – Supporting the Shift: Framework for the Effective Resettlement of Young People Leaving Custody.* Beyond Youth Custody. Retrieved November 29, 2017, from http://www.beyondyouthcustody.net/

wp-content/uploads/Now-all-I-care-about-is-my-future-Supporting-the-shift-full-research-report.pdf.

Hazenberg, R., Seddon, F., & Denny, S. (2014). Investigating the *Outcome* Performance of Work-integration Social Enterprises (WISEs): Do WISEs Offer 'Added Value' to NEETs? *Public Management Review, 16*(6), 876–899.

Higgins, G. E., Kirchner, E. E., Ricketts, M. L., & Marcum, C. D. (2013). Impulsivity and Offending from Childhood to Young Adulthood in the United States: A Developmental Trajectory Analysis. *International Journal of Criminal Justice Sciences, 8*(2), 182–187.

Hodkinson, P., Hodkinson, H., & Sparkes, A. (1996). *Triumphs and Tears.* London: David Fulton Publishers.

Hosser, D. A., Windzio, M., & Greve, W. (2008). Guilt and Shame as Predictors of Recidivism: A Longitudinal Study with Young Prisoners. *Criminal Justice and Behavior, 35*, 138–152.

Jolliffe, D., & Farrington, D. P. (2004). Empathy and Offending: A Systematic Review and Meta-analysis. *Aggressive Violent Behaviour, 9*, 441–476.

Judge, T. A., Locke, E. A., & Durham, C. C. (1997). The Dispositional Causes of Job Satisfaction: A Core Evaluation Approach, *Research in Organisational. Behaviour, 19*, 151–188.

Leider, R. J. (1994). *Life Skills: Taking Charge of Your Personal and Professional Growth*. Paramus: Prentice-Hall.

Leutenberg, E. A., & Liptak, J. J. (2009). *The Practical Life Skills Workbook.* Duluth: Whole Person.

Lewis, S., Maguire, M., Raynor, P., Vanstone, M., & Vennard, J. (2007). What Works in Resettlement? Findings from Seven Pathfinders for Short-term Prisoners in England and Wales. *Criminology and Criminal Justice, 7*(1), 33–53.

Liptak, J. J. (2007). *The Life Skills IQ Test.* New York: Penguin Publishing.

Liptak, J. J. (2008). *Career Quizzes.* Indianapolis: JIST Publishing.

Maruna, S. (2001). *Making Good: How Ex-Convicts Reform and Rebuild Their Lives.* Washington, DC: American Psychological Association.

Masten, A. S. (2001). Ordinary Magic: Resilience Processes in Development. *American Psychologist, 56*, 227–238.

Ministry of Justice. (2017). Proven Reoffending Statistics Quarterly Bulletin – October 2015 – December 2015. Retrieved January 8, 2018, from https://www.gov.uk/government/uploads/system/uploads/attachment_data/file/658379/proven-reoffending-bulletin-oct15-dec15.pdf.

Montgomery, P., Donkoh, C., & Underhill, K. (2006). Independent Living Programs for Young People Leaving the Care System: The State of the Evidence. *Children and Youth Services Review, 28*(12), 1435–1448.

Morris, T., & Morris, P. (1963). *Pentonville: A Sociological Study of an English Prison*. London: Routledge.

Muncie, J. (2014). *Youth and Crime*. London: Sage Publication Ltd.

Niven, S., & Stewart, D. (2005). *Resettlement Outcomes on Release from Prison in 2003*. London: Home Office.

Paterson-Young, C. (2018). *'Inspiring Futures' – How Social Impact Measurement as a Form of Organisational Performance Management Can Enhance Outcomes for Children and Young People in Custody*. University of Northampton. Thesis.

Paterson-Young, C., Hazenberg, R., Bajwa-Patel, M., & Denny, S. (2017). Developing a Social Impact Measurement Framework to Enhance Outcomes for Young People in Custody – What to Measure? *British Society of Criminology – Conference 2017*.

Pinkerton, J., Dolan, P., & Canavan, J. (2004). *Family Support in Ireland: Definition and Strategic Intent. A Paper for the Department of Health and Children*. Dublin: Stationery Office.

Pitts, J. (2007). *Young and Safe in Lambeth. The Deliberations of Lambeth Executive Commission on Children, Young People and Violent Crime*. London: London Borough Council.

Rutter, M. (1985). Resilience in the Face of Adversity: Protective Factors and Resistance to Psychiatric Disorder. *British Journal of Psychiatry, 147*(6), 589–611.

Schofield, G., & Simmonds, J. (Eds.). (2009). The Child Placement Handbook. Research, Policy and Practice. BAAF.

Schofield, G., Thoburn, J., Howell, D., & Dickens, J. (2005). The Search for Stability and Permanence: Modelling the Pathways of Long-stay Looked After Children. *British Journal of Social Work, 37*(4), 619–642.

Schwarzer, R. (Ed.). (1992). *Self-efficacy: Thought Control of Action*. Washington, DC: Hemisphere.

Schwarzer, R., & Jerusalem, M. (1995). *Generalized Self-Efficacy Scale*. In J. Weinman, S. Wright, & M. Johnston (Eds.), *Measures in Health Psychology: A User's Portfolio* (pp. 35–37). Windsor, UK: NFER-NELSON.

Tangney, J. P., Stuewig, J., & Martinez, A. G. (2014). Two Faces of Shame: Understanding Shame and Guilt in the Prediction of Jail Inmates' Recidivism. *Psychological Science, 25*, 799–805.

Taxman, F. (2004). The Offender and Re-entry: Supporting Active Participation in Reintegration. *Federal Probation, 68*(2), 31–35.

Umbreit, M., & Zehr, H. (1996). Restorative Family Group Conferences: Differing Models and Guidelines for Practice. *Federal Probation, 60*(3), 24–29.

Ungar, M. (2005). *Handbook for Working with Children and Youth: Pathways to Resilience Across Cultures and Contexts*. Los Angeles: Sage Publications.

Weber, M. (1978). *Economy and Society: An Outline of Interpretative Sociology*. Berkeley, CA: California University Press.

8

Rehabilitative Environment

Successful transition from custody relies on successful resettlement, which is a process that supports individuals in custody and on release to secure a smooth transition into the community, whilst ensuring communities are protected from harm and recidivism (HM Inspectorates of Prisons and Probation 2001). This is particularly important for young people who have been removed from the community while moving through key stages of their development; stages that support young people to develop the skills that allow for successful transition to adulthood. Halting this development in the community not only impacts on transition to adulthood, but also impacts on securing resources that are essential in adulthood. Young people in custodial environments express concerns over securing accommodation, obtaining employment or education, financial security, relationships, health, wellbeing and substance misuse (Local Government Association 2011; Paterson-Young et al. 2017). Developing sustainable and effective services that tackle the areas outlined above must be the longer-term goals of resettlement for young people accommodated in custody who, because of *"engaging in offending behaviour are particularly vulnerable to negative life outcomes (including unemployment, poor education, mental health, difficulties and social*

C. Paterson-Young et al., *The Social Impact of Custody on Young People in the Criminal Justice System*, https://doi.org/10.1007/978-3-030-18422-3_8

exclusions)" (Beal 2014: 63). This reflects recommendations proposed by the Audit Commission (1996, 1998) and the Taylor (2016) reports, and the STCs statement of purpose (2015) *"…staff are committed to helping sentenced young persons as they move into the community, supporting them to have appropriate accommodation and education and training on release"*.

Despite the fact current approaches theoretically aim to deliver the services required to support young people to develop resilience, stability and resources to support desistence, the limited provisions in STCs mean that these services are severely lacking. This chapter draws on analysis from the previous chapters exploring health and wellbeing, relationships, education, independence and attitudes to offending. By drawing together this analysis, and positioning it within a SIM framework, this chapter develops what can be termed the Resettlement Pyramid that outlines the crucial building blocks to achieving successful transitions. To fully understand this model, this chapter will outline the development stages for the rehabilitative environment, the foundations of the rehabilitative environment and the approaches to implementing the model.

8.1 Developing a Rehabilitative Environment

Unsurprisingly, an understanding of the impacts of custody can help with the design and implementation of effective resettlement schemes. The voices of young people are essential in providing this understanding; however, researchers examining transitions out of the secure estate to the community rarely explore their views (Beal 2014). The experiences and outcomes of young people aged 15–17 years, transitioning from Youth Offending Institutes were explored by Beal (2014), using an Interpretative Phenomenological Analysis (IPA), with results detailing that tailored support packages were essential for addressing the individual needs of young people. Beal's (2014) research highlights the importance of understanding the perceptions of young people accommodated in (and transitioning from) STCs, to help identify vulnerabilities and motivations. Research on the experiences of young people in custody suggests that custodial sentences decrease emotional stability, interrupt engagement in education and interrupt relationships with families and peers (Beal 2014).

Identifying integrated interventions that can holistically meet the individual needs of young people and that are outcomes focused (primarily around reducing recidivism), provides the best means for reducing reoffending rates and improving youth transitions to adulthood.

Building on the prior literature exploring custodial environments and the analysis of the data from the STC, a five-phase model of resettlement was developed (The Resettlement Pyramid). The Resettlement Pyramid outlines the factors that help young people build resilience and pro-social attitudes and hence promote positive outcomes. As outlined in earlier chapters, health, wellbeing and safety, relationships, education and independence all make up the crucial building blocks to successful transition. The Resettlement Pyramid compliments the work of Hazel et al. (2017) who proposed five key characteristics for effective and sustainable resettlement support: constructive (focused on identify-shift, strength-based approaches and empowerment); co-created (focused on inclusion of children, young people and supporters); customised (focused on individual and diverse support); consistent (focused on designing a seamless process from admission); and co-ordinated (focused on widespread partnership). The Resettlement Pyramid, positions ICAP theory and desistance approaches within a wider SIM framework, which provides the vital steps for introducing a model for measuring the wider impact of custody on young people. The inclusion of sub-elements within the Resettlement Pyramid (i.e. education and independence), provides professionals with an opportunity to monitor the impact of each stage on young people in custody (Fig. 8.1).

This model illustrates an environment that promotes positive outcomes for young people in custody by addressing key stages in the resettlement process. The foundations of the pyramid are explored in the next section; however, before exploring the foundations it is essential to recap the main elements of the pyramid: health, wellbeing and safety; relationships; education; independence and pro-social attitudes. The health inequalities and experiences of young people prior to entering custody impact on the development of emotional regulation, coping mechanisms and life satisfaction. Custodial environments play a pivotal role in developing interventions and services to support young people to understand and address the health and wellbeing issues that impact on positive

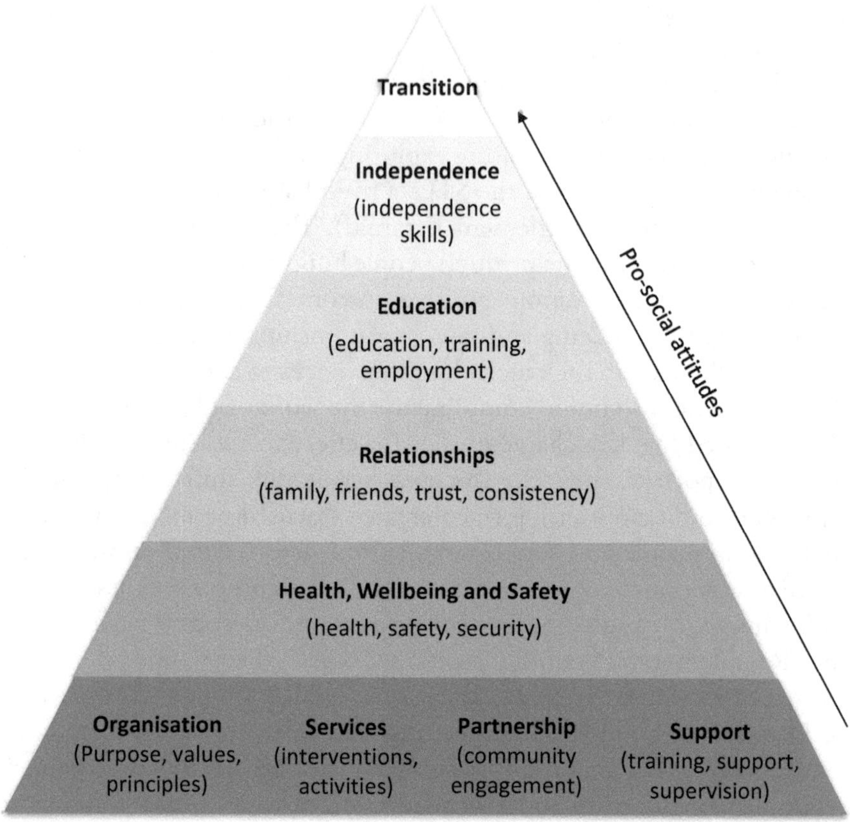

Fig. 8.1 Resettlement Pyramid (Authors' Own)

outcomes. Addressing health and wellbeing is vital to young people's progress; however, relationships are equally important. Young people in custody have often lived in challenging family environments (i.e. witnessing domestic violence; pro-criminal family members). Therefore, a focus on a young people's relationships within a holistic SIM framework that places the young people at the centre, acts as a powerful enabler of change, both within the STC (or other custodial environment) and beyond custody during resettlement. The development of positive, stable and trusting relationships within the STC, and with other individuals beyond custody (family, friends and those in the youth justice system), acts as both an enabler of positive social action for the young people and an inhibitor of those relationships that may otherwise draw the young people back into offending behaviours. Positive relationships allow the young people to engage in internalised change (Farrington and Ttofi 2014) and enable the self-reflexivity that is required to be able to resist negative influences and sustain desistance (Vaughan 2006; Maruna 1997, 2001). If young people develop positive relationships, then opportunities for achieving positive outcomes (and progressing within the pyramid) are maximised. Creating opportunities for achieving positive outcomes is pivotal for young people, but these opportunities do not simply come from health and wellbeing, or relationships.

Given the relationships between poor educational attainment and skills with crime, implementing effective and sustainable services to support the young people in education in the community and custody is paramount to reducing recidivism and improving their life chances of (often) severely disadvantaged young people. Custodial environments, such as STCs, should support young people to develop the essential skills required for achieving education and employment on release from custody (e.g. qualifications, improved literacy and numeracy skills, employment skills). Education plays a significant role in helping young people achieve positive outcomes, as well as reducing recidivism, but the isolation experienced by young people impacts on their transition from custody to the community (Farrington, Loeber, Yin and Anderson 2002; Farrington 2005, 2007; Montgomery et al. 2006). Developing interventions and services that support young people to develop independence is pivotal for supporting young people to transition from custody to the community. It also helps to develop resilience, which enables young people to deal with challenging situations, leading to empowerment and internalised locus of control (Goldsmith, Veum and Darity 1996). This empowerment and internalised locus of control has been shown in this chapter to be central to young people believing that their 'horizons for action' and ability to engage in 'social action' will develop. All of the elements within the pyramid are designed to help young people achieve positive outcomes and future-focused attitudes. Analysis of the qualitative and quantitative data for young people in the STC was used to identify several important social impact factors for measurement; an indicative list is outlined in Table 8.1.

Table 8.1 Social impact measurement factors for young people in STCs

Health and Wellbeing	Health and wellbeing encompass the state of physical, mental, social and spiritual wellbeing. This includes improving physical health; managing substance misuse; promoting good mental wellbeing and promoting a positive sense of self.	Physical Health (e.g. fitness test, BMI) Mental Wellbeing (e.g. Warwick-Edinburgh Wellbeing Scale) Substance use (e.g. Outcome Star) Sense of self and life satisfaction (e.g. Life-satisfaction survey)
Relationships	Relationships encompass the range of social, emotional and intimate needs of individuals. This includes promoting pro-social relationships; establishing trust and consistency; and the development of skills for re-building relationships.	Trust (e.g. self-reported views on relationships) Pro-social relationships (e.g. Pro-Social Tendency measure—Carlo and Randall 2002) Consistency (e.g. Staff Turnover) Attachment (e.g. self-reported views relationships)
Education, Training and/or Employment	Education encompasses the rights of access to education, training and/or employment. This includes promoting improvement in numeracy and literacy; qualification attainment; and promoting participation and engagement in meaningful activities.	Securing placement in education, training or employment (e.g. young people in education, training or employment) Numeracy and Literacy level (e.g. Numeracy and literacy skills assessment) Qualifications (e.g. highest MVQ equivalent) Meaningful activities (e.g. engagement in activities)
Independence	Independence encompasses access to secure and stable accommodation in a positive environment. This includes promoting understanding of basic living skills such as cooking and hygiene as well as providing the knowledge of accessing benefits and services.	Basic living skills (e.g. Independent Life Skills Test—Chap. 7) Essential life skills (e.g. Independent Life Skills Test—Chap. 7) Safe and secure accommodation (e.g. self-reports and support visits) Accessing benefits and services (e.g. Independent Life Skills Test—Chap. 7)

(*continued*)

Table 8.1 (continued)

Attitudes to offending	Attitudes to offending encompasses the personal narrative associated with criminal activity. This includes developing restorative attitudes; promoting attitudes to desistance; reducing the need for gang participation; and improving the views of services as effective and sustainable.	Restorative attitudes (e.g. self-reported views on crime) Views of services (e.g. beneficiaries satisfaction survey) Attitudes to crime (e.g. self-reported views on crime) Gang participation (e.g. police data, pre-sentence reports)

The Resettlement Pyramid not only focuses on developing positive outcomes for young people, but also on identifying the foundations for successful delivery. These foundations are based on findings from research with staff from all areas of the STC, and information on the strategic direction of STCs. The development of interventions and services are reliant on the strategic direction of the organisation, which is underpinned by its core principles and values. As discussed in Chap. 3, the STC requires a clear strategic direction to ensure staff members understand the purpose and principles of the custodial environment—information that is crucial for delivering effective and sustainable services. The development of a multi-stakeholder SIM framework for young people in STCs (and wider custodial environments) that places outcomes for the young people as the main performance indicator, can help to develop this understanding with staff and empower young people. Indeed, such measurement can be inputted into service design and delivery to ensure that interventions are effective (Clifford et al. 2014; Hazenberg and Clifford 2016; Hazenberg et al. 2014). Throughout this book, the factors contributing to successful resettlement and positive outcomes for young people were explored, but the questions that remains are 'do the current provisions in custody offer staff/professionals the level of information needed to provide effective and sustainable services?' and 'If not, then what information do they require and can staff also be empowered to deliver more effective services?'

8.2 Foundation of the Rehabilitative Model

Strengthening the foundations of the rehabilitative environment is essential for developing effective interventions and services for young people in STCs. The analyses of services throughout this book cover one element of the rehabilitative foundation. However, the other elements that require consideration require exploration: the organisation's purpose; support, supervision and training; and partnership working, so as to fully understand the current STC approach.

8.2.1 Organisational Purpose

Delivering effective and sustainable services relies on establishing the beliefs, assumptions and knowledge that underpin organisations. Knowlton and Phillips (2013) argue that as service delivery is rooted in assumptions, knowledge and beliefs, one must first understand these areas (through research and experience), before understanding service impact. Exploring the purpose of the STC is crucial to understanding 'how the organisation's values, aims, objectives and structure influenced the services offered to young people' The original purpose of STCs was *"accommodating trainees in a safe environment within secure conditions; and helping trainees prepare for their return to the outside community"* (Appendix A—STC Rules, 1998). Developments in STCs, following the deaths of the 17-year-olds Kevin Henson and David Dennis in custody in 2000 (Youth Justice Board 2014a), resulted in the introduction of a new Statement of Purpose (further updated in 2015). This new statement of purpose compliments and enhances the original 1998 rules. Although the Statement of Purpose (2015) was designed to enhance the 1998 rules, positioning safety and care as central to the purpose, the founding principles of STCs have remained consistent. This results in confusion for staff employed in STCs, who believe that the current values and principles are inappropriate for the centre today, as demonstrated in comments made by staff:

> *It's absolutely lost its way and vision… I was there from when it opened. The party line that we were given… was that the STC was set up by the Government to provide a short sharp shock to persistent offenders who were stealing cars and burglary and that kind of level. And it was very, very, rare that we would have a 15-year-old in custody as they went, automatically, to a Youth Offending Institution. Whereas obviously now we have kids just short of 18 at the point they are sentenced even, and the way that STC, the purpose and function has not changed to reflect that change.* (Jane, Staff Member)

> *I think some of the values need to change sometimes, especially with the older boys we have now. Seven years ago, we mostly had 13 and 14 year olds but now we have 16 17 and 15 year olds and I think we need to change with the times. I think they are still there, but it can be a bit of a grey area and we should change with the clientele of young people we have here now.* (Ella, Staff Member)

> *I mean the values and principles are clearly displayed around the centre and we receive information on our training, but I don't think they work in the centre at the moment. I haven't been here long but my understanding is that the kids we used to have here were much younger, like 13 and 14. Most of the kids, if you can call them kids that we have here now are like 16 and 17. The older kids are intense because they are set in their ways and don't want to listen to the rules… I think they need to change the values and principles to reflect our current kids.* (Val, Staff Member)

> *They are appropriate for the centre but not for our clientele, in terms of the young people. In terms of STC rules from 1998, so that's nearly 20 years now… We are still running around with the same rules, but we are not the same we were 20 years ago. Things have moved forward but unfortunately they haven't moved it and changed enough to deal with the young people we are dealing with now.* (Pat, Staff Member)

One area for concern, voiced by staff across all areas in the STC, relates to the changing cohort of young people accommodated in custodial environments. STCs were designed to accommodate young people aged 12 to

14 years-old receiving Secure Training Orders or Detention Training Orders. This changed, following a review into the deaths of Kevin Henson and David Dennis (Youth Justice Board 2014a), with young people aged 12 to 17 years-old now accommodated in STCs. Provisions also allow for accommodation to continue for those aged 18 years with additional vulnerabilities (Pitts 2001). Despite changes in the age and sentences of young people accommodated in STCs, the purpose and rules have remained largely static, which leaves staff members concerned that the environment is unable to cater to young people's needs. The needs of young people aged 16 years differs greatly from the needs of a 12-year-old, so how do these environments balance the different needs of young people?

The challenges for staff working with young people with different needs are evident in Chap. 6, with current educational provisions aimed at the younger cohort of young people. Indeed, the educational provisions in STCs have only undergone minor changes since its conception in 1998, with young people expressing frustration over the level of difficulty in education. With STCs accommodating older young people, the effectiveness of educational provisions requires significant overhaul to ensure the needs of all young people are met. For example, creating additional vocational provisions for young people to learn the key skills required to enter a profession (such as construction) on release. This would not only give young people meaningful activities in custody, but also create opportunities upon release.

Another area that requires significant overhaul to meet the needs of this changing cohort of young people is the delivery of skills aimed at independent living. Young people leave custody with limited skills for independent living, yet many are accommodated in hostel or semi-independent living environments immediately upon release. If the STC does not teach the necessary skills for independent living, then how can we expect young people to succeed upon release? It is clear that STCs are still organised to work with younger young people aged 12–14 years, and this means that they are unable to support older young people to manage their transitions to adulthood and into the community, especially when they are not moving back into familial or secure accommodation as younger young people would. Interventions that place the needs of the individual young person at the centre would help to overcome this, whilst the monitoring of social impact would provide evidence of efficacy.

Delivering effective service relies on staff members understanding the direction and purpose of the services. Staff participating in our research expressed concerns over the dissemination of information of changes in STCs, with 46% reporting limited information on changes to policies and/or procedures and 60% reporting limited information on changes to the STC structure and/or management team. The level of understanding of changes to policies and/or procedures was dependent on the role, with staff members in residential roles less likely to receive information on the changes to policies and/or procedures in the STC ($p < 0.05$). Researchers (Alexander et al. 1994; Magner et al. 1996; Labov 1997; Ongori 2007) argue that unstable and unpredictable environments impact negatively on job satisfaction and commitment to the organisation. The turnover in staff at STCs was evident during the research fieldwork, with the Managing Director of Children's Services and Director of Children's Services changing on three occasions between 2015 and 2017. These high turnover rates not only impact on the levels of morale amongst staff, but also on the development of the positive and trustful relationships that help young people succeed upon release (Clancy et al. 2006; Maguire and Raynor 2006). Given the past experiences of many of the young people, including their experience of trauma in its many forms (see Chap. 4), this high turnover in staff is unacceptable if young people are to be effectively supported to deal with this trauma.

Information from the research showed that 39% of staff were employed for less than 12 months, with 27% employed for less than 6 months. The length of service in roles was also dependant on role type, with staff in residential roles significantly more likely to have been employed for shorter periods ($p < 0.05$). Staff members employed for less than 12 months reported feelings of uncertainty, which can be explained by the changes to management and loss of experienced staff members. This uncertainty negatively impacts on young people's experiences, with a revolving door of professionals serving to disrupt the continuity of trust, impacting on their engagement with staff and their upwards progression within the Resettlement Pyramid.

8.2.2 Support, Supervision and Training

The changing needs of young people in custody and the high turnover rates, outline the need for effective support and supervision. Young people in custody come from diverse backgrounds, with information from case-analysis showing that: 64% experienced parental separation; 65% had exposure to pro-criminal family members; 51% were exposed to domestic abuse; 25% experienced bereavement; and 43% had experienced the care system. Staff accessing information on young people are often exposed to emotionally distressing information including detailed information on abuse. Furthermore, staff employed in custodial environments experience high-levels of violence (both physical and verbal) (Ofsted 2017). Ofsted's (ibid) report, outlining the levels of violence in secure estates, demonstrated an increase in levels of violence, with over 20 assaults on staff recorded over a six-month period. Violence against staff in custody can be serious and life changing, with one incident in 2017 resulting in a 21-year-old custody officer spending several days in a coma after an assault by five young people in an STC (BBC 2017). This illustrates the potential physical, psychological and emotional challenges that staff face in custodial environments. Exposure to physical, psychological and emotional violence may result in trauma for staff (Stanley and Goddard 2002); so supporting staff is pivotal for ensuring the effective and sustainable delivery of services (Ferguson 2005; Carpenter et al. 2012).

Research shows that effective support, supervision and training help with job satisfaction and organisational commitment, which reduces stress and reduces turnover (Stanley and Goddard 2002; Ferguson 2005; Carpenter et al. 2012). Staff participating in this research negatively reflected on support and supervision, seeing the support that they had received as inadequate:

> *…I have worked with kids for a long time and I have had quality supervision. The understanding of supervision in the local authority is very different from here. People will write the supervision before they have even met the staff here and get them to sign it. That's not what supervision is. But again, everybody has*

got so much to do and it's like, it's tokenistic, it's a tick box rather than something that people feel is a benefit for them and to aid their development and to support them. (Jane, Staff Member)

I used to have regular support and supervision until the manger left, the new manager isn't as good. I think we need support in this role but all you hear is "we are short staffed; we have to cancel your support sessions". There is always an excuse because of staffing. Some people attend support and supervision and just sign the notes, half of the time the notes were written before the support and supervision. It's a joke like. We need to start supporting staff. After the situation with R, all the staff on shift were really shook, but we barely got any support. It was a case of: "are you ok? Good". (Val, Staff Member)

No, I haven't had supervision for, I think I am going to say, 2 years… you don't know your weak area, you just might hear it through the grapevine that you are bad at that and staff look at deployment and think "OMG look what shit team I have to work with today". And if you had supervision, it could highlight the weak areas… (Rich, Staff Member)

In the beginning yeah, I wouldn't say as much lately because it's constantly always changing. Somebody who was once your manager is now something else. And you don't always have the same managers, so you don't have supervisions and you don't get kept up to date with a lot of the stuff so probably not, no. (Abi, Staff Member)

I don't think I get, nah…I think the supervision policy on paper sounds really good. If it was followed and practiced it would be very beneficial but a lot of reasons why it probably doesn't happen as it should. (Pat, Staff Member)

No. Not all the time, no. It's a challenging environment so we need more support and supervision, more than we have now. (Martha, Staff Member)

The negative impact of the inadequate and irregular supervisory support described by staff above on both their wellbeing and motivation, will undoubtedly be affecting provision for young people and the success of the STC. Levels of supervision related directly to staff roles, with staff engaging directly with young people on a daily basis (i.e. the residential staff) reporting lower levels of support and supervision than those in health or resettlement roles:

> *Absolutely, yes…100 per cent, my managers are fantastic. I have supervision every month and I am very much 'wear my heart on my sleeve'. They know if I am having a bad day, my managers will notice and invite me to talk to them.* (Karen, Staff Member)

> *Yeah so, my manager is good, and he does meet with us once a month. And we can just catch up regularly, if he can't catch up with me officially then he will come and check on the staff and see if we are alright. I'm quite good though, I will go and speak to him if I have any issues and he will sort it out. I feel education is good because we are a small team and there are only 30 of us, it's different from the rest of the site where there are over 100 staff.* (Ella, Staff Member)

> *Healthcare, we get good support from our manager and my supervisor has just given me recent supervision, so yeah. We get regular supervision.* (Charlie, Staff Member)

These discrepancies were also evident from the staff questionnaires, with residential staff members significantly more likely to indicate that support and supervision was inadequate. Indeed, statistically significant differences were identified in the levels of support, with staff in residential roles less likely to receive adequate support and supervision ($p < 0.01$). Staff members in residential roles have exposure to higher levels of violence, so you would expect these staff members to receive a higher level of support and supervision (clearly this is not the case). Staff should be offered consistent and regular support and supervision to help promote good health and wellbeing, which will then help to ensure the effective delivery of services. This support should be offered by a visible and supportive management team alongside effective training, clear guidance, regular reviews and open organisational cultures.

With limited support offered to staff members, the delivery of effective training and experience is crucial. Experience working with young people should be essential for working in this type of environment; however, 42% of staff members reported having no prior experience working with young people. The level of experience was dependent on the role, with staff in non-residential roles significantly more likely to have experience working with children than those working in residential roles. This could be due to the fact that many staff members in non-residential roles moved from residential roles. There is however, a mandatory seven-week Initial Training Course (ITC) (approved by the Youth Justice Board) for all staff members recruited by the STC, covering security, first aid, safeguarding, interpersonal skills, substance misuse and Managing and Minimising Physical Restraint (MMPR). During this research, the researchers had the opportunity to attend the ICT (except for MMPR), noting that essential training such as safeguarding is covered in three hours, with only basic information on adverse childhood experiences and child abuse. Of more concern, was the fact that there was no training on trauma (for example, engaging with young people after trauma), which is essential for supporting young people who have experienced adverse experiences. The level of training was discussed by staff members participating in the research:

> *I think that you don't learn enough about being on the job. I think what they do is fantastic, and they teach you some things. But it needs to be more practical… what the young people do from 7am–9pm, you don't learn that on ICT or how to manage a shift… I managed to learn from someone that had 10 years' experience. You don't get that anymore. We don't have staff that long in service anymore. It makes it difficult. You have new staff training new staff.* (Karen, Staff Member)

> *I want to say yes because we do have like 8 weeks of training at the beginning but, not really. The training we get is good, but it doesn't really prepare you for what happens on the floor. You hear about the stuff that can go wrong in here, but the training doesn't really prepare you.* (Val, Staff Member)

> *When I became an officer it was really hard because I learnt all about the laws and yeah, the CNR training then no PCC when I first started (MMPR). We learned that, and we learned first aid and the laws. But what they didn't actually tell you, is that when you go on the unit, we talk about when the young person gets up, they do this, and they do that.* (Rich, Staff Member)

These members of staff felt that the training they received was not practical enough and did not adequately prepare them for their roles.

> *.... for mine personally, yes. I feel that when I came on board my managers helped me out a lot. They are just two brilliant managers. One has a lot of knowledge behind her, especially within residential and resettlement...* (Sam, Staff Member)

Sam was fortunate to have two experienced managers that were able to support and train her when she joined. However, for others this was not the case and further on-the-job training and work-shadowing were proposed:

> *I think the new staff here are just dropped in the deep end. Yes, they do the training out there and read stuff and that's fine but when you are actually out on the units doing this, it's completely different. I think they should have a good week or two where they should be shadowing someone that's been here. Rather than taking trainees to and from healthcare, I don't think they should be counted as a person and should just be given the chance to do shadowing.* (Abi, Staff Member)

> *So legally, to be a custody officer here you have to fulfil 294 hours of training throughout the ITC... It's really hard to train in a classroom; they say, "this is what you need to do" and then they are expected to do it 7 weeks later. It doesn't work. Training on the ground needs to happen a lot more... it's a really surreal environment and you can't really be trained as much on.* (Naz, Staff Member)

More on the job training and shadowing would allow new staff to get hands on experience, before beginning on their own in what is without doubt a difficult and 'surreal' workplace. The disparity in knowledge and practice highlighted by the staff quotes is significant, with staff members' requests for additional training ignored/overlooked, which impacts on their ability to deliver effective and sustainable services. Again, members of staff employed in residential roles were significantly more likely to report negative views on the adequacy of training. Research on the impact of training showed that adequate training provisions motivate employees to deliver effective services, increase job satisfaction and reduce stress (Vroom 1964; Griffin 2001; Lambert and Paoline 2005). One's ability to effectively deliver services is hindered by poor training and supervision, which may explain the reasons for high staff turnover in the STC (Lambert et al. 2009).

8.2.3 Partnership Working

Partnership working enhances service delivery and opportunities for young people, an essential part of the criminal justice system (Taylor 2016). But how does this work in custody? The rehabilitation of young people relies on partnership working, with effective coordination of services crucial for building relationships and continuity (Taylor 2016). Custodial environments are designed to deliver multi-agency partnership approaches, with multiple services available to young people. Despite the availability of services in custody, staff members reflected on the lack of continuity on release:

> *It's really difficult because, I think, to complete a good piece of work and an in-depth piece of work, it might not be in the kids' best interest to start it here… There needs to be more work done with the local authority around them taking ownership [around] what needs to happen and will continue [on release].* (Jane, Staff Member)

> *But at the same time, for external, they can come in. I always say that to youth offending team workers that they can come in and do work with their young people. Some will agree in the plans, but they don't come in and do any work. This is one thing I always say in meetings, is there any work that you can provide for the young people because they have built those relationships. So, in an ideal world, it would be good for them to come in and do work with them… but mostly of the time they say 'no'.* (Sam, Staff Member)

Management of custodial sentences for young people sits jointly with the secure estate and Youth Offending Teams (Youth Offending Team) (Youth Justice Board 2014a). Information collected from analysing case-notes and interviewing staff members working in the secure estate suggests that Youth Offending Team case-managers only attend meetings to review transition plans, and have limited contact with young people outside these review meetings. This illustrates the passing of responsibility between the Youth Offending Team and the secure estate, with expectations that the secure estate deal with young people until release. The problem with this approach is that young people do not build up relationships with Youth Offending Team workers, which negatively impacts on successful transitions from custody. Young people participating in research expressed negative views of Youth Offending Team, stating that Youth Offending Team workers *"talk at you"* and *"don't listen"*. Research conducted by Phoenix and Kelly (2013) support this, finding that young people believed Youth Offending Team workers are uncaring.

The failure to engage with young people in custody impacts on the development of positive relationships, which impacts on successful resettlement (Bateman and Hazel 2013). The window for empowering, motivating and engaging young people on release from custody, is limited (Hazel et al. 2002; Bateman and Hazel 2013). Thus, developing relationships in custody is of paramount importance in supporting successful transitions, as well as empowering and motivating change. Indeed, it is not only partnership working throughout the custodial journey, but outreach services and community groups that are essential for reducing offending behaviour (McAra and McVie 2010). The previous chapters have shown that the empowerment of young people, through an individual outcomes-based approach is critical to improving their health, wellbeing, education, independence and resilience. However, this cannot be carried out in isolation within the STC, but has to be carried out holistically with the very institutions and individuals whose support is crucial to the young people upon release.

8.3 Using the Rehabilitative Environment Model

Resettlement and desistance are the most important social impacts of youth custody and it is perhaps here that the lack of power that young people have is the most evident and the need for a SIM framework the most apparent. Young people from disadvantaged backgrounds, who form a large proportion of those in custody, are disadvantaged economically, socially and psychologically; therefore, when little has been done to address these areas within the STC, they are unlikely to be able to be successfully resettled or desist. If we want to support young people in successful resettlement and desistance from crime, then we must empower them within the youth justice system by introducing a process that is led through an outcomes-based approach. By developing a combined theoretical approach, through an analytical lens centred upon Weberian (1978) conceptions of power, the Resettlement Pyramid has been developed with a focus on the bidirectional flow of resources. Consequently, social action and the consequent resource flows mediate both the development journey of the young people and the existent structures within the STC, as well as the behaviours of all stakeholders within this ecosystem. As identified in Chap. 3, engaging stakeholders in the resettlement process is also critical if recidivism is to be reduced and young people successfully integrated into communities. Empowering young people using a SIM framework and placing them at the centre of resettlement is the most effective way to ensure successful transition, reduce recidivism and safeguard human rights.

However, the rehabilitative environment is not a linear process, with progression based on the individual needs of young people; certainly, it is not an 'all or nothing' scenario. Monitoring and reviewing the foundations of the rehabilitative environment allows organisations to determine the effectiveness and sustainability of their approach. This allows organisations to identify issues and challenges in the foundations of the rehabilitative environment, which if not addressed will negatively impact young people's progression (and the safety and wellbeing of staff). Monitoring and reviewing young people's progress through each stage of the rehabilitative environment, allows organisations to measure the outcomes at each stage and to feed these back into service design and delivery through an evidence-based approach (Hazenberg et al. 2014; Clifford et al. 2014). If satisfactory outcomes are not achieved for young people, then organisations can employ new, innovative approaches based on individual needs. Even if satisfactory outcomes are achieved for young people, organisations must monitor and review any situational changes (i.e. staff turnover), which may result in regression. Creating an environment that empowers staff and young people, supports the development of effective services, which in turn supports positive outcomes for young people.

8.4 The Rehabilitative Environment Model and Social Impact

This chapter has to date explored the Resettlement Pyramid and how this can be utilised to reduce recidivism. In Chap. 3 we also explored social impact measurement theory, to build the 'young people Centred, Theory-led SIM Framework for Youth Offending' (see Fig. 3.2), which combines SIM theory with ICAP theory. In the chapters that followed, we then explored the various factors that influence offending behaviour before, within and post- incarceration. These include health and wellbeing, education, relationships, independence and resilience. The purpose of these chapters was to both identify the underlying causes of offending and therefore to identify measurement tools that could be used as outcome variables for the SIM. The measurement of outputs, impacts and especially outcomes[1], is critical in providing a holistic assessment of SIM and developing an increasingly robust 'theory of change' (Clifford et al. 2014; Hazenberg and Clifford 2016). Through the identification of the economic, relational and psychological factors that underpin offending behaviour, we were able to develop the Resettlement Pyramid and identify the relevant social impact measurement factors for young people within STCs that were discussed earlier in this chapter (see Fig. 8.1 and Table 8.1). This therefore provides a 'roadmap' of the important outcome variables to be assessed in intervention design and evaluation in STCs.

Throughout the book, social impact measurement and the identification of these variables has been posited as beneficial, due to the way that it allows the young people to be placed at the centre of youth justice interventions. This approach is grounded in Weberian concepts of empowerment, in which social and institutional factors act to inhibit the 'social action' of young people in STCs, both during their incarceration and post-release (Weber 1978). Without such a young person centred approach, the reality is that the very social and institutional conditions that led to their offending behaviour previously, will be recreated within the STC and in their post-release environments. This evidently leads to

[1] See Section 3.4 for a detailed overview of these concepts within SIM theory. Also see McLoughlin et al. (2009) for a detailed overview of the concepts.

reoffending and the re-entry of the young people into the Criminal Justice System, with the human costs (to the young people and the victims) and the financial costs (to society) that are then incurred. The empowerment of the young people therefore, and the widening of what Hodkinson et al. (1996) termed their 'Horizons for Action', are critical if the cycle of offending amongst young offenders is to be broken. This is why multi-stakeholder approaches to intervention design, evaluation and re-design are therefore so critical (Hazenberg et al. 2014), especially when trying to solve the 'wicked problems' that have troubled policy-makers since the 1970s (Rittel and Webber 1973). Indeed, it is only by identifying the key factors underpinning offending as we have done in the Resettlement Pyramid, but then applying it holistically on an individually tailored basis to young people in custody (and post-release), that a truly multi-intervention pathway can be created that will reduce reoffending and create measurable social impact (Hazenberg et al. 2014).

The key element to our model and the original contribution that it makes, is that embedded within this multi-stakeholder, multi-intervention design for supporting positive outcomes for young people in STCs, are three different, but complimentary theoretical approaches (ICAP; Desistance; and SIM theories). The embedding of: ICAP's three key elements (economic, relational and psychological factors) (Farrington and Ttofi 2014); the three elements of desistance theory (age, social bond and personal narrative) (Maruna 2001); and the core measurement principles of SIM theory (outputs, outcomes, impacts, deadweight, alternative attribution and drop-off) (McLoughlin et al. 2009; Clifford et al. 2014; Hazenberg and Clifford 2016); combine to provide a holistic overview of how young people should be supported and how this can be effectively measured. In addition, the importance placed on multi-stakeholder identification and engagement (Clifford et al. 2014; Hazenberg et al. 2014), with specific focus on young people as the primary beneficiary, means that the Resettlement Pyramid increases empowerment of young people in a way that can lead to reduced offending.

Nevertheless, there are still inherent risks in the approach that we articulate in this book. First, social impact remains a poorly defined and nebulous concept, which is therefore open to misinterpretation or deliberate manipulation by relevant stakeholders. Indeed, this can best be evidenced by the fetish in policy circles for demonstrating the fiscal savings that can be produced by interventions, the so called 'Social Return on Investment', over and above the equally important (but often ignored) softer outcomes. As Voltan and Hervieux (2017) discussed, SIM can be manipulated by those with power in a system, as they can force or incentivise stakeholders to measure specific variables. This can act as a powerful shaper of behaviour and potentially lead interventions away from being focused on young people. Indeed, from our Weberian (1978) perspective, this is precisely what is most likely to occur if not guarded against, as the young people are the actors with the least power in the system.

8.5 Summary

Developing a SIM framework that measures independence factors contributing to recidivism and desistance is crucial to developing effective and sustainable services. As discussed previously, developing personal and social independence skills allows young people to make a successful transition to adulthood. The expectation of early-transition with limited support for young people leaving custody presents barriers to positive outcomes (Cashmore and Paxman 1996; Morrow and Richards 1996; Montgomery et al. 2006). As young people in the STC receive limited opportunities to learn independence skills and develop resilience (both crucial building blocks in the Resettlement Pyramid), the impact on reducing recidivism will be negative.

To measure the impact of custody on the development of independence, developing an impact measurement approach is crucial. For example, measuring young people's understanding of financial management from arrival to post-release (6-month to 24-month follow-up) would allow professionals to identify changes in understanding of financial management. This approach acknowledges the key questions proposed by Nevill and Lumley (2011) (see Section 3.2) underpinned by theory of change foundations discussed in Section 3.3. By introducing this approach, the organisation can identify the resources and activities required for supporting young people (for example, restorative justice interventions) and the outputs, outcomes and impact achieved from such interventions. This implementation of interval measurement throughout the young person's journey allows the STC, Youth Justice Board and professionals to assess improvements or challenges to developing pro-social attitudes.

The rehabilitate environment model outlines the essential steps for introducing a SIM model for measuring the social impact of STCs on young people. To embed the rehabilitative environment model within the SIM framework, a significant overhaul of the current STC model is required. Evidence from this research shows that the STC fails to empower young people to achieve positive outcomes due to inadequate and/or limited service provisions (i.e. limited development of independence) and inadequate direction, support and training for staff. Significant overhaul is required to deal with the issues highlighted in this research. Specifically, there is a need to:

1. Explore the needs of young people with acknowledgement of factors outlined in the rehabilitative environment.
2. Review the purpose, values and principles of Secure Training Centres to establish relevant service targets that relate to activities and outcomes as part of a Theory of Change.
3. Develop interventions and services based on the individual needs of young people entering Secure Training Centres.
4. Increase psychology, substance misuse and trauma-informed mental health services for young people in STCs (and in general).
5. Introduce appropriate support, supervision, training and development for staff members employed in Secure Training Centres.
6. Empower STC staff members with a view to increasing job satisfaction, efficacy and reducing staff turnover.
7. Develop a process that promotes cohesive partnership working and community engagement between the STC and communities.

Considering the extensive changes outlined above that are required to make STCs more efficacious in reducing reoffending, the question remains: should we overhaul or replace the current approach to imprisonment for young people? Is it time to stop locking children up out of sight and bring them into plain view and provide them with the help and support they so desperately need and deserve?

References

Alexander, J., Bloom, J., & Nichols, B. (1994). Nursing Turnover and Hospital Efficiency: An Organization-Level Analysis. *Industrial Relations, 33*(4), 505–520.

Audit Commission. (1996). *Misspent Youth: Young People and Crime Summary.* London: Audit Commission.

Audit Commission. (1998). Misspent Youth '98 – The Challenge for Youth Justice. Retrieved April 12, 2018, from http://webarchive.nationalarchives.gov.uk/20090415152538/http://www.auditcommission.gov.uk/Products/NATIONAL-REPORT/7C38F5A0-C744-4362-A6C6-90A12D52258D/archive_misyth98.pdf.

Bateman, T., & Hazel, N. (2013). Engaging Young People in Resettlement: Research Report. London: Nacro/Beyond Youth Custody. Retrieved June 5, 2016, from http://www.beyondyouthcustody.net/wp-content/uploads/Engaging-young-people-in-resettlement.pdf.

BBC. (2017). *Custody Office Attacked by Five Boys at Young Offender Unit.* Retrieved December 20, 2017, from http://www.bbc.co.uk/news/uk-england-beds-bucks-herts-39293479.

Beal, C. (2014). Insider Accounts of the Move to the Outside: Two Young People Talk About Their Transitions from Secure Institutions. *Journal of Youth Justice, 13*(1), 63–75.

Carlo, G., & Randall, B. (2002). The Development of a Measure of Prosocial Behaviors for Late Adolescents. *Journal of Youth and Adolescence, 33(1), 31–44.*

Carpenter, J., Webb, C., Bostock, L., & Coomber, C. (2012). *Effective Supervision in Social Work and Social Care.* Social Care Institute for Excellent – Research Briefing 43.

Cashmore, J., & Paxman, M. (1996). *Wards Leaving Care: A Longitudinal Study.* Sydney, Australia: New South Wales Department of Community Services.

Clancy, A., Hudson, K., Maguire, M., Peake, R., Raynor, P., Vanstone, M., & Kynch, J. (2006). *Getting Out and Staying Out: Results of the Prisoner Resettlement Pathfinders.* Bristol: Policy Press.

Clifford, J., Hehenberger, L., & Fantini, M., (2014, June). *Proposed Approaches to Social Impact Measurement in European Commission Legislation and in Practice Relating to: EuSEFs and the EaSI*, European Commission Report 140605. Retrieved from http://ec.europa.eu/internal_market/social_business/docs/expert-group/social_impact/140605-sub-group-report_en.pdf and http://ec.europa.eu/social/main.jsp?catId=738&langId=en&pubId=7735&type=2&furtherPubs=yes.

Farrington, D. (2005). *Integrated Developmental and Life-Course Theories of Offending. Advances in Criminological Theory*. New Brunswick, NJ: Transaction.

Farrington, D. (2007). Origins of Violent Behaviour over the Life Span. In D. J. Flannery, A. T. Vazsonyi, & I. D. Waldman (Eds.), *The Cambridge Handbook of Violent Behavior and Aggression*. Cambridge: Cambridge University Press.

Farrington, D., & Ttofi, M. (2014). Developmental and Life-Course Theories of Offending. In H. Morizot & L. Kazemian (Eds.), *The Development of Criminal and Antisocial Behaviour*. New York: Springer.

Farrington, D., Loeber, R., Yin, Y., & Anderson, S. J. (2002). Are Within-Individual Causes of Delinquency the Same as Between-Individual Causes? *Criminal Behaviour and Mental Health, 12*(1), 53–68.

Ferguson, H. (2005). Working with Violence, the Emotions and the Psycho-social Dynamics of Child Protection: Reflection on the Victoria Climbie Case. *The International Journal of Social Work Education, 24*(7), 781–795.

Goldsmith, A. H., Veum, J. R., & Darity, W., Jr. (1996). The Psychological Impact of Unemployment & Joblessness. *Journal of Socio-Economics, 25*(3), 333–358.

Griffin, M. (2001). Job Satisfaction Among Detention Officers: Implications for Understanding a System. *Criminal Justice Studies, 19*, 225–239.

Hazel, N., Hagell, A., Liddle, M., Archer, D., Grimshaw, R., & King, J. (2002). *Assessment of the Detention and Training Order and Its Impact on the Secure Estate Across England and Wales*. London: Youth Justice Board.

Hazel, N., Goodfellow, P., Liddle, M., Bateman, T., & Pitts, J. (2017). *"Now All I Care About Is My Future" – Supporting the Shift: Framework for the Effective Resettlement of Young People Leaving Custody*. Beyond Youth Custody. Retrieved November 29, 2017, from http://www.beyondyouthcustody.net/wp-content/uploads/Now-all-I-care-about-is-my-future-Supporting-the-shift-full-research-report.pdf.

Hazenberg, R., & Clifford, J. (2016). GECES and the Valid Measurement of Social Impact in the VCSE Sector. In R. Gunn & C. Durkin (Eds.), *Social Entrepreneurship: A Skills Approach* (2nd ed.). Bristol: Policy Press.

Hazenberg, R., Seddon, F., & Denny, S. (2014). Programme Recruitment and Evaluation: The Effect of an Employability Enhancement Programme on the General Self-efficacy Levels of Unemployed Graduates. *Journal of Education and Work, 28*(3), 273–300.

HM Inspectorate of Prisons. (2001). *Through the Prison Gate – A Joint Thematic Review by HM Inspectorates of Prisons and Probation*. Retrieved February 26, 2016, from https://www.justiceinspectorates.gov.uk/hmiprisons/wp-content/uploads/sites/4/2014/08/Through-The-Prison-Gate-2001-ao.pdf.

Hodkinson, P., et al. (1996). *Triumphs & Tears: Young People, Markets & the Transition from School to Work*. London: David Fulton.

Knowlton, L. W., & Phillips, C. C. (2013). *The Logic Model Guidebook: Better Strategies for Great Results* (2nd ed.). London: Sage Publications.

Labov, B. (1997). Inspiring Employees the Easy Way. *Incentive, 171*(10), 114–118.

Lambert, E., & Paoline, E. (2005). The Impact of Medical Issues and Job Satisfaction of Jail Staff. *Punishment and Society, 7, 259–275.*

Lambert, E. G., Hogan, N. L., Moore, B., Tucker, K., Jenkins, M., Stevenson, M., & Jiang, S. (2009). The Impact of the Work Environment on Prison Staff: The Issue of Consideration, Structure, Job Variety and Training. *American Journal of Criminal Justice, 34*, 166–180.

Magner, N., Welker, R., & Johnson, G. (1996). The Interactive Effects of Participation and Outcome Favourability in Performance Appraisal on Turnover Intentions and Evaluations of Supervisors. *Journal of Occupational Organisation Psychology, 69*, 135–143.

Maguire, M., & Raynor, P. (2006). How the Resettlement of Prisoners Promotes Desistence from Crime: Or Does It? *Criminology and Criminal Justice, 6*(1), 19–38.

Maruna, S. (1997). Going Straight: Desistance from Crime and Life Narratives of Reform. *The Narrative Study of Lives, 5*, 59–93.

Maruna, S. (2001). *Making Good: How Ex-Convicts Reform and Rebuild Their Lives*. Washington: American Psychological Association.

McAra, L., & McVie, S. (2010). Youth Crime and Justice: Key Messages from the Edinburgh Study of Youth Transitions and Crime. *Criminology and Criminal Justice, 10*(2), 179–209.

McLoughlin, J., Kaminski, J., Sodagar, B., Khan, S., Harris, R., Arnaudo, G., & McBrearty, S. (2009). A Strategic Approach to Social Impact Measurement of Social Enterprises: The SIMPLE Methodology. *Social Enterprise Journal, 5*(2), 154–178.

Montgomery, P., Donkoh, C., & Underhill, K. (2006). Independent Living Programs for Young People Leaving the Care System: The State of the Evidence. *Children and Youth Services Review, 28*, 1435–1448.

Morrow, V., & Richards, M. (1996). *Transitions to Adulthood: A Family Matter*. London: Joseph Rowntree Foundation.

Nevill, C., & Lumley, T. (2011). *Impact Measurement in the Youth Justice Sector.* [online]. Retrieved September 9, 2015, from http://www.thinknpc.org/publications/measuring-together/.

Ofsted. (2017). *Inspection of Secure Training Centres – Inspection of Oakhill Secure Training Centre.* Retrieved February 12, 2018, from https://reports.ofsted.

gov.uk/sites/default/files/documents/secure-training-centre-reports/oakhill/OakhillSTC_January2017.pdf.

Ongori, H. (2007). A Review of the Literature on Employee Turnover. *African Journal of Business Management,* 049–054.

Paterson-Young, C., Hazenberg, R., Bajwa-Patel, M., & Denny, S. (2017). Developing a Social Impact Measurement Framework to Enhance Outcomes for Young People in Custody – What to Measure? *British Society of Criminology – Conference 2017.*

Phoenix, J., & Kelly, L. (2013). You Have to Do It for Yourself – Responsibilization in Youth Justice and Young People's Situated Knowledge of Youth Justice Practice. *British Journal of Criminology, 53*, 419–437.

Pitts, J. (2001). *The New Politics of Youth Crime: Discipline or Solidarity*. Dorset: Russell House Publishing.

Rittel, H. W. J., & Webber, M. M. (1973). Dilemmas in the General Theory of Planning. *Policy Sciences, 4*, 155–169.

Stanley, J., & Goddard, C. (2002). *In the Firing Line: Violence and Power in Child Protection Work*. Chichester: Wiley.

STC. (1998). Rules [Online]. Retrieved June 8, 2016, from http://www.legislation.gov.uk/uksi/1998/472/contents/made.

Taylor, C. (2016). An Interim Report of Emerging Findings from the Review of the Youth Justice System. Retrieved July 1, 2016, from https://www.gov.uk/government/news/review-of-the-youth-justice-system.

The Local Government Association. (2011). Resettlement of Youth Offenders: How Local Initiatives Can Make a Difference. L11–565.

Vaughan, B. (2006). The Internal Narrative of Desistance. *British Journal of Criminology, 47*(3), 390–404.

Voltan, A., & Hervieux, C. (2017). Social Impact Assessment of a Community Engagement Initiative, *Paper presented at the 9th International Social Innovation Research Conference,* 12th–14th December 2017, Swinburne University of Technology, Melbourne.

Vroom, V. H. (1964). *Work and Motivation*. San Francisco: Jossey-Bass.

Weber, M. (1978). *Economy and Society: An Outline of Interpretative Sociology*. Berkeley, CA: California University Press.

Youth Justice Board. (2014a). *Deaths of Children in Custody: Action Take, Lessons Learnt.* Retrieved June 30, 2016, from https://www.gov.uk/government/uploads/system/uploads/attachment_data/file/362715/deaths-children-in-custody.pdf.

9

The Future of Youth Justice Rehabilitation

9.1 The Youth Justice Contradiction

The issues surrounding youth justice are complex and often contradictory, with a public desire to lock-away the 'problems' that society has created, but also a recognition that rehabilitation is the only long-term solution to reducing recidivism and hence overall crime. This clash of punitive and welfare logics, alongside the complexity of causation behind youth offending, has created a youth justice system that neither benefits the young people at its heart, nor wider society. Instead, it has created a system that reproduces the inequalities and disadvantage in society, which have directly led to the offending behaviours of the young people in the first place. Traditionally, there has been little incentive for politicians to act to reform this despite their oft-repeated desire to do so, due to public perceptions that are centred on both 'threatening' young people and rose-tinted views of a safer past (Pearson 1983). This removes any electoral incentive for action. A second-class of youth citizen is therefore created, trapped in a punitive cycle of deprivation that has its origins in familial and societal failures.

C. Paterson-Young et al., *The Social Impact of Custody on Young People in the Criminal Justice System*, https://doi.org/10.1007/978-3-030-18422-3_9

Throughout this book we have sought to articulate an alternative vision for youth justice, one that is centred on the young people's holistic needs, in a manner that deals with the *underlying causes* of their criminal behaviour (abuse, trauma, education, and personal agency to name a few discussed in this book). In doing so, the arguments presented are closely aligned with those made in the Taylor Report (2016) in that what is required are multi-stakeholder and multi-agency responses to youth justice in which the young people are placed at the centre of a rehabilitative framework. Such a framework focused upon the diverse needs of the young people and including health and wellbeing, positive relationships, education and personal agency (independence, attitudes and behaviours); is crucial to reducing recidivism and delivering a more just society. Furthermore, whilst a significant proportion of the focus of this book has been on delivering this within custodial settings (i.e. Secure Training Centres), it is clear that such a focus should also be undertaken both pre-offending (for those identified as 'at risk'), and in the community (i.e. community justice interventions and transitions from custody). What differentiates our arguments from those made before however, is the creation of our rehabilitative framework, grounded in philosophical arguments focused on Weberian conceptions of empowerment (Weber 1978), and embedded in social impact theory exploring the measurement of young person centred outcomes (and fiscal impact for society). One can only hope that if (as history suggests) politicians are incapable of grasping the youth justice nettle for moral reasons, that arguments centred on how reducing reoffending can save the Exchequer money might have more resonance!

Our focus on providing a philosophical underpinning to youth justice is critical because, as Case (2018) articulates, we currently have a youth justice system in England that is devoid of any philosophical approach to welfare and justice. This absence of strategic thinking towards the causes of criminal behaviour in young people and how to prevent such behaviours in the first place, whilst also reducing recidivism afterwards, is symptomatic of the clash of punitive and rehabilitative logics outlined earlier. Indeed, to borrow from Kuhnian (1996) conceptions of paradigmatic thought, if there is a dominant paradigm in youth justice at the present time it is one of confusion and obfuscation. This can be perhaps best evidenced by the 1990s New Labour political mantra of being tough on crimes antecedents (McLaughlin et al. 2001). Indeed, when the causes of crime include abuse, trauma, poor education and social disadvantage, it is difficult to see how being 'tough' is the best approach to dealing with such complex issues. Such is the logical confusion at the centre of policy and practice in youth justice! In order to overcome this incoherence, it is critical to develop rehabilitative frameworks that are centred upon positive outcomes for young people, so as to empower them in their transitions to adulthood.

9.2 Empowering Young People Through Positive Outcomes Measurement

The central tenet of this book is that the empowerment of young people is crucial to reducing recidivism, and in developing our framework and Resettlement Pyramid we borrow from the work of Weber (1978) in relation to empowerment and social action. As was discussed in Chap. 3, Weber focuses on how power in social structures mediates resource-flow, shapes personal agency (and hence social action), and creates discourse around topics that entrench power imbalances. Analysing youth justice through a Weberian lens therefore, reveals a system in which institutional logics are confused, with a *de jure* focus on welfare, but a *de facto* focus on punishment. This creates tensions within institutions (especially STCs) whereby their alleged raison-d'être is to educate and rehabilitate young people; but where their physical design, funding and contractual arrangements (as well as the narrative surrounding them), is one of incarceration to a minimum acceptable standard. However, Weber (ibid) also argues that power is mediated by class structures, whereby those with power create institutions that entrench this power, by ensuring that the status quo is maintained. In such systems, young people from disadvantaged backgrounds (as many young people in STCs are) are overlooked by the system, as they have the least amount of power and influence. Social impact measurement offers the opportunity to overcome these power deficits, by forcing those with power within the system to acknowledge and focus upon positive outcomes for young people.

The measurement of outcomes can provide the mechanism that empowers young people in the youth justice system, by placing them at the centre of intervention design and evaluation and allowing them to direct (mediated by other expert stakeholders) the support and outcomes that will be most beneficial to them in reducing recidivism and guiding successful transitions to adulthood. In this way SIM provides the mechanism for shaping institutional behaviour, changing discourse and narratives (creating what Kuhn would describe as a paradigmatic shift in the field) (Kuhn 1996), as well as embedding social and relational networks in ways that support the transitions of the young people. Nevertheless, the key here is to ensure that the outputs, outcomes and impacts (see Chap. 3 for a detailed discussion of these) identified for measurement within the youth justice system, are genuinely young people centred, as otherwise SIM becomes just another mechanism with which those with power in the system can shape behaviour (Voltan and Hervieux 2017).

9.3 The Resettlement Pyramid

In Chap. 8 we introduced the Resettlement Pyramid as part of our resettlement model (see Fig. 8.1), which detailed the pathway and areas of focus for supporting young people to desist from offending and to provide them with the skills required to make successful transitions to adulthood beyond the STC (and the youth justice system more broadly). Our model details the need for holistic support across the youth justice spectrum in relation to health and wellbeing, relationships, education, independence and during transitions. This holistic support must be present throughout the youth justice system (and beyond), including the organisational purpose within STCs (or other residential custodial settings). Indeed, this provision must be embedded in the purpose and values of the: organisations themselves; interventions delivered (whether in custody or beyond); in the community through partnership working between agencies; and through support for young people including training, assistance (i.e. employment, housing etc.) and supervision. It is not the focus of this chapter to reiterate an in-depth overview of this model here, full detail is included in Chap. 8; however, here there will now be an exploration of the key factors within each of the main areas (health, wellbeing, and safety; relationships; education; independence; and attitudes to offending).

The health, wellbeing and safety of young people is the first critical area of focus when seeking to reduce recidivism, enhance youth transitions and ensure that the duty of care towards young people is carried out. Indeed, without in-depth work in this area young people cannot progress up the pyramid towards transition. Whilst there is an abundance of literature in relation to the health and wellbeing of young people in the youth justice system (Khan 2010; Murray 2012; Hughes et al. 2012); our focus in Chap. 4 was on trauma, and specifically the role that experiences of abuse, bereavement and violence have on young people's development (Kitzman et al. 2003; Holt et al. 2008; Cohen et al. 2017). The narrative of trauma is a powerful one in explaining young people's offending behaviours, and without acknowledgement of this and support to overcome this, such traumas are repeated in custody and beyond, reinforcing (understandably) the cycle of offending and anti-social behaviour. Without appropriate emotional support to cope with this trauma, and an environment that allows young people to build up trust in those supporting them, young people will continue to struggle with emotional regulation and proactive coping. It is critical that this support continues beyond custody when the young people go back to their communities to continue their transitions to adulthood. Currently, this is not the case and so we as a society are presented with a situation where young people have been incarcerated in environments that may exacerbate their trauma with little support and are then released back into the community with little continuing assistance. Indeed, without the ability to emotionally regulate and cope with everyday life, further support such as education and training will have little impact and the offending cycle of the young people will continue.

Assuming that appropriate support is provided to cope with trauma, then support around developing positive relationships is the next element of the Resettlement Pyramid. It is worth noting that elements in the Pyramid are not linear and that positive relationships can help support young people to cope with trauma. Relationships for young people are an essential factor in the decisions and choices that they make in life, including the groups they join, peers they associate with and their decisions to engage in criminality (Young et al. 2007). Prior research has demonstrated that young people in care or custody want support from professionals/staff members who have genuine concern and empathy for them, want to spend time with them and who are open and honest with them (Fletcher 1993; Baldry and Kemmis 1998; Bell 2002; Morgan 2006; McLeod 2008). It is therefore clear from the body of prior research conducted with young people that positive relationships can support young people to survive custody, engage with resettlement, positively transition from custody to the community and adulthood, and desist from offending (Clancy et al. 2006; Maguire and Raynor 2006; Bateman and Hazel 2014). Therefore, supporting young people to engage in positive relationships with staff in the STC, and to ensure that these relationships are not broken upon release without an appropriate transition period, is critical. If this is done then the young people can engage in and process internalised change (Farrington and Ttofi 2014) and self-reflexivity (Vaughan 2007; Maruna 1997, 2001), which optimises their chances of then successfully engaging in the education that is meant to be a core part of the STC programme.

Providing young people with skills and qualifications provides the next step in the Resettlement Pyramid, and one that can support their transitions to adulthood, especially in relation to employment. Chapter 6 illustrated the links between social disadvantage, SEND, and BAME with school exclusions, and how this then feeds into the likelihood of a young people ending up in custody. Indeed, the educational attainment age of young people in custody is generally lower than average, with research for the Communities that Care (2005) report demonstrating a link between youth offending and low educational achievement. McNeill et al. (2012) highlighted the role that education and training plays in holistic programmes of support for supporting young people to desist, whilst the Taylor Report (2016) also recognised this. Young people in STCs require in-depth and individually tailored educational support that recognises their educational history and needs (i.e. SEND), and that also then supports them to achieve qualifications that open up further/higher education avenues post-custody. If this is provided, then the opportunities to promote desistance increase and hence the social impact of custodial sentences is improved. It remains to be seen whether the Secure Schools being established in the wake of the Taylor (2016) report can provide this.

The final element of the Resettlement Pyramid prior to transitions relates to independence and attitudes, and specifically the development of personal and social skills that enable successful transitions to adulthood (Montgomery et al. 2006). In addition, the changing of attitudes to offending is also important in reducing recidivism. Developing independence in young people through the development of skills including communication, emotional management, employment, financial management, securing accommodation and accessing services (Montgomery et al. 2006); provides a key element to reducing the loneliness that research has shown affects young people during their transition from custody (Farrington and Loeber 2002; Farrington 2005, 2007; Montgomery et al. 2006). Such skills promote resilience and can form an integral part of the educational offer in STCs, which can help reduce recidivism and promote positive transitions to adulthood. Such resilience can lead to internalised locus of control (Goldsmith et al. 1996), which empowers young people and broadens their horizons for action (Hodkinson et al. 1996).

9.4 Resettlement and Effective Transitions

Having engaged with young people in STCs (and youth justice interventions more generally) through the Resettlement Pyramid, the foundations for successful resettlement and transition both into the community and adulthood are therefore laid. This means that the low expectations of young people upon transition and the lack of support that they are given during it (Cashmore and Paxman 1996; Morrow and Richards 1996; Montgomery et al. 2006) can be overcome. However, to ensure that positive progress is made with the young people across the key areas of the Resettlement Pyramid, it is crucial that longitudinal measures of this progress are identified and captured during young people's time in custody and beyond. This is what we presented in the previous chapter in Table 8.1, where we began to identify the relevant areas for measurement and possible specific measures for these that could be used (i.e. the Warwick/Edinburgh Wellbeing Scale). The application of these measures across the youth justice sector and certainly within STCs, and the linking of these outcome measures to performance management frameworks, provides the mechanism from which young people can be placed at the centre of policy, practice and evaluation. This empowerment of the young people can then help to reduce recidivism, generate social impact (and cost-savings for the government) and lead to truly multi-intervention pathways that can create sustainable social impact (Hazenberg et al. 2014). Based upon this, the authors propose seven key recommendations for the effective rehabilitation of young people in STCs (albeit this could also be applied elsewhere in youth justice as well). These are listed below:

1. Explore the needs of young people with acknowledgement of factors outlined in the rehabilitative environment.
2. Review the purpose, values and principles of STCs to establish relevant service targets that relate to activities and outcomes as part of a ToC.
3. Develop interventions and services based on the individual needs of young people entering STCs.
4. Increase psychology, substance misuse and trauma-informed mental health services for young people in STCs (and in general).
5. Introduce appropriate support, supervision, training and development for staff members employed in STCs.
6. Empower STC staff members with a view to increasing job satisfaction, efficacy and reducing staff turnover.
7. Develop a process that promotes cohesive partnership working and community engagement between the STC and communities.

Throughout this book we have sought to demonstrate both the complexity of the causes of youth offending and attempts to promote desistance/reduce recidivism. We do not intend that this book should over-simplify these issues or to suggest that there are easy fixes to reoffending patterns. Nor do we wish to suggest that SIM provides a 'holy grail' solution to youth offending and its causes. Indeed, the issue of youth offending is one of the key 'wicked problems' (Rittel and Webber 1973) that have faced policy-makers for decades, as its causes are complex and based within family breakdown, abuse and trauma, educational failure, institutional barriers, funding and the personal agency of the young people. However, we do believe that SIM provides an opportunity to begin to reframe the debates and narratives within youth justice towards a young person centred focus on welfare and rehabilitation, rather than punitive approaches to what society sees as 'problem' children. It is only through the creation of holistic frameworks of support that make institutions and stakeholders within the system accountable for the outcomes achieved by young people, that reoffending can be reduced and positive transitions for young people achieved. Additionally, it is only by empowering young people to overcome past negative experiences and to develop hopes and aspirations for the future, that they can be enabled to engage in Weber's (1978) positive social action and to lead fulfilling lives.

References

Baldry, S., & Kemmis, J. (1998). What Is It Like to Be Looked After by a Local Authority? *British Journal of Social Work, 28*, 129–136.

Bateman, T., & Hazel, N. (2014). *Youth Justice Timeline*. Retrieved from http://www.beyondyouthcustody.net/wp-content/uploads/youth-justice-timeline.pdf.

Bell, M. (2002). Promoting Children's Rights Through the Use of Relationship. *Child and Family Social Work, 7*, 1–11.

Case, S. (2018). *Youth Justice: A Critical Introduction*. Oxon: Routledge.

Cashmore, J., & Paxman, M. (1996). *Wards Leaving Care: A Longitudinal Study*. Sydney, Australia: New South Wales Department of Community Services.

Clancy, A., Hudson, K., Maguire, M., Peake, R., Raynor, P., Vanstone, M., & Kynch, J. (2006). *Getting Out and Staying Out: Results of the Prisoner Resettlement Pathfinders*. Bristol: Policy Press.

Cohen, J. A., Mannarino, A. P., & Deblinger, E. (2017). *Treating Trauma and Traumatic Grief in Children and Adolescents* (2nd ed.). London: The Guildford Press.

Communities that Care. (2005). *Risk and Protective Factors*. London: Youth Justice Board.

Farrington, D. (2005). *Integrated Developmental and Life-Course Theories of Offending. Advances in Criminological Theory*. New Jersey: Transaction.

Farrington, D. (2007). Origins of Violent Behaviour Over the Life Span. In D. J. Flannery, A. T. Vazsonyi, & I. D. Waldman (Eds.), *The Cambridge Handbook of Violent Behavior and Aggression*. Cambridge: Cambridge University Press.

Farrington, D., Loeber, R., & Yin, Y. (2002). Are Within-individual Causes of Delinquency the Same as Between-Individual Causes? *Criminal Behaviour and Mental Health, 12*(1), 53–68.

Farrington, D., & Ttofi, M. (2014). Developmental and Life-Course Theories of Offending. In H. Morizot & L. Kazemian (Eds.), *The Development of Criminal and Antisocial Behaviour*. New York: Springer.

Fletcher, B. (1993). *Not Just a Name: The Views of Young People in Residential and Foster Care. Who Cares?* London: National Consumer Council.

Goldsmith, A. H., Veum, J. R., & Darity, W., Jr. (1996). The Psychological Impact of Unemployment & Joblessness. *Journal of Socio-Economics, 25*(3), 333–358.

Hazenberg, R., Seddon, F., & Denny, S. (2014). Programme Recruitment and Evaluation: The Effect of an Employability Enhancement Programme on the General Self-efficacy Levels of Unemployed Graduates. *Journal of Education and Work, 28*(3), 273–300.

Hodkinson, P., Hodkinson, H., & Sparkes, A. (1996). *Triumphs and Tears*. London: David Fulton Publishers.

Hughes, N., Williams, H., Chitsabesan, P., Davies, R., & Mounce, L. (2012). *Nobody Made the Connection: The Prevalence of Neuro-disability in Children and Young People Who Offend*. London: Children's commissioner.

Khan, L. (2010). *Reaching Out, Reaching in: Promoting Mental Health and Emotional Well-being in Secure Settings*. Centre for Mental Health. Retrieved September 28, 2017, from http://www.ohrn.nhs.uk/resource/policy/Reachingoutreachingin.pdf.

Kitzman, K., Gaylord, N., Holt, A., & Kenney, E. (2003). Child Witnesses to Domestic Violence: A Meta-Analytic Review. *Journal of Consulting and Clinical Psychology, 71*(2), 229–235.

Kuhn, T. (1996). *The Structure of Scientific Revolutions* (3rd ed.). London: University of Chicago Press.

Maguire, M., & Raynor, P. (2006). How the Resettlement of Prisoners Promotes Desistence from Crime: Or Does It? *Criminology and Criminal Justice, 6*(1), 19–38.

Maruna, S. (1997). Going Straight: Desistance from Crime and Life Narratives of Reform. In *The Narrative Study of Lives* (Vol. 5, pp. 59–93).

Maruna, S. (2001). *Making Good: How Ex-Convicts Reform and Rebuild their Lives*. Washington, DC: American Psychological Association Books.
McLaughlin, E., Muncie, J., & Hughes, G. (2001). The Permanent Revolution: New Labour, New Public Management and the Modernization of Criminal Justice. *Criminology and Criminal Justice, 1*(3), 301–318.
McLeod, A. (2008). 'A Friend and an Equal': Do Young People in Care Seek the Impossible from Their Social Workers? *British Journal Social Work*, Advance Access, 1–17.
Montgomery, P., Donkoh, C., & Underhill, K. (2006). Independent Living Programs for Young People Leaving the Care System: The State of the Evidence. *Children and Youth Services Review, 28*, 1435–1448.
Morgan, R. (2006). Young People and Offending (Foreword). In M. Stephenson (Ed.), *Young People and Offending – Education, Youth Justice and Social Inclusion*. London: Routledge.
Morrow, V., & Richards, M. (1996). *Transitions to Adulthood: A Family Matter*. London: Joseph Rowntree Foundation.
Murray, R. (2012). *Children and Young People in Custody 2011/12: An Analysis of the Experiences of 15–18 Year Olds in Prisons*. London: HMIP/the Youth Justice Board.
Pearson, G. (1983). *Hooligan: A History of Respectable Fears*. London: Macmillan.
Taylor, C. (2016). *An Interim Report of Emerging Findings from the Review of the Youth Justice System*. London: Ministry of Justice.
Vaughan, B. (2007). The Internal Narrative of Desistance. *British Journal of Criminology, 47*, 390–404.
Voltan, A., & Hervieux, C. (2017). Social Impact Assessment of a Community Engagement Initiative, *Paper presented at the 9th International Social Innovation Research Conference*, 12th–14th December 2017, Swinburne University of Technology, Melbourne
Weber, M. (1978). *Economy and Society: An Outline of Interpretative Sociology*. Berkeley, CA: California University Press.
Young, T., Fitzgerald, M., Hallsworth, S., & Joseph, I. (2007). *Groups, Gangs and Weapons*. London: Youth Justice Board.

Epigraph

"It is right that children who break the law are dealt with differently to adults. Children act impulsively and often do not appreciate the consequences of their actions; they are not emotionally developed and may struggle to communicate effectively. This is particularly true of so many of the children who offend, who often have learning or speech and communication problems. But children also have great strengths on which to build and are capable of rapid and extraordinary change. There needs to be a shift in the way society, including central and local government, thinks about youth justice so that we see the child first and the offender second. Offending should not mean forfeiting the right to childhood. If children who offend are to become successful and law-abiding adults, the focus must be on improving their welfare, health and education—their life prospects—rather than simply imposing punishment" (Taylor, 2016: 3).

C. Paterson-Young et al., *The Social Impact of Custody on Young People in the Criminal Justice System*, https://doi.org/10.1007/978-3-030-18422-3

Appendix A: Secure Training Centre Rules 1998 (STC 1998)

Statement of Purpose

1. The aims of a centre shall be—

    a. to accommodate trainees in a safe environment within secure conditions; and
    b. to help trainees prepare for their return to the outside community.

2. The aim mentioned in paragraph (1)(b) above shall be achieved, in particular, by—

    a. providing a positive regime offering high standards of education and training;
    b. establishing a programme designed to tackle the offending behaviour of each trainee and to assist in his development;
    c. fostering links between the trainee and the outside community; and
    d. co-operating with the services responsible for the trainee's supervision after release.

C. Paterson-Young et al., *The Social Impact of Custody on Young People in the Criminal Justice System*, https://doi.org/10.1007/978-3-030-18422-3

3. A statement of the aims mentioned in paragraph (1) above and how they are to be achieved shall be prepared and displayed in each centre and shall be made available on request—

    a. to trainees;
    b. to any person visiting the centre; and
    c. to any person inspecting the centre.

Appendix B: Secure Training Centre Statement of Purpose (2015)

1. (…) Secure Training Centre works with young people aged 12–17 years who are either sentenced or remanded. Sentenced young persons (trainees) are detained either under Section 100 of the Powers of the Criminal Court (Sentencing) Act 2000 to a Detention and Training Order or, for more serious offences, under Sections 90, 91, 228 or 226 of the same Act. Remanded young persons are remanded to Youth Detention Accommodation as nominated by the Secretary of State under Sections 90–107 of the Legal Aid Sentencing and Punishment of Offenders Act 2012.
2. The Centre is committed to looking after and accommodating all sentenced and remanded young persons in safe and secure conditions. The Centre provides high-quality standards of care for all young persons, by providing well-maintained living conditions and positive staff relationships, as well as helping to promote social, emotional and physical needs, based on the principles of dignity, privacy and respect.
3. Every member of staff at the Secure Training Centre is committed to maintaining the highest standards of care, control, good order and discipline, protecting vulnerable or disruptive young persons from themselves and/or others.

C. Paterson-Young et al., *The Social Impact of Custody on Young People in the Criminal Justice System*, https://doi.org/10.1007/978-3-030-18422-3

4. The Centre will treat all young persons as individuals and award them dignity and respect by promoting their cultural and religious needs, respecting gender, disability and diversity, ensuring the Centre promotes anti-discriminatory and anti-racist behaviour.
5. The Centre is committed to providing every young person with a positive regime offering high standards of education, healthcare, anti-offending programmes aimed at preventing re-offending and preparing young people for their return to the community.
6. All sentenced young persons will be presented with challenging programmes to tackle offending behaviour, confront them with the effects of their actions, making them realise the consequences for themselves and society.
7. All remanded young persons will be provided with education, regime activities and citizenship programmes which will not compromise their inherent right to innocence.
8. The Centre is committed to having a comprehensive complaints and representations procedure where complaints are taken seriously and responded to within agreed timescales. The Centre works proactively with the Youth Justice Board Monitor and Barnardos in promoting children's rights linked to their responsibilities to act in an appropriate way.
9. The Centre will work positively in partnership with Youth Offending Teams and other external agencies to support and enhance the transition for all the young people into the community on their release.
10. All young persons' Planning Meetings will involve the young persons, their parents and/or carers. Programmes will be based on initial and ongoing assessment to ensure that the programmes fully meet the needs of the young person when in custody or on remand and promote ongoing work in the community.
11. The Centre is committed to supporting all young persons, their families and/or carers, to maintain contact and to help them work in partnership with the Centre's staff team. Help in supporting families and carers, offering advice and assistance is essential to the Centre's work.

12. Centre staff are committed to helping sentenced young persons as they move into the community, supporting them to have appropriate accommodation and education and training on release. The Centre staff are committed to the continued work with the Youth Offending Team, education establishments, parents and carers, while offering post release advice and support, by contributing to the community review and follow up communication.

References

Chapter 1

Cohen, S. (1972). *Folk Devils and Moral Panics: The Creation of the Mods and Rockers*. London: Routledge.
Farrington, D. (2005). *Integrated Developmental and Life-Course Theories of Offending. Advances in Criminological Theory*. New Jersey: Transaction.
Franklin, B., & Petley, J. (1996). Killing the Age of Innocence: Newspaper Reporting of the Death of James Bulger. In J. Picler & S. Wagg (Eds.), *Thatcher's Children? Politics, Childhood and Society on the 1980s and the 1990s*. London: Falmer Press.
Montgomery, P., Donkoh, C., & Underhill, K. (2006). Independent Living Programs for Young People Leaving the Care System: The State of the Evidence. *Children and Youth Services Review, 28*, 1435–1448.
Muncie, J., Hughes, G., & McLaughlin, E. (2002). *Youth Justice: Critical Reading*. London: Sage.
Paterson-Young, C. (2018). *'Inspiring Futures' – How Social Impact Measurement as a Form of Organisational Performance Management Can Enhance Outcomes for Young People in Custody*. PhD Thesis, University of Northampton.
Pearson, G. (1983). *Hooligan: A History of Respectable Fears*. London: Macmillan.
Smith, R. (2007). *Youth Justice: Ideas, Policy, Practice*. Devon: Willan Publishing.

C. Paterson-Young et al., *The Social Impact of Custody on Young People in the Criminal Justice System*, https://doi.org/10.1007/978-3-030-18422-3

Taylor, C. (2016). *An Interim Report of Emerging Findings From the Review of the Youth Justice System*. London: Ministry of Justice.
Weber, M. (1978). *Economy and Society: An Outline of Interpretative Sociology*. Berkley, CA: California University Press.

Chapter 2

Audit Commission. (1996). *Misspent Youth: Young People and Crime Summary*. London: Audit Commission.
Audit Commission. (1998). Misspent Youth '98 – The Challenge for Youth Justice. Retrieved April 12, 2018, from http://webarchive.nationalarchives.gov.uk/20090415152538/http://www.audit-commission.gov.uk/Products/NATIONAL-REPORT/7C38F5A0-C744-4362-A6C6-90A12D52258D/archive_misyth98.pdf.
Bateman, T. (2017). *The State of Youth Justice 2017 – An Overview of Trends and Developments*. National Association for Youth Justice – Justice for Children in Trouble.
Bateman, T., & Hazel, N. (2014). *Youth Justice Timeline*. Retrieved June 5, 2016, from http://www.beyondyouthcustody.net/wp-content/uploads/youth-justice-timeline.pdf.
BBC. (2016). *Teenage Prison Abuse Exposed*. Retrieved September 12, 2016, from http://www.bbc.co.uk/programmes/b06ymzly.
Cameron, D. (2008). *Fixing Our Broken Society*. Retrieved February 28, 2019, from https://www.webarchive.org.uk/wayback/archive/20080907225219/http://www.conservatives.com/tile.do?def=news.story.page&obj_id=145626&speeches=1.
Case, S. (2018). *Youth Justice: A Critical Introduction*. Oxon: Routledge.
Cohen, J. A., Mannarino, A. P., & Deblinger, E. (2017). *Treating Trauma and Traumatic Grief in Children and Adolescents* (2nd ed.). London: The Guildford Press.
Department of Education. (2017). *Children Accommodated in Secure Children's Homes at 31 March 2017: England and Wales*. SFR 23/2017.
Goldson, B. (2002). Children, Crime and the State. In B. Goldson, M. Lavalette, & J. McKechnie (Eds.), *Children, Welfare and the State*. London: Sage.
Graham, J., & Moore, C. (2008). *Beyond Welfare Versus Justice: Juvenile Justice England and Wales*. In J. Junger-Tas & S. H. Decker (Eds.), *International Handbook of Juvenile Justice*. New York: Springer.

Hendrick, H. (1997). Constructions and Reconstructions of British Childhood: An Interpretative Survey, 1800 to the Present. In A. James & A. Prout (Eds.), *Constructing and Reconstructing Childhood: Contemporary Issues in the Sociological Study of Childhood* (pp. 33–60). London: Routledge.

Hendrick, H. (2006). Histories of Youth Crime and Justice. In B. Goldson & J. Muncie (Eds.), *Youth Crime and Justice*. London: Sage Publications.

Holt, S., Buckley, H., & Whelan, S. (2008). The Impact of Exposure to Domestic Violence on Children and Young People: A Review of the Literature. *Child Abuse & Neglect, 32*(8), 797–810.

Kitzmann, K., Gaylord, N., Holt, A., & Kenney, E. (2003). Child Witnesses to Domestic Violence: A Meta-Analytic Review. *Journal of Consulting and Clinical Psychology, 71*(2), 339–352.

Lawson, K. M., Back, S. E., Hartwell, K. J., Maria, M. M., & Brady, K. T. (2013). A Comparison of Trauma Profiles among Individuals with Prescription Opioid, Nicotine, or Cocaine Dependence. *The American Journal on Addictions, 22*(2), 127–131.

Ministry of Justice. (2010). *Breaking the Cycle: Effective Punishment, Rehabilitation and Sentencing of Offenders*. London: Ministry of Justice.

Muncie, J. (2009). *Youth and Crime* (3rd ed.). Oxford: Sage Publication Ltd.

Muncie, J. (2015). *Youth and Crime* (4th ed.). Oxford: Sage Publication Ltd.

Muncie, J., Hughes, G., & McLaughlin, E. (2002). *Youth Justice: Critical Reading*. London: Sage.

Paterson-Young, C. (2018). *'Inspiring Futures' – How Social Impact Measurement as a Form of Organisational Performance Management Can Enhance Outcomes for Young People in Custody*. PhD Thesis, University of Northampton.

Paterson-Young, C., Hazenberg, R., Bajwa-Patel, M., & Denny, S. (2017). *Developing a Social Impact Measurement Framework to Enhance Outcomes for Young People in Custody—What to Measure?* British Society of Criminology – Conference 2017.

Pearson, G. (1983). *Hooligan: A History of Respectable Fears*. London: Macmillan.

Pitts, J. (2001). *The New Politics of Youth Crime: Discipline or Solidarity*. Dorset: Russell House Publishing.

STC. (1998). Rules [Online]. Retrieved June 8, 2016, from http://www.legislation.gov.uk/uksi/1998/472/contents/made.

Taylor, C. (2016). *Review of the Youth Justice System in England and Wales*. London: Ministry of Justice, The Parliamentary Office of Science and Technology (2016) *Education in Youth Custody*. Post note: 524.

The Lammy Review. (2017). *An Independent Review into the Treatment of, and Outcomes for Black, Asian and Minority Ethnic individuals in the Criminal*

Justice System. Retrieved June 26, 2018, from https://assets.publishing.service.gov.uk/government/uploads/system/uploads/attachment_data/file/643001/lammy-review-final-report.pdf.
Youth Justice Board. (2011). *Youth Justice Statistics 2009/10 – England and Wales.* London: Youth Justice Board.
Youth Justice Board. (2014a). *Deaths of Children in Custody: Action Take, Lessons Learnt.* London: Youth Justice Board.
Youth Justice Board. (2014b). *AssetPlus Model Document.* London: Youth Justice Board.
Youth Justice Board. (2015a). *Youth Justice Statistics 2013/2014.* London: Youth Justice Board.
Youth Justice Board. (2015b). *Youth Offending Teams: Making the Difference for Young People, Victims and Communities.* London: Youth Justice Board.
Youth Justice Board. (2018). *Youth Justice Statistics 2016/2017.* London: Youth Justice Board.

Chapter 3

Bersani, B. E., Laub, J. H., & Nieuwbeerta, P. (2009). Marriage and Desistance from Crime in the Netherlands: Do Gender and Socio-historical Context Matter? *Journal of Quantitative Criminology, 25*, 3–24.
Burdge, R., & Vanclay, F. (1996). Social Impact Assessment: A Contribution to the State of the Art Series. *Impact Assessment, 14*, 59–86.
Chen, H., & Rossi, P. H. (1980). *The Multi-Goal Theory Driven Approach to Evaluation: A Model Linking Basic & Applied Social Science. Social Forces, 59*(1), 106–122.
Clifford, J., Markey, K., & Malpani, N. (2013). *Measuring Social Impact in Social Enterprise: The State of Thought and Practice in the UK*, London, E3M. Retrieved from http://ec.europa.eu/internal_market/social_business/docs/expert-group/social_impact/presentation-e3m_en.pdf.
Clifford, J., Hehenberger, L., & Fantini, M. (2014). *Proposed Approaches to Social Impact Measurement in European Commission Legislation and in Practice Relating to: EuSEFs and the EaSI*, European Commission Report 140605 (June 2014). Retrieved from http://ec.europa.eu/internal_market/social_business/docs/expert-group/social_impact/140605-sub-group-report_en.pdf and http://ec.europa.eu/social/main.jsp?catId=738&langId=en&pubId=7735&type=2&furtherPubs=yes.

Emerson, J. (2000). *The Nature of Returns: A Social Capital Markets Inquiry into Elements of Investment and The Blended Value Proposition*, Harvard Working Paper Series, No. 17 Social Enterprise Series, Boston, MA. Retrieved from http://www.blendedvalue.org/wp-content/uploads/2004/02/pdf-nature-of-returns.pdf.

Farrall, S., & Bowling, B. (1999). Structuration, Human Development and Desistance from Crime. *British Journal of Criminology, 39*(2), 252–267.

Farrington, D. (2003). Key results from the First 40 Years of the Cambridge Study in Delinquent Development. In T. P. Thornberry & M. D. Krohn (Eds.), *Taking Stock of Delinquency: An Overview of Findings from Contemporary Longitudinal Studies*. New York: Kluwer.

Farrington, D. (2005). *Integrated Developmental and Life-Course Theories of Offending. Advances in Criminological Theory*. New Jersey: Transaction.

Farrington, D. (2007). Origins of Violent Behaviour Over the Life Span. In D. J. Flannery, A. T. Vazsonyi, & I. D. Waldman (Eds.), *The Cambridge Handbook of Violent Behavior and Aggression*. Cambridge: Cambridge University Press.

Farrington, D., & Ttofi, M. (2014). Developmental and Life-Course Theories of Offending. In H. Morizot & L. Kazemian (Eds.), *The Development of Criminal and Antisocial Behaviour*. New York: Springer.

Giordano, P. C., Cernkovich, S. A., & Rudolph, J. L. (2002). Gender, Crime and Desistance: Toward a Theory of Cognitive Transformation. *American Journal of Sociology, 107*, 990–1064.

Glueck, S., & Glueck, E. (1937). *Later Criminal Careers*. New York: Kraus.

Goring, C. (1919). *The English Convict*. London: His Majesty's Stationary Office.

Hazenberg, R., & Clifford, J. (2016). GECES and the Valid Measurement of Social Impact in the VCSE Sector. In R. Gunn & C. Durkin (Eds.), *Social Entrepreneurship: A Skills Approach* (2nd ed.). Bristol: Policy Press.

Hazenberg, R., Seddon, F., & Denny, S. (2014). Programme Recruitment & Evaluation: The Effect of an Employability Enhancement Programme on the General Self-efficacy Levels of Unemployed Graduates. *Journal of Education & Work, 28*(3), 273–300.

Hehenberger, L., Harling, A-M., & Scholten, P. (2013). A Practical Guide to Measuring and Managing Impact. Brussels, European Venture Philanthropy Association: 124. Retrieved from http://evpa.eu.com/publication/guide-measuring-and-managing-impact-2015/.

Hirschi, T. (1969). *The Causes of Delinquency*. Berkeley: The University of California Press.

Hirschi, T., & Gottfredson, M. (1983). Age and the Explanation of Crime. *American Journal of Sociology, 89*, 552–584.

Jain, P. (2018). *Conceptualising Social Value: Perspectives of the Public, Private and Third Sectors in the UK.* PhD Thesis, University of Northampton.

Maruna, S. (2001). *Making Good: How Ex-Convicts Reform and Rebuild their Lives*. Washington: American Psychological Association.

McLoughlin, J., Kaminski, J., Sodagar, B., Khan, S., Harris, R., Arnaudo, G., & McBrearty, S. (2009). A Strategic Approach to Social Impact Measurement of Social Enterprises: The SIMPLE Methodology. *Social Enterprise Journal, 5*(2), 154–178.

McNeill, F. (2002). *Beyond 'What Works': How and Why Do People Stop Offending?* CJSW Briefing (Paper 5).

McNeill, F., Farrall, S., Lightowler, C., & Maruna, S. (2012). *How and Why People Stop Offending: Discovering Desistance, Insights: Evidence Summaries to Support Social Services in Scotland* (Vol. 15). Glasgow: IRISS.

Millar, R., & Hall, K. (2013). Social Return on Investment (SROI) and Performance Measurement. *Public Management Review, 15*(6), 923–941.

Moloney, M., MacKenzie, K., Hunt, G., & Joe-Laidler, K. (2009). The Path and Promise of Fatherhood for Gang Member. *British Journal of Criminology, 49*(3), 305–325.

Nicholls, A. (2009). We Do Good Things Don't We? Blended Value Accounting in Social Entrepreneurship. *Accounting, Organizations and Society, 34*(6–7), 755–769.

Paterson-Young, C. (2018). *'Inspiring Futures' – How Social Impact Measurement as a Form of Organisational Performance Management Can Enhance Outcomes for Young People in Custody*, PhD Thesis, University of Northampton.

Sairinen, R., & Kumpulainen, S. (2006). Assessing the Social Impact in Urban Waterfront Regeneration. *Environmental Impact Assessment Review, 26*, 120–135.

Sampson, R., & Laub, J. (1993). *Crime in the Making: Pathways and Turning Points Through Life*. Cambridge, MA: Harvard University Press.

Soothill, K., Ackerley, E., & Francis, B. (2004). Profiles of Crime Recruitment. *British Journal of Criminology, 44*, 401–418.

Voltan, A., & Hervieux, C. (2017). Social Impact Assessment of a Community Engagement Initiative, *Paper presented at the 9th International Social Innovation Research Conference*, 12th–14th December 2017, Swinburne University of Technology, Melbourne.

Weber, M. (1978). *Economy and Society: An Outline of Interpretative Sociology*. Berkeley, CA: California University Press.

Chapter 4

Argyle, M. (2001). *The Psychology of Happiness* (2nd ed.). Hove: Methuen and Co.

Chitsabesan, P., Kroll, L., Bailey, S., Kenning, C., Sneider, S., MacDonald, W., Theodosiou, L., et al. (2006). Mental Health Needs of Young Offenders in Custody and in the Community. *British Journal of Psychiatry, 188*, 534–540.

Chitsabesan, P., Lennox, C., Theodosiou, L., Law, H., Bailey, S., & Shaw, J. (2014). The Development of the Comprehensive Health Assessment Tool for Young Offenders within the Secure Estate. *Journal of Forensic Psychiatry and Psychology, 25*, 1–25.

Cohen, J. A., Mannarino, A. P., & Deblinger, E. (2017). *Treating Trauma and Traumatic Grief in Children and Adolescents* (2nd ed.). London: The Guildford Press.

Eaton, J., & Paterson-Young, C. (2018). *The Little Orange Book*. Derby: Victim Focus.

Golzari, M., Hunt, S. J., & Anoshiravani, A. (2006). The Health Status of Youth in Juvenile Detention Facilities. *Journal of Adolescent Health, 38*(6), 776–782.

Hanson, R. K., & Harris, A. J. R. (2000). Where Should We Intervene? Dynamic Predictors of Sexual Offense Recidivism. *Criminal Justice and Behavior, 27*, 6–35.

Harrison, P. A., Fulkerson, J. A., & Beebe, T. J. (1997). Multiple Substance Use Among Adolescent Physical and Sexual Abuse Victims. *Child Abuse and Neglect, 21*, 529–539.

HM Chief Inspector of Prisons. (1999). *Suicide Is Everyone's Concern: A Thematic Review by HM Chief Inspector of Prisons for England and Wales*. London: Home Office.

Hughes, N., Williams, H., Chitsabesan, P., Davies, R., & Mounce, L. (2012). *Nobody Made the Connection: The Prevalence of Neuro-disability in Children and Young People Who Offend*. London: Children's commissioner.

Jacobson, J., Bhardwa, B., Gyateng, T., Hunter, G., & Hough, M. (2010). *Punishing Disadvantage: A Profile of Children in Custody*. London: Prison Reform Trust.

Khan, L. (2010). *Reaching Out, Reaching in: Promoting Mental Health and Emotional Well-Being in Secure Settings*. Centre for Mental Health. Retrieved September 28, 2017, from http://www.ohrn.nhs.uk/resource/policy/Reachingoutreachingin.pdf.

Kinner, S. A., Degenhardt, L., & Coffey, C. (2014). Complex Health Needs in the Youth Justice System: A Survey of Community-Based and Custodial Offenders. *Journal of Adolescent Health, 54*, 521–526.

Lader, D., Singleton, N., & Meltzer, H. (1997). *Psychiatric Morbidity Among Young Offenders in England and Wales*. London: Office for National Statistics.

Lader, D., Singleton, N., & Meltzer, H. (2003). Psychiatric Morbidity Among Young Offenders in England and Wales. *International Review of Psychiatry, 15*, 144–147.

Laws, B., & Crewe, B. (2016). Emotional Regulation Among Male Prisoners. *Theoretical Criminology, 20*(4), 529–547.

Lawson, K. M., Back, S. E., Hartwell, K. J., Maria, M. M., & Brady, K. T. (2013). A Comparison of Trauma Profiles Among Individuals with Prescription Opioid, Nicotine, or Cocaine Dependence. *American Journal on Addictions, 22*(2), 127–131.

Layard, R. (2005). *Happiness: Lessons from a New Science*. London: Penguin.

Lennox, C. (2014). The Health Needs of Young People in Prison. *British Medical Bulletin, 112*(1), 17–25.

Murray, R. (2012). *Children and Young People in Custody 2011/12: An Analysis of the Experiences of 15–18 Year Olds in Prisons*. London: HMIP/the Youth Justice Board.

NHS. (2016). *Health Survey for England 2015: Health, Social Care and Lifestyles*. NHS Digital and Office for National Statistics.

Ofsted. (2007). Establishing Successful Practice in Pupil Referral Units and Local Authorities. Retrieved from http://dera.ioe.ac.uk/6542/1/Pupil%20referral%20units%20establishing%20successful%20practice%20in%20pupil%20referral%20units%20and%20local%20authorities%20PDF%20format%29.doc.pdf.

Ofsted. (2018). *Inspection of Secure Training Centres – Inspection of Oakhill Secure Training Centre*. Retrieved October 1, 2018, from https://reports.ofsted.gov.uk/sites/default/files/documents/secure-training-centre-reports/oakhill/Oakhill%20STC%20June%202018%20report.pdf.

Parker, H., Aldridge, J., & Measham, F. (1998). *Illegal Leisure. The Normalization of Adolescent Recreational Drug Use*. London: Routledge.

Paterson-Young, C. (2018). *'Inspiring Futures' – How Social Impact Measurement as a Form of Organisational Performance Management Can Enhance Outcomes for Young People in Custody*. PhD Thesis, University of Northampton.

Planalp, S. (1999). *Communicating Emotion: Social, Moral, and Cultural Processes*. Cambridge: Cambridge University Press.

Public Health England. (2017). Health Inequalities: Reducing Inequalities in Local Areas.

University of Manchester. (2013). The Comprehensive Health Assessment Tool. Retrieved September 23, 2018, from http://www.ohrn.nhs.uk/OHRNResearch/CHATManualV32013.pdf.

Wright, S., Liddle, M., & Goodfellow, P. (2016). Young Offenders and Trauma: Experience and Impact: A Practitioner's Guide. Beyond Youth Custody. Retrieved from http://www.beyondyouthcustody.net/wp-content/uploads/BYC-Trauma-experience-and-impact-practitioners-guide.pdf.

Youth Justice Board & Ministry of Justice. (2019). Youth Justice Statistics 2017/18. England and Wales. Retrieved from https://assets.publishing.service.gov.uk/government/uploads/system/uploads/attachment_data/file/774866/youth_justice_statistics_bulletin_2017_2018.pdf.

Zamble, E., & Quinsey, V. L. (2001). *The Criminal Recidivism Process*. London: Cambridge University Press.

Chapter 5

Abrams, L. S. (2007). From Corrections to Community: Youth Offenders' Perceptions of the Challenges of Transition. *Journal of Offender Rehabilitation, 44*, 31–53.

Aspy, C. B., Oman, R. F., Vesely, S. K., McLeroy, K., Rodine, S., & Marshall, L. (2004). Adolescent Violence: The Protective Effects of Youth Assets. *Journal of Counseling and Development, 82*(3), 268–276.

Baldry, S., & Kemmis, J. (1998). What Is It Like to Be Looked After by a Local Authority? *British Journal of Social Work, 28*, 129–136.

Bateman, T., & Hazel, N. (2014). *Youth Justice Timeline*. Retrieved from http://www.beyondyouthcustody.net/wp-content/uploads/youth-justice-timeline.pdf.

Bell, M. (2002). Promoting Children's Rights Through the Use of Relationship. *Child and Family Social Work, 7*, 1–11.

Beyond Youth Custody. (2017, April). *Lessons from Youth in Focus: Research Report*, Big Lottery Fund. Retrieved from http://www.beyondyouthcustody.net/wp-content/uploads/Lessons-from-Youth-in-Focus-Research-Report.pdf.

Bronfenbrenner, U. (1979). *The Ecology of Human Development*. Cambridge, MA: Harvard University Press.

Cid, J., & Martí, J. (2012). Turning Points and Returning Points: Understanding the Role of Family Ties in the Process of Desistance. *European Journal of Criminology, 9*(6), 603–620. https://doi.org/10.1177/1477370812453102.

Clancy, A., Hudson, K., Maguire, M., Peake, R., Raynor, P., Vanstone, M., & Kynch, J. (2006). *Getting Out and Staying Out: Results of the Prisoner Resettlement Pathfinders*. Bristol: Policy Press.

Ellis, L. (1988). The Victimful-victimless Crime Distinction, and Seven Universal Demographic Correlates of Victim Criminal Behaviour. *Personality & Individual Difference.*

Farrington, D. P. (1993). Childhood Origins of Teenage Antisocial Behaviour and Adult Social Dysfunction. *Journal of the Royal Society of Medicine*. 86.

Farrington, D. (2005). *Integrated Developmental and Life-Course Theories of Offending. – Advances in Criminological Theory*. New Jersey: Transaction.

Farrington, D., & Ttofi, M. (2014). Developmental and Life-Course Theories of Offending. In H. Morizot & L. Kazemian (Eds.), *The Development of Criminal and Antisocial Behaviour*. New York: Springer.

Fletcher, B. (1993). Not Just a Name: The Views of Young People in Residential and Foster Care. Who Cares? National Consumer Council, London.

Goodfellow, P., Wilkinson, S., Hazel, N., Bateman, T., Liddle, M., Wright, S., & Factor, F. (2015). *Effective Resettlement of Young People*. London: Nacro/ Beyond Youth Custody.

Hart, D. (2015). Correction or Care? The Use of Custody for Children in Trouble. *Prison Reform Trust.*

Hazel, N., Goodfellow, P., Liddle, M., Wright, S., Lockwood, K., McAteer, L., Francis, V., & Wilkinson, S. (2016). *The Role of Family Support in Resettlement.* Beyond Youth Custody. Retrieved from http://www.beyondyouthcustody.net/wp-content/uploads/The-role-of-family-support-in-resettlement-a-practitioners-guide.pdf.

Hazel, N., Goodfellow, P., Liddle, M., Bateman, T., & Pitts, J. (2017). *"Now All I Care About Is My Future": Supporting the Shift – Framework for the Effective Resettlement of Young People Leaving Custody*, Beyond Youth Custody. Retrieved from http://www.beyondyouthcustody.net/wp-content/uploads/Now-all-I-care-about-is-my-future-Supporting-the-shift-full-research-report.pdf.

Holt, S., Buckley, H., & Whelan, S. (2006). The Impact of Exposure to Domestic Violence on Young People: A Review of the Literature. *Journal of Child Abuse and Neglect, 32*, 797–810.

House of Commons. (2007). Young Black People and the Criminal Justice System, House of Commons Home Affairs Committee, Second Report of Session 2006–07 Volume I. Retrieved from https://publications.parliament.uk/pa/cm200607/cmselect/cmhaff/181/181i.pdf.

Kidson, H. (2013). Reducing Recidivism Amongst Young People in Custody Through Welfare Lead Rehabilitation. Winston Churchill Memorial Trust. Retrieved from https://www.wcmt.org.uk/sites/default/files/migrated-reports/1189_1.pdf.

Kitzmann, K., Gaylord, N., Holt, A., & Kenney, E. (2003). Child Witnesses to Domestic Violence: A Meta-Analytic Review. *Journal of Consulting and Clinical Psychology., 71*(2), 229–235.

Liddle, M. (2016). *Resettlement Work with Young People: Using Individual Case-studies to Assess Costs and Benefits*, Beyond Youth Custody. Retrieved from http://www.beyondyouthcustody.net/wp-content/uploads/Resettlement-work-with-young-people-using-individual-case-studies-to-assess-costs-and-benefits.pdf.

Lipsey, M. W., & Derzon, J. H. (1998). Predictors of Violent or Serious Delinquency in Adolescence and Early Adulthood, A Synthesis of Longitudinal Research. In R. Loeber & D. P. Farrington (Eds.), *Serious and Violent Juvenile Offenders: Risk Factors and Successful Interventions*. Thousand Oaks, CA: Sage.

Local Government Association. (2017). *Councils Call for Urgent Action to Improve Safety in Youth Offending Institutions.* Retrieved January 10, 2019, from http://www.beyondyouthcustody.net/wp-content/uploads/The-role-of-family-support-in-resettlement-a-practitioners-guide.pdf.

Maguire, M., & Raynor, P. (2006). How the Resettlement of Prisoners Promotes Desistence from Crime: Or Does It? *Criminology and Criminal Justice, 6*(1), 19–38.

Maruna, S. (1997). Going Straight: Desistance from Crime and Life Narratives of Reform. *The Narrative Study of Lives, 5*, 59–93.

Maruna, S. (2001). *Making Good: How Ex-Convicts Reform and Rebuild Their Lives*. Washington, DC: American Psychological Association Books.

Matsueda, R. L. (1988). The Current State of Differential Association Theory. Crime and Delinquency. Retrieved from http://cad.sagepub.com/cgi/content/abstract/34/3/277.

McLeod, A. (2008). 'A friend and An Equal': Do Young People in Care Seek the Impossible from Their Social Workers? British Journal Social Work, Advance Access, 1–17.

Moore, T., McArthur, M., & Saunders, V. (2013). Young People Talk About Transitioning from Youth Detention to the Community: Making Good. *Australian Social Work, 66*, 328–343.

Morgan, R. (2006). Young People and Offending (Foreword). In M. Stephenson (Ed.), *Young People and Offending – Education, Youth Justice and Social Inclusion*. London: Routledge.

Mulvey, E. P., et al. (2004). Theory and Research on Desistance from Antisocial Activity Among Serious Adolescent Offenders. *Youth Violence and Juvenile Justice, 2*(3), 213–236. https://doi.org/10.1177/1541204004265864.

NHS England. (2017). Just Health: An Enquiry into the Emotional Health and Wellbeing of Young People in the Youth Justice System, Peer Power Research. Retrieved from http://www.peerpower.org.uk/wp-content/uploads/2017/01/Just%20Health%20Report%20(for%20Web).pdf.

Ofsted. (2017). Inspection of Secure Training Centres – Inspection of Oakhill Secure Training Centre. Retrieved February 12, 2018, from https://reports.ofsted.gov.uk/sites/default/files/documents/secure-training-centre-reports/oakhill/OakhillSTC_January2017.pdf.

Partridge, S. (2004). *Examining Case Management Models for Community Sentences*. Home Office Online Report 17/04. London: Home Office.

Phoenix, J., & Kelly, L. (2013). 'You Have to Do it for Yourself' – Responsibilization in Youth Justice and Young People's Situated Knowledge of Youth Justice Practice. *British Journal of Criminology, 53*, 419–437.

Rogers, R. (2011). 'Instant Adulthood' and the Transition of Young People Out of State Care. *Journal of Sociology, 47*(4), 411–426.

Sampson, R., & Laub, J. (1993). *Crime in the Making: Pathways and Turning Points Through Life*. Cambridge, MA: Harvard University Press.

Umberson, D., & Montez, J. (2010). Social Relationships and Health: A Flashpoint for Health Policy. *Journal of Health and Social Behavior, 51*, S54–S66.

Vaughan, B. (2007). The Internal Narrative of Desistance. *British Journal of Criminology, 47*, 390–404.

Weber, M. (1978). *Economy and Society: An Outline of Interpretative Sociology*. Berkeley, CA: California University Press.

West, D. J., & Farrington, D. P. (1973). *Who Becomes Delinquent?* London: Heinemann.

Whitebook, M., & Sakai, L. (2003). Turnover Begets Turnover: An Examination of Job and Occupational Instability Among Child Care Center Staff. *Early Childhood Research Quarterly, 18*(3), 273–293.

Young, T., Fitzgerald, M., Hallsworth, S., & Joseph, I. (2007). *Groups, Gangs and Weapons*. London: Youth Justice Board.

Chapter 6

Bailey, R. (2009). Well-Being, Happiness and Education. *British Journal of the Sociology of Education, 30*(6), 795–802.

Bajwa, M. (2014). Parental Choice and School Placement – Issues for Parents of Children with Statements of Special Educational Needs. Doctoral thesis.

University of Northampton. Retrieved from http://nectar.northampton.ac.uk/8847/.

Bajwa-Patel, M., & Devecchi, C. (2014). 'Nowhere That Fits': The Dilemma of School Choice for Children with Statements of Special Educational Needs in England. *SFL, 29*(2), 117–135.

Barton, L. (1998). Developing an Emancipatory Research Agenda: Possibilities and Dilemmas. In P. Clough & L. Barton (Eds.), *Articulating with Difficulty: Research Voices in Inclusive Education*. London: Paul Chapman.

Casey, L. (2016). The Casey Review: A Review into Opportunity and Integration, December 2016.

Daniels, H., Cole, T., Sellman, E., Sutton, J., Visser, J., & Bedward, J. (2003). Study of Young People Permanently Excluded from School. London: DfES. Research Report No 405.

Department for Education (DfE). (2011). Getting the Simple Things Right: Charlie Taylor's Behaviour Checklists. Retrieved from https://assets.publishing.service.gov.uk/government/uploads/system/uploads/attachment_data/file/571640/Getting_the_simple_things_right_Charlie_Taylor_s_behaviour_checklists.pdf.

Department for Education (DfE). (2017a). Permanent and Fixed-Period Exclusions in England: 2015 to 2016. Retrieved from https://assets.publishing.service.gov.uk/government/uploads/system/uploads/attachment_data/file/645075/SFR35_2017_text.pdf.

Department for Education (DfE). (2017b). Exclusion from Maintained Schools, Academies and Pupil Referral Units in England Statutory Guidance for Those with Legal Responsibilities in Relation to Exclusion. Retrieved from https://assets.publishing.service.gov.uk/government/uploads/system/uploads/attachment_data/file/641418/20170831_Exclusion_Stat_guidance_Web_version.pdf.

DfE. (2018a). Promoting the Guidance of Looked After Children and Previously Looked After Children. Statutory Guidance for Local Authorities. Retrieved from https://assets.publishing.service.gov.uk/government/uploads/system/uploads/attachment_data/file/683556/Promoting_the_education_of_looked-after_children_and_previously_looked-after_children.pdf.

DfE. (2018b). Permanent and Fixed Period Exclusions in England: 2016 to 2017. Retrieved from https://assets.publishing.service.gov.uk/government/uploads/system/uploads/attachment_data/file/726741/text_exc1617.pdf.

DfE. (2018c). Special Educational Needs in England: January 2018. https://assets.publishing.service.gov.uk/government/uploads/system/uploads/attachment_data/file/729208/SEN_2018_Text.pdf.

Dodge, K. A., Bai, Y., Ladd, H. F., Muschkin, C. G. (2016). Impact of North Carolina's Early Childhood Development Programmes and Policies on Educational Outcomes in Elementary School. https://doi.org/10.1111/cdev.12645.

Evans, C., & Hardaker, G. (2015). Understandings and Applications of Resilience. *Journal for Multicultural Education, 9*(3), 1.

Evans, J., & Vincent, C. (1997). Parental Choice and Special Education. In G. Glatter, P. A. Woods, & C. Bagley (Eds.), *Choice and Diversity in Schooling: Perspectives and Prospects*. London: Routledge.

Farrington, D. (1996). Understanding and Preventing Youth Crime. Report retrieved from https://www.jrf.org.uk/report/understanding-and-preventing-youth-crime.

Gallipoli, G., & Fella, G. (2007). Education and Crime Over the Life Cycle. Rimini Centre for Economic Analysis, Working Paper Series. 81. https://doi.org/10.1093/restud/rdu014.

Gewirtz, S., Ball, S. J., & Bowe, R. (1995). *Markets, Choice and Equity in Education*. Buckingham: Open University Press.

Gorard, S., Taylor, C., & Fitz, J. (2003). *Schools, Markets and Choice Policies*. London: Routledge Falmer.

Harris, A., & Ranson, S. (2005). The Contradictions of Education Policy: Disadvantage and Achievement. *British Educational Research Journal,* ***31***(2), 571–587.

Hart, D. (2006). *Tell Them Not to Forget About Us*. London: National Children's Bureau.

Heckman, J. J. (2006). Skill Formation and the Economics of Investing in Disadvantaged Children. *Science, 312*(5782), 1900–1902. https://doi.org/10.1126/science.1128898.

HM Chief Inspector of Prisons for England and Wales. (2017). *Annual Report 2016–17*. London: HMIP.

HM Government. (2018). The Site for the First Secure School. Retrieved from https://assets.publishing.service.gov.uk/government/uploads/system/uploads/attachment_data/file/752377/site-brochure.pdf.

Home Office Research, Development and Statistics Directorate. (2004). The Role of Education in Enhancing Life Chances and Preventing Offending. London: Home Office. Retrieved from https://webarchive.nationalarchives.gov.uk/20081107201453/http://www.crimereduction.homeoffice.gov.uk/youth/youth55.htm.

House of Lords. (2018). Written Answers. https://www.parliament.uk/written-questions-answers-statements/written-question/lords/2018-04-26/HL7326.

Houses of Parliament. (2016). POSTNOTE: Education in Youth Custody. Number 524. May 2016.

Howard League for Penal Reform. (2010). *Access to Justice Denied*. London: Howard League for Penal Reform.

IfL. (2013). Retrieved from https://set.et-foundation.co.uk/media/796985/2013_05_IfL_Transforming-Education-in-Youth-Custody.pdf.

Lanskey, C. (2011). Promise or Compromise? Education for Young People in Secure Institutions in England. *Youth Justice Journal, 11*(1), 47–60.

Lazar, I., Darlington, R., Murray, H., Royce, J., & Snipper, A. (1982). The Lasting Effects of Early Education: A Report from the Consortium for Longitudinal Studies, Monographs of the Society for Research in Child Development, 47 (2–3), serial no. 195.

Lochner, L., & Moretti, E. (2004). The Effect of Education on Crime: Evidence from Prison Inmates, Arrests, and Self-Reports. *The American Economic Review, 94*(1), 155–189.

Machin, S., Marie, O., & Vuji¢, S. (2010). The Crime Reducing Effects of Education, CEP Discussion Paper No 979.

McAra, L., & McVie, S. (2010). Youth Crime and Justice: Key Messages from the Edinburgh Study of Youth Transitions and Crime. *Criminology and Criminal Justice, 10*(*2*), 179–209. https://doi.org/10.1177/174889580936097.

McCrone, T., & Morris, M. (2004). Research into the Impact of pre-16 Vocational Education. Report published by NFER, July 2004. Retrieved from http://cep.lse.ac.uk/research/skills/Skills_Publications/McCrone_Morris_2004.pdf.

McNeil, F. (2006). A Deslstance Paradigm for Offender Management. *Criminology and Criminal Justice, 6*(1), 37–60.

Meghir, C., Palme, M., & Schnabel, M. (2011). The Effect of Education Policy on Crime: An Intergenerational Perspective. Institute for Fiscal Studies Working Paper W11/11. Retrieved from, https://doi.org/10.1111/cdev.12645.

Ministry of Justice. (2013). Analysis of Education Funding Agency Administrative Data, published in Transforming Youth Custody. Retrieved from https://www.gov.uk/government/consultations/transforming-youth-custodyputting-education-at-the-heart-of-detention.

Ministry of Justice and DfE. (2016). Understanding Educational Background of Young Offenders. Full report. Retrieved from https://assets.publishing.service.gov.uk/government/uploads/system/uploads/attachment_data/file/577542/understanding-educational-background-of-young-offenders-full-report.pdf.

Moffitt, T. E. (1993). Adolescence-limited and Life-Course-Persistent Antisocial Behaviour: A Developmental Taxonomy. *Psychological Review, 100*(4), 674–701.

Morgan, R. (2006). *Stephenson, M. (2011). Young People and Offending: Education, Youth Justice and Social Inclusion*. Oxon: Routledge.

Mortimore, P., Sammons, P., Stoll, L., Lewis, D., & Ecob, R. (1988). *School Matters: The Junior Years*. Wells: Open Books.

OFSTED. (2007). Establishing Successful Practice in Pupil Referral Units and Local Authorities. Retrieved from http://dera.ioe.ac.uk/6542/1/Pupil%20referral%20units%20establishing%20successful%20practice%20in%20pupil%20referral%20units%20and%20local%20authorities%20PDF%20format%29.doc.pdf.

OFSTED report. (2018). Inspection of Oakhill STC. Retrieved from https://files.api.ofsted.gov.uk/v1/file/50010313.

ONS. (2017). Young People Not in Education, Employment or Training (NEET), UK: March 2018. Retrieved from https://www.ons.gov.uk/employmentandlabourmarket/peoplenotinwork/unemployment/bulletins/youngpeoplenotineducationemploymentortrainingneet/march2018.

Prison Reform Trust. (2017). In Care, Out of Trouble. How the Life Chances of Children in Care Can Be Transformed by Protecting Them from Unnecessary Involvement in the Criminal Justice System—Impact Report, London: PRT. Retrieved from http://www.prisonreformtrust.org.uk/Portals/0/Documents/Care%20review%20impact%20report%20Jan%202017%20UPDATE%20FINAL.pdf.

Runswick- Cole, K. (2011). Time to End the Bias Towards Inclusive Education? *British Journal of Special Education, 38*(3), 112–119.

Rutter, M. (1985). Family and School Influences on Cognitive Development. *Journal of Child Psychology and Psychiatry, 26*(5), 683–704.

Rutter, M., Maughan, B., Mortimore, P., & Ouston, J. (1979). *Fifteen Thousand Hours: Secondary Schools and Their Effects on Children*. London: Open Books.

Sutherland, A., Merrington, S., Jones, S., & Baker, K. (2005). *The Role of Risk and Protective Factors*. London: Youth Justice Board for England and Wales.

Sylva, K. (1994). The Impact of Early Learning on Children's Later Development. In C. Ball (Ed.), *Start Right: The Importance of Early Learning*. London: The Royal Society for the Encouragement of Arts, Manufacturers and Commerce.

Taylor, C. (2016). *An Interim Report of Emerging Findings from the Review of the Youth Justice System*. London: Ministry of Justice. Retrieved July 1, 2016, from https://www.gov.uk/government/news/review-of-the-youth-justice-system.

Utting, D. (1996). *Reducing Criminality Among Young People: A Sample of Relevant Programmes in the United Kingdom. Home Office Research Study 161*. London: Home Office.

Watt, B., Howells, K., & Delfabbro, P. (2004). Juvenile Recidivism: Criminal Propensity, Social Control and Social Learning Theories. *Psychiatry, Psychology and Law, 11*(1), 141–153.

Youth Justice Board. (2005). Risk and Protective Factors. Retrieved from http://mws-73973.mws3.csx.cam.ac.uk/people/academic_research/david_farrington/riskprot.pdf

Youth Justice Board. (2006). Engagement in Education, Training and Employment. Retrieved from http://dera.ioe.ac.uk/7999/1/Barriers%20to%20ETE%20report%20FINAL.pdf.

Youth Justice Board. (2016). Youth Custody Report January 2016. Ministry of Justice.

Youth Justice Board and Ministry of Justice. (2018). Youth Justice Statistics 2016/17. England and Wales. Statistics Bulletin. Retrieved from https://assets.publishing.service.gov.uk/government/uploads/system/uploads/attachment_data/file/676072/youth_justice_statistics_2016-17.pdf.

Chapter 7

Beal, C. (2014). Insider Accounts of the Move to the Outside: Two Young People Talk About Their Transitions from Secure Institutions. *Journal of Youth Justice, 13*(1), 63–75.

Bortner, M. A., & Williams, L. M. (1997). *Youth in Prison*. New York: Routledge.

Braithwaite, J. (2002). *Restorative Justice and Response Regulation*. New York: Oxford University Press.

Case, S., & Haines, K. (2009). *Understanding Youth Offending: Risk Factor Research, Policy and Practice*. Cullompton: Willan.

Defoe, I. N., Farrington, D. P., & Loeber, R. (2013). Disentangling the Relationship Between Delinquency and Hyperactivity, Low Achievement, Depression, and Low Socio-economic Status: Analysis of Repeated Longitudinal Data. *Journal of Criminal Justice, 41*, 100–107.

Dickens, J., Howell, D., Thoburn, J., & Schofield, G. (2007). Children Starting to Be Looked After by Local Authorities in England: An Analysis of Inter-authority Variation and Case-centred Decision-making. *British Journal of Social Work, 37*, 597–617.

Dixey, R., & Woodall, J. (2011). Prison Staff and the Health Promoting Prison. *International Journal of Prisoner Health, 7*, 8–16.

Farrington, D. (1990). Implications of Criminal Career Research for the Prevention of Offending. *Journal of Adolescence, 13*(2), 93–113.

Farrington, D. (1992). Juvenile Delinquency. In J. C. Coleman (Ed.), *The School Years* (2nd ed., pp. 123–116). London: Routledge.

Farrington, D. (2005). *Integrated Developmental and Life-Course Theories of Offending. Advances in Criminological Theory*. New Jersey: Transaction.

Farrington, D. (2007). Origins of Violent Behaviour over the Life Span. In D. J. Flannery, A. T. Vazsonyi, & I. D. Waldman (Eds.), *The Cambridge handbook of Violent Behavior and Aggression*. Cambridge: Cambridge University Press.

Farrington, D., & Ttofi, M. (2014). Developmental and Life-Course Theories of Offending. In H. Morizot & L. Kazemian (Eds.), *The Development of Criminal and Antisocial Behaviour*. New York: Springer.

Farrington, D., & West, D. (1995). Effects of Marriage, Separation, and Children on Offending by Adult Males. In Z. Blau & J. Hagan (Eds.), *Current Perspectives on Aging and the Life Cycle*. Greenwich: JAI Press.

Farrington, D., Loeber, R., Yanming, Y., & Anderson, S. (2002). Are Within-Individual Causes of Delinquency the Same as Between-Individual Causes? *Criminal Behaviour and Mental Health, 12*(1), 53–68.

Goldsmith, A. H., Veum, J. R., & Darity, W., Jr. (1996). The Psychological Impact of Unemployment & Joblessness. *Journal of Socio-Economics, 25*(3), 333–358.

Harper, G., & Chitty, C. (2005). The Impact of Correction on Re-offending: A Review of 'what works'. *Home Office Research Study* 291.

Hazel, N., Goodfellow, P., Liddle, M., Bateman, T., & Pitts, J. (2017). *"Now All I Care About Is My Future" – Supporting the Shift: Framework for the Effective Resettlement of Young People Leaving Custody*. Beyond Youth Custody. Retrieved November 29, 2017, from http://www.beyondyouthcustody.net/wp-content/uploads/Now-all-I-care-about-is-my-future-Supporting-the-shift-full-research-report.pdf.

Hazenberg, R., Seddon, F., & Denny, S. (2014). Investigating the *Outcome* Performance of Work-integration Social Enterprises (WISEs): Do WISEs Offer 'Added Value' to NEETs? *Public Management Review, 16*(6), 876–899.

Higgins, G. E., Kirchner, E. E., Ricketts, M. L., & Marcum, C. D. (2013). Impulsivity and Offending from Childhood to Young Adulthood in the United States: A Developmental Trajectory Analysis. *International Journal of Criminal Justice Sciences, 8*(2), 182–187.

Hodkinson, P., Hodkinson, H., & Sparkes, A. (1996). *Triumphs and Tears*. London: David Fulton Publishers.

Hosser, D. A., Windzio, M., & Greve, W. (2008). Guilt and Shame as Predictors of Recidivism: A Longitudinal Study with Young Prisoners. *Criminal Justice and Behavior, 35*, 138–152.

Jolliffe, D., & Farrington, D. P. (2004). Empathy and Offending: A Systematic Review and Meta-analysis. *Aggressive Violent Behaviour, 9*, 441–476.

Judge, T. A., Locke, E. A., & Durham, C. C. (1997). The Dispositional Causes of Job Satisfaction: A Core Evaluation Approach, *Research in Organisational. Behaviour, 19*, 151–188.

Leider, R. J. (1994). *Life Skills: Taking Charge of Your Personal and Professional Growth*. Paramus: Prentice-Hall.

Leutenberg, E. A., & Liptak, J. J. (2009). *The Practical Life Skills Workbook*. Duluth: Whole Person.

Lewis, S., Maguire, M., Raynor, P., Vanstone, M., & Vennard, J. (2007). What Works in Resettlement? Findings from Seven Pathfinders for Short-term Prisoners in England and Wales. *Criminology and Criminal Justice, 7*(1), 33–53.

Liptak, J. J. (2007). *The Life Skills IQ Test*. New York: Penguin Publishing.

Liptak, J. J. (2008). *Career Quizzes*. Indianapolis: JIST Publishing.

Maruna, S. (2001). *Making Good: How Ex-Convicts Reform and Rebuild Their Lives*. Washington, DC: American Psychological Association.

Masten, A. S. (2001). Ordinary Magic: Resilience Processes in Development. *American Psychologist, 56*, 227–238.

Ministry of Justice. (2017). Proven Reoffending Statistics Quarterly Bulletin – October 2015 – December 2015. Retrieved January 8, 2018, from https://www.gov.uk/government/uploads/system/uploads/attachment_data/file/658379/proven-reoffending-bulletin-oct15-dec15.pdf.

Montgomery, P., Donkoh, C., & Underhill, K. (2006). Independent Living Programs for Young People Leaving the Care System: The State of the Evidence. *Children and Youth Services Review, 28*(12), 1435–1448.

Morris, T., & Morris, P. (1963). *Pentonville: A Sociological Study of an English Prison*. London: Routledge.

Muncie, J. (2014). *Youth and Crime*. London: Sage Publication Ltd.

Niven, S., & Stewart, D. (2005). *Resettlement Outcomes on Release from Prison in 2003*. London: Home Office.

Paterson-Young, C. (2018). *'Inspiring Futures' – How Social Impact Measurement as a Form of Organisational Performance Management Can Enhance Outcomes for Children and Young People in Custody*. University of Northampton. Thesis.

Paterson-Young, C., Hazenberg, R., Bajwa-Patel, M., & Denny, S. (2017). Developing a Social Impact Measurement Framework to Enhance Outcomes for Young People in Custody – What to Measure? *British Society of Criminology – Conference 2017*.

Pinkerton, J., Dolan, P., & Canavan, J. (2004). *Family Support in Ireland: Definition and Strategic Intent. A Paper for the Department of Health and Children*. Dublin: Stationery Office.

Pitts, J. (2007). *Young and Safe in Lambeth. The Deliberations of Lambeth Executive Commission on Children, Young People and Violent Crime*. London: London Borough Council.

Rutter, M. (1985). Resilience in the Face of Adversity: Protective Factors and Resistance to Psychiatric Disorder. *British Journal of Psychiatry, 147*(6), 589–611.

Schofield, G., & Simmonds, J. (Eds.). (2009). The Child Placement Handbook. Research, policy and practice. BAAF.

Schofield, G., Thoburn, J., Howell, D., & Dickens, J. (2005). The Search for Stability and Permanence: Modelling the Pathways of Long-stay Looked After Children. *British Journal of Social Work, 37*(4), 619–642.

Schwarzer, R. (Ed.). (1992). *Self-efficacy: Thought Control of Action*. Washington, DC: Hemisphere.

Schwarzer, R., & Jerusalem, M. (1995). *Generalized Self-Efficacy Scale*. In J. Weinman, S. Wright, & M. Johnston (Eds.), *Measures in Health Psychology: A User's Portfolio* (pp. 35–37). Windsor, UK: NFER-NELSON.

Tangney, J. P., Stuewig, J., & Martinez, A. G. (2014). Two Faces of Shame: Understanding Shame and Guilt in the Prediction of Jail Inmates' Recidivism. *Psychological Science, 25*, 799–805.

Taxman, F. (2004). The Offender and Re-entry: Supporting Active Participation in Reintegration. *Federal Probation, 68*(2), 31–35.

Umbreit, M., & Zehr, H. (1996). Restorative Family Group Conferences: Differing Models and Guidelines for Practice. *Federal Probation, 60*(3), 24–29.

Ungar, M. (2005). *Handbook for Working with Children and Youth: Pathways to Resilience Across Cultures and Contexts*. Los Angeles: Sage Publications.

Weber, M. (1978). *Economy and Society: An Outline of Interpretative Sociology*. Berkeley, CA: California University Press.

Chapter 8

Alexander, J., Bloom, J., & Nichols, B. (1994). Nursing Turnover and Hospital Efficiency: An Organization-level Analysis. *Industrial Relations, 33*(4), 505–520.

Audit Commission. (1996). *Misspent Youth: Young People and Crime Summary*. London: Audit Commission.

Audit Commission. (1998). Misspent Youth '98 – The Challenge for Youth Justice. Retrieved April 12, 2018, from http://webarchive.nationalarchives.gov.uk/20090415152538/http://www.auditcommission.gov.uk/Products/NATIONAL-REPORT/7C38F5A0-C744-4362-A6C6-90A12D52258D/archive_misyth98.pdf.

Bateman, T., & Hazel, N. (2013). Engaging Young People in Resettlement: Research Report. London: Nacro/Beyond Youth Custody. Retrieved June 5, 2016, from http://www.beyondyouthcustody.net/wp-content/uploads/Engaging-young-people-in-resettlement.pdf.

BBC. (2017). *Custody Office Attacked by Five Boys at Young Offender Unit.* Retrieved December 20, 2017, from http://www.bbc.co.uk/news/uk-england-beds-bucks-herts-39293479.

Beal, C. (2014). Insider Accounts of the Move to the Outside: Two Young People Talk About Their Transitions from Secure Institutions. *Journal of Youth Justice, 13*(1), 63–75.

Carlo, G., & Randall, B. (2002). The Development of a Measure of Prosocial Behaviors for Late Adolescents. *Journal of Youth and Adolescence, 33*(*1*), *31–44*.

Carpenter, J., Webb, C., Bostock, L., & Coomber, C. (2012). *Effective Supervision in Social Work and Social Care.* Social Care Institute for Excellent – Research Briefing 43.

Cashmore, J., & Paxman, M. (1996). *Wards Leaving Care: A Longitudinal Study.* Sydney, Australia: New South Wales Department of Community Services.

Clancy, A., Hudson, K., Maguire, M., Peake, R., Raynor, P., Vanstone, M., & Kynch, J. (2006). *Getting Out and Staying Out: Results of the Prisoner Resettlement Pathfinders.* Bristol: Policy Press.

Clifford, J., Hehenberger, L., & Fantini, M., (2014, June). *Proposed Approaches to Social Impact Measurement in European Commission Legislation and in Practice Relating to: EuSEFs and the EaSI*, European Commission Report 140605. Retrieved from http://ec.europa.eu/internal_market/social_business/docs/expert-group/social_impact/140605-sub-group-report_en.pdf and http://ec.europa.eu/social/main.jsp?catId=738&langId=en&pubId=7735&type=2&furtherPubs=yes.

Farrington, D. (2005). *Integrated Developmental and Life-Course Theories of Offending. Advances in Criminological Theory.* New Brunswick, NJ: Transaction.

Farrington, D. (2007). Origins of Violent Behaviour over the Life Span. In D. J. Flannery, A. T. Vazsonyi, & I. D. Waldman (Eds.), *The Cambridge Handbook of Violent Behavior and Aggression.* Cambridge: Cambridge University Press.

Farrington, D., & Ttofi, M. (2014). Developmental and Life-Course Theories of Offending. In H. Morizot & L. Kazemian (Eds.), *The Development of Criminal and Antisocial Behaviour.* New York: Springer.

Farrington, D., Loeber, R., Yin, Y., & Anderson, S. J. (2002). Are Within-Individual Causes of Delinquency the Same as Between-Individual Causes? *Criminal Behaviour and Mental Health, 12*(1), 53–68.

Ferguson, H. (2005). Working with Violence, the Emotions and the Psycho-social Dynamics of Child Protection: Reflection on the Victoria Climbie Case. *The International Journal of Social Work Education, 24(7), 781–795.*

Goldsmith, A. H., Veum, J. R., & Darity, W., Jr. (1996). The Psychological Impact of Unemployment & Joblessness. *Journal of Socio-Economics, 25*(3), 333–358.

Griffin, M. (2001). Job Satisfaction Among Detention Officers: Implications for Understanding a System. *Criminal Justice Studies, 19*, 225–239.

Hazel, N., Hagell, A., Liddle, M., Archer, D., Grimshaw, R., & King, J. (2002). *Assessment of the Detention and Training Order and Its Impact on the Secure Estate Across England and Wales*. London: Youth Justice Board.

Hazel, N., Goodfellow, P., Liddle, M., Bateman, T., & Pitts, J. (2017). *"Now All I Care About Is My Future" – Supporting the Shift: Framework for the Effective Resettlement of Young People Leaving Custody.* Beyond Youth Custody. Retrieved November 29, 2017, from http://www.beyondyouthcustody.net/wp-content/uploads/Now-all-I-care-about-is-my-future-Supporting-the-shift-full-research-report.pdf.

Hazenberg, R., & Clifford, J. (2016). GECES and the Valid Measurement of Social Impact in the VCSE Sector. In R. Gunn & C. Durkin (Eds.), *Social Entrepreneurship: A Skills Approach* (2nd ed.). Bristol: Policy Press.

Hazenberg, R., Seddon, F., & Denny, S. (2014). Programme Recruitment and Evaluation: The Effect of an Employability Enhancement Programme on the General Self-efficacy Levels of Unemployed Graduates. *Journal of Education and Work, 28*(3), 273–300.

HM Inspectorate of Prisons. (2001). *Through the Prison Gate – A Joint Thematic Review by HM Inspectorates of Prisons and Probation.* Retrieved February 26, 2016, from https://www.justiceinspectorates.gov.uk/hmiprisons/wp-content/uploads/sites/4/2014/08/Through-The-Prison-Gate-2001-ao.pdf.

Hodkinson, P., et al. (1996). *Triumphs & Tears: Young People, Markets & the Transition from School to Work*. London: David Fulton.

Knowlton, L. W., & Phillips, C. C. (2013). *The Logic Model Guidebook: Better Strategies for Great Results* (2nd ed.). London: Sage Publications.

Labov, B. (1997). Inspiring Employees the Easy Way. *Incentive, 171*(10), 114–118.

Lambert, E., & Paoline, E. (2005). The Impact of Medical Issues and Job Satisfaction of Jail Staff. *Punishment and Society, 7, 259–275.*

Lambert, E. G., Hogan, N. L., Moore, B., Tucker, K., Jenkins, M., Stevenson, M., & Jiang, S. (2009). The Impact of the Work Environment on Prison Staff: The Issue of Consideration, Structure, Job Variety and Training. *American Journal of Criminal Justice, 34*, 166–180.

Magner, N., Welker, R., & Johnson, G. (1996). The Interactive Effects of Participation and Outcome Favourability in Performance Appraisal on Turnover Intentions and Evaluations of Supervisors. *Journal of Occupational Organisation Psychology, 69*, 135–143.

Maguire, M., & Raynor, P. (2006). How the Resettlement of Prisoners Promotes Desistence from Crime: Or Does It? *Criminology and Criminal Justice, 6*(1), 19–38.

Maruna, S. (1997). Going Straight: Desistance from Crime and Life Narratives of Reform. *The Narrative Study of Lives, 5*, 59–93.

Maruna, S. (2001). *Making Good: How Ex-Convicts Reform and Rebuild Their Lives*. Washington: American Psychological Association.

McAra, L., & McVie, S. (2010). Youth Crime and Justice: Key Messages from the Edinburgh Study of Youth Transitions and Crime. *Criminology and Criminal Justice, 10*(2), 179–209.

McLoughlin, J., Kaminski, J., Sodagar, B., Khan, S., Harris, R., Arnaudo, G., & McBrearty, S. (2009). A Strategic Approach to Social Impact Measurement of Social Enterprises: The SIMPLE Methodology. *Social Enterprise Journal, 5*(2), 154–178.

Montgomery, P., Donkoh, C., & Underhill, K. (2006). Independent Living Programs for Young People Leaving the Care System: The State of the Evidence. *Children and Youth Services Review, 28*, 1435–1448.

Morrow, V., & Richards, M. (1996). *Transitions to Adulthood: A Family Matter*. London: Joseph Rowntree Foundation.

Nevill, C., & Lumley, T. (2011). *Impact Measurement in the Youth Justice Sector*. [online]. Retrieved September 9, 2015, from http://www.thinknpc.org/publications/measuring-together/.

Ofsted. (2017). *Inspection of Secure Training Centres – Inspection of Oakhill Secure Training Centre*. Retrieved February 12, 2018, from https://reports.ofsted.gov.uk/sites/default/files/documents/secure-training-centre-reports/oakhill/OakhillSTC_January2017.pdf.

Ongori, H. (2007). A Review of the Literature on Employee Turnover. *African Journal of Business Management*, 049–054.

Paterson-Young, C., Hazenberg, R., Bajwa-Patel, M., & Denny, S. (2017b). Developing a Social Impact Measurement Framework to Enhance Outcomes for Young People in Custody – What to Measure? *British Society of Criminology – Conference 2017*.

Phoenix, J., & Kelly, L. (2013). You Have to Do It for Yourself– Responsibilization in Youth Justice and Young People's Situated Knowledge of Youth Justice Practice. *British Journal of Criminology, 53*, 419–437.

Pitts, J. (2001). *The New Politics of Youth Crime: Discipline or Solidarity*. Dorset: Russell House Publishing.

Rittel, H. W. J., & Webber, M. M. (1973). Dilemmas in the General Theory of Planning. *Policy Sciences, 4*, 155–169.

Stanley, J., & Goddard, C. (2002). *In the Firing Line: Violence and Power in Child Protection Work*. Chichester: Wiley.

STC. (1998). Rules [Online]. Retrieved June 8, 2016, from http://www.legislation.gov.uk/uksi/1998/472/contents/made.

Taylor, C. (2016). An Interim Report of Emerging Findings from the Review of the Youth Justice System. Retrieved July 1, 2016, from https://www.gov.uk/government/news/review-of-the-youth-justice-system.

The Local Government Association. (2011). Resettlement of Youth Offenders: How Local Initiatives Can Make a Difference. L11–565.

Vaughan, B. (2006). The Internal Narrative of Desistance. *British Journal of Criminology, 47*(3), 390–404.

Voltan, A., & Hervieux, C. (2017). Social Impact Assessment of a Community Engagement Initiative, *Paper presented at the 9th International Social Innovation Research Conference*, 12th–14th December 2017, Swinburne University of Technology, Melbourne.

Vroom, V. H. (1964). *Work and Motivation*. San Francisco: Jossey-Bass.

Weber, M. (1978). *Economy and Society: An Outline of Interpretative Sociology*. Berkeley, CA: California University Press.

Youth Justice Board. (2014). *Deaths of Children in Custody: Action Take, Lessons Learnt.* Retrieved June 30, 2016, from https://www.gov.uk/government/uploads/system/uploads/attachment_data/file/362715/deaths-children-in-custody.pdf.

Chapter 9

Baldry, S., & Kemmis, J. (1998). What Is It Like to Be Looked After by a Local Authority? *British Journal of Social Work, 28*, 129–136.

Bateman, T., & Hazel, N. (2014). *Youth Justice Timeline*. Retrieved from http://www.beyondyouthcustody.net/wp-content/uploads/youth-justice-timeline.pdf.

Bell, M. (2002). Promoting Children's Rights Through the Use of Relationship. *Child and Family Social Work, 7*, 1–11.

Case, S. (2018b). *Youth Justice: A Critical Introduction*. Oxon: Routledge.

Cashmore, J., & Paxman, M. (1996). *Wards Leaving Care: A Longitudinal Study*. Sydney, Australia: New South Wales Department of Community Services.

Clancy, A., Hudson, K., Maguire, M., Peake, R., Raynor, P., Vanstone, M., & Kynch, J. (2006). *Getting Out and Staying Out: Results of the Prisoner Resettlement Pathfinders*. Bristol: Policy Press.

Cohen, J. A., Mannarino, A. P., & Deblinger, E. (2017). *Treating Trauma and Traumatic Grief in Children and Adolescents* (2nd ed.). London: The Guildford Press.

Communities that Care. (2005). *Risk and Protective Factors*. London: Youth Justice Board.

Farrington, D. (2005). *Integrated Developmental and Life-Course Theories of Offending. Advances in Criminological Theory*. New Jersey: Transaction.

Farrington, D. (2007b). Origins of Violent Behaviour Over the Life Span. In D. J. Flannery, A. T. Vazsonyi, & I. D. Waldman (Eds.), *The Cambridge Handbook of Violent Behavior and Aggression*. Cambridge: Cambridge University Press.

Farrington, D., Loeber, R., & Yin, Y. (2002). Are Within-individual Causes of Delinquency the Same as Between-Individual Causes? *Criminal Behaviour and Mental Health, 12*(1), 53–68.

Farrington, D., & Ttofi, M. (2014). Developmental and Life-Course Theories of Offending. In H. Morizot & L. Kazemian (Eds.), *The Development of Criminal and Antisocial Behaviour*. New York: Springer.

Fletcher, B. (1993). *Not Just a Name: The Views of Young People in Residential and Foster Care. Who Cares?* London: National Consumer Council.

Goldsmith, A. H., Veum, J. R., & Darity, W., Jr. (1996). The Psychological Impact of Unemployment & Joblessness. *Journal of Socio-Economics, 25*(3), 333–358.

Hazenberg, R., Seddon, F., & Denny, S. (2014). Programme Recruitment and Evaluation: The Effect of an Employability Enhancement Programme on the General Self-efficacy Levels of Unemployed Graduates. *Journal of Education and Work, 28*(3), 273–300.

Hodkinson, P., Hodkinson, H., & Sparkes, A. (1996). *Triumphs and Tears*. London: David Fulton Publishers.

Hughes, N., Williams, H., Chitsabesan, P., Davies, R., & Mounce, L. (2012). *Nobody Made the Connection: The Prevalence of Neuro-disability in Children and Young People Who Offend*. London: Children's commissioner.

Khan, L. (2010). *Reaching Out, Reaching in: Promoting Mental Health and Emotional Well-Being in Secure Settings*. Centre for Mental Health. Retrieved September 28, 2017, from http://www.ohrn.nhs.uk/resource/policy/Reachingoutreachingin.pdf.

Kitzmann, K., Gaylord, N., Holt, A., & Kenney, E. (2003). Child Witnesses to Domestic Violence: A Meta-Analytic Review. *Journal of Consulting and Clinical Psychology, 71*(2), 229–235.

Kuhn, T. (1996). *The Structure of Scientific Revolutions* (3rd ed.). London: University of Chicago Press.

Maguire, M., & Raynor, P. (2006). How the Resettlement of Prisoners Promotes Desistence from Crime: Or Does It? *Criminology and Criminal Justice, 6*(1), 19–38.

Maruna, S. (1997). Going Straight: Desistance from Crime and Life Narratives of Reform. In *The Narrative Study of Lives* (Vol. 5, pp. 59–93).

Maruna, S. (2001). *Making Good: How Ex-Convicts Reform and Rebuild their Lives*. Washington, DC: American Psychological Association Books.

McLaughlin, E., Muncie, J., & Hughes, G. (2001). The Permanent Revolution: New Labour, New Public Management and the Modernization of Criminal Justice. *Criminology and Criminal Justice, 1*(3), 301–318.

McLeod, A. (2008). 'A Friend and an Equal': Do Young People in Care Seek the Impossible from Their Social Workers? *British Journal Social Work*, Advance Access, 1–17.

Montgomery, P., Donkoh, C., & Underhill, K. (2006). Independent Living Programs for Young People Leaving the Care System: The State of the Evidence. *Children and Youth Services Review, 28*, 1435–1448.

Morgan, R. (2006). Young People and Offending (Foreword). In M. Stephenson (Ed.), *Young People and Offending – Education, Youth Justice and Social Inclusion*. London: Routledge.

Morrow, V., & Richards, M. (1996). *Transitions to Adulthood: A Family Matter*. London: Joseph Rowntree Foundation.

Murray, R. (2012). *Children and Young People in Custody 2011/12: An Analysis of the Experiences of 15–18 Year Olds in Prisons*. London: HMIP/the Youth Justice Board.

Pearson, G. (1983). *Hooligan: A History of Respectable Fears*. London: Macmillan.

Taylor, C. (2016). *An Interim Report of Emerging Findings from the Review of the Youth Justice System*. London: Ministry of Justice.

Vaughan, B. (2007). The Internal Narrative of Desistance. *British Journal of Criminology, 47*, 390–404.

Voltan, A., & Hervieux, C. (2017). Social Impact Assessment of a Community Engagement Initiative, *Paper presented at the 9th International Social Innovation Research Conference*, 12th–14th December 2017, Swinburne University of Technology, Melbourne

Weber, M. (1978). *Economy and Society: An Outline of Interpretative Sociology*. Berkeley, CA: California University Press.

Young, T., Fitzgerald, M., Hallsworth, S., & Joseph, I. (2007). *Groups, Gangs and Weapons*. London: Youth Justice Board.

Index[1]

A

Abuse, 4, 18, 22, 50–52, 55, 92, 133, 150, 153, 168, 169, 171, 175
Accommodation, 5, 16, 17, 54, 78, 109, 111–115, 117, 119, 135, 139, 140, 148, 173, 185
Alternative attribution, 31, 32, 35, 41, 159
Alternative provisions, 92, 93, 96
Anti-social behaviour, 36, 51, 64, 66, 86, 87, 98–99, 128, 171
Anti-social potential, 3, 36, 130
Attitudes, 2, 5, 28, 65, 72, 74, 109–135, 140, 141, 143, 161, 168, 173

B

Belonging, 4, 64, 130
Bereavement, 22, 50, 67, 150, 171

C

Care system, 22, 28, 150
Child-focused, 3, 23
Childhood, 7, 9, 23, 50, 51, 78, 86, 119, 153
Complex needs, 17, 92, 102
Confidence, 9, 110
Coping mechanism, 4, 22, 50–53, 58, 141
Crime, 14, 19, 20, 37, 38, 41, 64, 69, 70, 75, 86, 87, 93, 98, 102, 134, 143, 156, 167, 169

[1] Note: Page numbers followed by 'n' refer to notes.

C. Paterson-Young et al., *The Social Impact of Custody on Young People in the Criminal Justice System*, https://doi.org/10.1007/978-3-030-18422-3

Criminalising, 2
Criminality, 37, 172
Criminal Justice System, 13, 14, 22, 23, 37, 48, 63, 70, 74, 119, 132, 155, 159
Criminological perspective, 36
Custodial environments, 5, 48, 51, 53–56, 58, 59, 71, 78, 114, 119, 134, 139, 141–143, 145, 147, 150, 155
Custody, 1–5, 10, 12, 13, 16–23, 29, 47, 48, 55–59, 63, 69, 71, 72, 74, 76–78, 83, 87–102, 109–111, 113–129, 131, 133–135, 139–143, 146, 148, 150, 155, 156, 159, 160, 168, 170–173

D

Deadweight, 31, 32, 34, 41, 159
Deprived areas, 64
Desistance, 1, 3–5, 32, 33, 36–39, 41, 42, 59, 63–65, 78, 97, 103, 109, 111, 112, 120, 128, 131, 132, 134, 141, 143, 156, 159, 160, 172, 174
Disadvantage, 3, 21, 28, 36, 47, 48, 63, 83, 85, 86, 101, 102, 143, 156, 167, 169, 172
Diverse needs, 2, 168
Domestic abuse, 22, 78, 150
Drop-off, 31, 35, 41, 159

E

Education, 1, 2, 4, 5, 7, 14, 17, 19, 49, 50, 54, 55, 57, 58, 64, 78, 79, 83–103, 109–111, 113, 115–120, 129, 130, 139–141, 143, 148, 152, 156, 158, 168–172, 175, 181, 184, 185
Effectiveness, 15, 31, 59, 134, 148, 157
Emotional regulation, 5, 50, 51, 58, 112, 118, 141, 171
Empowerment, 5, 27–29, 76, 77, 109, 111, 118, 129, 135, 141, 143, 156, 158, 159, 168, 169, 174
England, 1, 2, 8–10, 12, 15, 16, 21, 53, 54, 56, 64, 84, 87, 88, 90, 91, 93, 101, 168
Evaluation, 31–34, 41, 77, 158, 159, 170, 174
Evidence-based, 1, 22, 157
Exclusion, 4, 66, 84–87, 92–94, 97, 99, 102, 103, 172
Experiences, 1, 2, 4, 19, 22, 23, 29, 32, 36–39, 47–59, 65, 66, 70, 72, 74, 75, 78, 92, 94, 95, 97, 102, 109, 113, 119, 128, 131, 133, 140, 141, 146, 149, 150, 152–154, 171, 175

F

Friendship, 70, 75

G

Gang, 21, 69, 75, 92, 129–131
Government, 7, 9, 10, 12, 14, 19, 23, 30, 83, 84, 92, 99, 101, 147, 174

H

Health and wellbeing, 2, 4, 5, 47–59, 77, 78, 110, 140–143, 152, 158, 168, 170, 171

Health problems, 49, 52, 53
Holistic, 3, 5, 15, 23, 32, 39, 74, 78, 142, 158, 159, 168, 170, 172, 175

I

Identity, 2, 11, 38, 70, 71, 76, 77, 95
Impact, 1–3, 1n1, 5, 7–23, 27–42, 47, 50, 51, 55, 58, 65, 67, 74–76, 78, 86, 101, 111, 113, 114, 119, 128, 129, 131, 132, 135, 139–141, 143, 146, 149, 151, 154–161, 168, 170–172, 174
Incarceration, 5, 16, 64–66, 68, 77, 158, 169
Independence, 2, 5, 109–135, 140, 141, 143, 156, 158, 160, 161, 168, 170, 171, 173
Inequalities, 4, 47–53, 55, 59, 85, 99, 131, 141, 167
Innovation, 30
Integrated Cognitive Anti-social Potential (ICAP), 1, 3, 5, 27, 28, 33, 36, 37, 39–42, 65, 77, 141, 158, 159
Intervention, 3, 12, 14, 15, 20, 21, 23, 28–35, 37, 39, 42, 48, 57–59, 70, 74–77, 98, 110, 111, 129, 131, 132, 134, 135, 141, 143, 145, 146, 148, 158–161, 168, 170, 173, 174
Isolation, 4, 23, 51, 71, 113, 118, 129, 135, 143, 156

L

Labelling, 22
Life satisfaction, 50, 54, 55, 58, 120, 141
Life skills inventory, 120

M

Meaningful activities, 130, 148
Mental health, 17, 48–50, 53, 56, 69, 100, 102, 139, 161, 174
Motivation, 37, 39, 71, 75, 109–111, 113, 114, 120, 128, 129, 140, 151
Multi-agency, 7, 11, 12, 84, 155, 168

O

Offending, 2–4, 7, 10, 12–14, 17, 20, 21, 28, 35, 36, 41, 50, 63–66, 68, 70, 71, 74–78, 86, 87, 98, 98n3, 101, 120, 128–132, 134, 135, 140, 143, 156, 158, 159, 167, 170–174, 181, 184
Outcomes, 1n1, 2, 3, 5, 8, 15, 20, 23, 28, 29, 31–37, 39, 41, 42, 48, 50, 54, 55, 58, 59, 71, 76, 78, 83, 84, 94, 95, 99, 101, 110, 111, 120, 135, 139–143, 145, 157–161, 168–170, 174, 175
Outputs, 31–35, 39, 41, 42, 158–160, 170

P

Personal narrative, 3, 38, 41, 120, 159
Physical health, 49, 49n2, 50, 52, 54, 56
Poverty, 3, 37, 64, 92, 131

Power, 2, 3, 11, 27–32, 39, 41, 42, 65, 131, 156, 157, 160, 169, 170
Power imbalances, 29, 65, 131, 169
Powerlessness, 133
Pro-criminal, 22, 65, 66, 77, 112, 132, 133, 142, 150
Prosocial identity, 38, 76, 77
Punishment, 8, 13, 14, 23, 37, 47, 101, 118, 169
Punitive, 2, 8–13, 15–23, 118, 167, 168, 175

R

Recidivism, 2, 4, 8, 13, 23, 28, 29, 31–33, 39, 41, 59, 64, 66, 70, 76–78, 83, 87, 98, 109, 111–113, 119, 120, 128, 129, 131, 132, 134, 135, 139, 141, 143, 157, 158, 160, 167–171, 173, 174
Rehabilitation, 3, 4, 6, 19, 32, 64, 65, 73, 76–78, 132, 167, 174, 175
Relationships, 2, 4, 33, 37, 54–56, 63–79, 87, 100, 109, 110, 113, 114, 128, 129, 132, 139–143, 149, 155, 156, 158, 168, 170–172, 183
Release, 4, 17, 48, 59, 63, 66–68, 70, 71, 77, 78, 99, 101, 111–115, 117–119, 128, 139, 140, 143, 148, 149, 155, 156, 172, 181, 184, 185
Remorse, 131–134
Reoffending, 5, 42, 75, 76, 83, 87, 133, 141, 159, 161, 168, 174, 175
Resettlement, 2, 4, 5, 42, 63, 64, 68, 69, 71, 76–78, 111, 118, 128, 129, 139–142, 145, 151, 154, 156, 157, 170, 172–175
Resettlement Pyramid, 5, 27, 32, 77, 78, 140–142, 145, 149, 157–160, 169, 173–175
Resilience, 5, 22, 50, 99, 109–111, 110n1, 118, 120, 128, 129, 135, 140, 141, 143, 156, 158, 160, 173
Responsibilisation, 12–14
Risk factors, 3, 37, 86, 87

S

Schooling, 5, 64, 85, 87, 92, 96, 102
Secure Children's Homes, 12, 15–18, 100n4
Secure schools, 3, 4, 101, 173
Secure Training Centre (STC), 1, 11, 27, 49, 64, 84, 110, 140, 169
Self-efficacy, 99, 110, 110n1
Self-esteem, 95, 110
Self-harm, 19, 49, 53
Sentencing, 14, 87, 183
Social action, 27, 29, 30, 39, 41, 76, 77, 111, 118, 131, 135, 143, 157, 158, 169, 175
Social disadvantage, 21, 169, 172
Social Impact Measurement (SIM), 1–3, 1n1, 5, 23, 27–42, 59, 76–78, 110n1, 140–142, 144–145, 156–161, 170, 174, 175
Social institutions, 2
Social problem, 9
Social structures, 2–3, 27, 28, 39, 169
Special educational needs, 90, 102

Stakeholders, 14, 28–30, 32, 35, 36, 41, 41n1, 59, 157, 159, 160, 170, 175
Strain, 37, 38
Substance use, 14, 22, 23, 49, 51, 52, 133
Success, 13, 31, 99, 151
Support network, 70

T
Theory of change, 33–36, 39, 41, 158, 160, 161
Transitions, 4, 5, 21, 23, 29, 59, 63–66, 71, 78, 86, 97, 98, 109–112, 114, 119, 120, 135, 139–141, 143, 148, 155–157, 160, 168–175
Trauma, 4, 22, 23, 50–53, 55, 58, 59, 109, 118, 133, 149, 150, 153, 168, 169, 171, 175
Trusting relationships, 64, 71, 74, 77, 78

U
Uncertainty, 112, 113, 128–131, 134, 149

V
Victimisation, 133
Violence, 50, 55, 58, 65, 75, 97, 128, 131, 133, 142, 150, 152, 171
Vocational qualifications, 95
Vulnerable, 2, 3, 16, 19, 23, 57, 63, 69, 70, 84, 91, 96, 98, 139, 183

W
Weberian, 3, 27, 28, 41, 157, 158, 160, 168, 169

Y
Young offenders, 10, 11, 14, 51, 76, 77, 89, 90, 159
Youth Justice Board (YJB), 11–15, 17, 18, 21, 49, 53, 59, 83, 86–89, 96, 97, 99–102, 148, 153, 161, 184
Youth Justice System, 2, 3, 5, 7–16, 18, 23, 27, 30, 41, 64, 76, 83, 87, 98, 101, 142, 156, 167, 168, 170, 171
Youth offending, 2, 3, 14, 21, 28, 35–40, 66, 77, 86, 167, 172, 174
Youth Offending Institutions, 10, 12, 15, 16, 18, 49, 100, 140, 147
Youth Offending Team (YOT), 11–13, 69, 70, 131, 155, 156, 185

Kolibri 360 GmbH
Ferdinand-Jühlke-Straße 7
99095 Erfurt, Deutschland
produktsicherheit@kolibri360.de